RHODODENDRONS

COLOUR PLATE 1

1 *R. arboreum*
2 *R. lindleyi*
3 *R. dichroanthum*
  ssp. *scyphocalyx*
4 *R. augustinii*
5 *R. orbiculare*

RHODODENDRONS

*Their history, geographical
distribution, hybridization
and culture*

Gerd Krüssmann

*Director of the Botanical Gardens in
Dortmund-Brunninghausen*

WARD LOCK LIMITED · LONDON

Ward Lock Limited
Warwick House, 116 Baker St., W1M 2BB

SBN 7063 1114 0

Printed in Great Britain
By Richard Clay (The Chaucer Press), Ltd.,
Bungay, Suffolk

CONTENTS

INTRODUCTION

This book is the result of many years of visiting the most famous parks and gardens in England, Scotland, Ireland, Germany and Holland—almost twenty years in all. So it is not surprising that I presume to offer to my readers a 'new approach' to rhododendrons. As the reader will soon realize, this is a very personal book. I have my own views on many aspects of rhododendron growing, and these do not always coincide with official pronouncements from testing stations and nurseries. Among other things, I do not see why amateurs should not be encouraged to see and learn about the most beautiful varieties of rhododendrons and azaleas, even if these are not available from their immediate vicinity.

Today it is possible for the lover of rhododendrons—or of nature generally—to visit all the treasures which are available on the market, even if it means spending a whole weekend doing so. He should enjoy rhododendrons without always wishing to possess them all; but if he does wish to buy any, this book will show him the way.

The numerous photographs taken by the author which appear in this book were augmented by further pictures taken in China, Japan, North America and the Caucasus. Grateful thanks are extended to all those who supplied these photographs. Another addition is the collection of line drawings by D. Holmgreen, copied in part from the author's originals.

RHODODENDRON—AZALEA

Right at the beginning it would be helpful to explain the two words, rhododendron and azalea, which many gardeners, both amateur and professional, use without fully understanding their meaning. The reason is quite simple, for nowadays there is no longer any division between them. Today the azaleas belong to the rhododendron family, being grouped together under the subspecies anthodendron. I should like to start by casting a brief look back over the history of these names.

The book *Species Plantarum* by the great botanist Karl Linnaeus, published in 1753, provided the basis for the modern method of scientifically naming plants. Through him, innumerable plants were given names which for the most part are still valid today. The first mention of the term 'azalea' occurs on page 150 of his book, and under this family name coined by Linnaeus come the varieties known at that time: *Azalea indica, A. pontica, A. lutea, A. viscosa, A. lapponica* and *A. procumbens*. Linnaeus coined this family name from the Greek word 'azaléos', which means roughly the same as 'dry', or 'arid'. This promptly gave rise to the belief that these plants grew in dry places—which was in fact not true.

On page 392 of the same book we find the name 'rhododendron', once again a Greek word, and which, literally translated, means 'rose tree'. Here, too, the known varieties were listed: *R. ferrugineum, R. dauricum, R. hirsutum, R. chamaecistus* and *R. maximum*, of which *R. ferrugineum* will be used as a model. Strangely enough, the word rhododendron already existed in the Greek language, for Dioscorides used it in his book *Materia Medica* during the first century A.D. to describe the oleander.

In 1754 there appeared a further book from Linnaeus which is still valuable today; it is titled *Genera Plantarum* (plant families). Naturally, the names rhododendron and azalea appear once again in this book, but with one difference—for this time Linnaeus wrote 'rhododendrum'. Of course, this name is as correctly constructed, philologically speaking, as rhododendron. Some later botanists went so far as to maintain that the name with the Latin ending 'um' was more correct and was to be preferred. Happily, modern botanical rules state that, in cases where Linnaeus provided two equally correct versions, the older of the two is the right one: and so we are left with rhododendron.

Richard A. Salisbury, an English botanist, in 1796 was the first to take the view that azaleas and rhododendrons could not remain as two separated genera, but must be grouped together. Many years went by, until, in 1834, G. Don grouped all the known varieties of azaleas under the heading rhododendron in his book *General System of Gardening and Botany* (Volume III, page 843). But by no means all

botanists followed his example, let alone all gardeners. Only after the appearance in 1870 in St. Petersburg of Karl Johann Maximowicz's book *Rhododendron Asiae Orientalis*, in which the author brilliantly described each of the eastern Asiatic varieties, has the use of the name azalea decreased. For the past 100 years or so only the name rhododendron has been used in serious botanical publications.

It is to be regretted that, for formal reasons too complicated to go into here, it was impossible to keep the old word azalea, to which gardeners have clung so tightly, at least to denote a subspecies. An attempt not many years ago to reinstate the azalea as the name of a subspecies was unsuccessful. So the name lives on only because of its daily use by gardeners and other enthusiasts.

It is interesting at this stage to return to Linnaeus and his two classifications, and to find out what still remains of them.

Azalea indica L. is now called *R. indicum* (L.) SWEET and must in no circumstances be confused with the gardeners' 'Indian azalea', correctly called *R. simsii* PLANCHON. There are now only three varieties of the above-named *R. indicum* being grown today, 'Macrantha' (which flowers in June/July), 'Balsaminaeflora' (a dwarf strain) and 'Kotin-shita' (which grows almost along the ground). All three are rather sensitive to frost.

Azalea pontica L. is now called *R. luteum* SWEET.
Azalea lutea L. is now called *R. calendulaceum* (MICHX) TORR.
Azalea viscosa L. is now called *R. viscosum* (L.) TORR.
Azalea lapponica L. is now called *R. lapponicum* (L.) WAHLEMB.
Azalea procumbens L. is now called *Loiseleuria procumbens* (L.) DESVAUX.
Rhododendron ferrugineum L. remains unchanged.
Rhododendron dauricum L. remains unchanged.
Rhododendrum hirsutum L. remains unchanged.
Rhododendron maximum L. remains unchanged.
Rhododendron chamaecistus in now called *Rhodothamnus chamaecistus* (L.) REICHENB.

In the two hundred years and more which have elapsed since Linnaeus's day our knowledge about the rhododendron family has grown enormously. Whereas there were then eleven known varieties, of which two must be discounted, since they can no longer be considered as belonging to the same genus, there are now between 800 and 1,000 known wild varieties. And since gardeners have been crossing the different species—that is, since the beginning of the nineteenth century—the number of hybrid varieties has grown to an estimated 7,000 or 8,000, if you take the trouble to consult the official Rhododendron Register and start counting.

Just one more word about the recognition of azaleas. In Linnaeus's time only deciduous azaleas were known, since his *A. lapponica* and *A. procumbens* were not correctly listed. These last-mentioned varieties lose their leaves in autumn and bloom from spring through till early summer, at the same time as, or just after, the formation of the new leaves. This is the case with most garden azaleas which occur under the headings 'Pontica' hybrids, 'Mollis-Sinensis' hybrids, 'Viscosa' hybrids and so on.

To these belong also the evergreens known as 'Japanese' azaleas. All these varieties, together with the countless garden varieties,

have dimorphous leaves, namely spring and summer leaves. The first appear at the same time as the blossoms, or shortly after, and are larger, paler green and thinner than the summer leaves, which do not appear until late summer after the spring leaves have nearly fallen off. The summer leaves are smaller, a darker green and coarser, and quite frequently they are also a different shape.

All rhododendrons which normally shed their leaves in late autumn, or which grow summer leaves, can be termed 'azaleas'. When dealing with practical gardeners, this is in many ways better, for misunderstandings can be avoided.

GEOGRAPHICAL DISTRIBUTION

The area of distribution of rhododendrons extends mainly across the northern hemisphere (Fig. 1). Curiously enough, there are no rhododendrons in either South America or in Africa, and in Australia there is one variety only. It is only in recent times that the tropical varieties have been studied in depth and brought more or less into general cultivation. The total number of known varieties is around 800–1,000. It is not possible to count more exactly, because botanists are not always agreed among themselves on how to classify the many varieties and the different kinds to be found under each variety.

The richest source of rhododendrons is in the western and south-western part of China, where almost half of all the known varieties originate. A further 300 varieties occur in South-East Asia, including around 190 in New Guinea alone. In the rest of Asia—northern and eastern China, Korea, Siberia and Japan—there are hardly 100 varieties, mostly deciduous azaleas (Fig. 2). America yields even fewer. Apart from the variety *Rhododendron catawbiense*, now so well established in our own gardens, there is just one evergreen and seventeen deciduous natural varieties (Fig. 5).

Europe, unfortunately, boasts so few varieties that they can be counted on the fingers of one hand: *R. lapponicum* in the far

North, then *R. ferrugineum* and *R. hirsutum* in the Alps, *R. kotschyi* in the Transsylvanian Alps and in northern Bulgaria. Of course, the few wild varieties found in the Caucasus come under this group, namely *R. ponticum*, *R. caucasicum*, *R. smirnowii*, *R. ungernii* and *R. luteum*, much better known as *Azalea pontica*; and finally comes the link between Asia and North America, *R. camtschaticum*.

West and south-west China

As we have seen, this area—the west and north-west parts of the province of Yunnan, the north, west and south parts of the province of Setschuan, south-east Tibet and northern Burma—is uniformly rich in wild varieties of all kinds. What is more, as the territory is about the same size as West Germany and France together, the reader will be astonished to learn that such a small area has not yet been thoroughly explored. This is because it is mountainous country which is very difficult of access, with great differences in altitude. The mountain ranges are comparatively young in relation to the Earth's history, very precipitous, and the climate varies considerably from

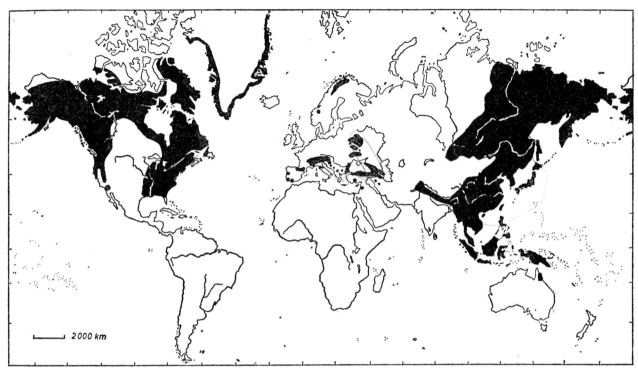

Fig. 1. World distribution of the rhododendron family. (After E. Jäger, 1968 and H. Sleumer, 1966.)

place to place. The flora and fauna of four different types of area coincide here. There is, therefore, an incredible variety of both plants and animals, whose number is barely exceeded by the rich tropical rain forests. Eminent botanists and plant-collectors have travelled over this area, but most foreigners have not been allowed access—as is still the case today.

Handel-Mazzetti and E. H. Wilson explored only the edge of this territory, but George Forrest and F. Kingdon Ward penetrated somewhat further. F. J. Rock, an American botanist of Austrian origin, was able to point to the existence of no less than 500 kinds of rhododendrons in the Yuling-Shan mountains alone. Particularly interesting is the report of Ernest Schäfer, who in 1931 was scientific leader of the second Brooke-Dolan expedition. In his own words:

'Coming from the east, that is from Yunnan or Szechwan, as soon as you have left behind you the subtropical flatlands and the low-lying hills, and have begun to penetrate into the mountainous areas, you find yourself in the range of distribution of the alpine rose, which stretches on the one side from the deeply incised valleys up to the boundaries of the everlasting snows, and on the other side to the area of the Tibetan plateaux whose average height is around 4,500 m./ 13,500 ft. With the exception of the arid scrub-covered dry valleys (at an altitude of around 1,000–2,000 m./3,000–7,800 ft.) the tundra (5,300 m./15,900 ft.) and the continental steppes of central Tibet, there are rhododendrons in almost unbelievable quantities. The optimum environment for the alpine rose lies in the high mountain regions thickly covered by dense subtropical jungle. Known as the "Hsifan" region, this area stretches from a height of 1,000 m./ 3,000 ft. right up to the 7,500 m./22,500 ft.-high peaks of the chain of mountains which all summer long are subject to the constant influence

of the rain-bearing monsoon winds blowing from the south.

'Further to the south, as for example in the mountainous regions near the rain forests, the steep, productive jungle loses its subtropical or purely tropical character and becomes dry savannah. To the north and the west the optimum environment for rhododendrons decreases along with the gradual disappearance of the so-called "Dwarf Bush Region" (which corresponds roughly to our dwarf pine zone). In any case, the distribution range of rhododendrons spreads northwards, far beyond the tree-line to where cushion-shaped, intertwined dwarf varieties join with dwarf willows in a tight mesh in the middle of the steppes.

'If you disregard the systematic classification of rhododendrons, the variations between the many types of east Tibetan alpine roses which are the results of climatic differences, are clearly discernible. As well as those variations which are the result of climate and the condition of the soil, the characteristics of the actual bloom—for example, *when* the plant flowers and how long they last—indicate the existence of many radically different biotopes. I found three different types of growth which had in many cases encroached on to each other's territory.

'I should like to make these three types the basis of my system, so as to achieve a uniformity of description. For just as it is difficult to fix exactly the boundaries surrounding the distribution zone of the species of animals to be found in any given area of inquiry, nature does not allow fixed boundaries to be set on the distribution of rhododendrons. In this connection I shall only attempt to give a clear overall picture which should by no means be taken as the ultimate and conclusive pronouncement on the subject, or as always correct in every detail. It is only intended to encourage and stimulate any botanist aspiring to carry out further research in that difficult territory

Geographical distribution

in order to add newer, rarer and more beautiful examples to the mysterious world of ornamental plants.

'The first of these rhododendrons, one which is moreover most typical of the humid primeval forests of Hsifan Mountain regions, is the tree-shaped variety most often found in the upper jungle areas. In the lower jungle (around 1,200–2,000 m./3,600–6,000 ft.) the tree-shaped rhododendrons crop up only rarely and never as the chief variety, although in this area individual specimens reach their greatest size, so that I was time and time again able to measure trees 15 m./45 ft. high, having trunks up to 40 cm./16 in. in diameter. Here the alpine roses might grow right in the middle of the forest, densely surrounded by firs, pines and various deciduous trees. They stretch straight up towards the light and thereby develop tall slim outlines. Their canopy of leaves does not begin to spread out until it is 5 or 6 m./15 or 18 ft. above the ground. Only in those areas where there are open spaces higher up are bush-shaped rhododendrons to be found in the jungle. Two important varieties found in this area are *Rhododendron denudatum* and *R. bureavii* (also common in bamboo jungle). According to my observations, the flowering period of these mainly deep red, but always richly coloured alpine roses lasts through the summer months from May until the end of August. But even in October I have come across flowering rhododendrons deep in the heart of the jungle.

'The higher we climb the more uniform and compact the stands of rhododendrons become until when they approach the tree-line (4,200–4,700 m./12,600–13,400 ft.) they achieve a dominant character. But at the same time the tree-shaped plants gradually give way to the densely-matted bush-shaped varieties. This shape remains constant throughout the geographical region of Tibet where trees occur at all. So it happens that the rhododendron belt, spreading out above the tree-line, and following the contour of the valleys, reaches back a long way into Tibet. Whereas the stems of alpine roses in the south and south-east—regions heavily influenced by the monsoons—mainly lie pressed horizontally on the ground because of their winter burden of snow, and only turn up their leafy end-twigs towards the light, the rhododendrons growing in the less snowy regions of Tibet usually stand upright, even when locked in impenetrable thickets.

'In the subtropical Hsifan Mountain regions, clumps of alpine roses reaching altitudes of between 3,000 and 4,500 m./9,000 and 13,500 ft. sometimes spread thickly over an area miles wide. When seen in full bloom during May or June, they present a breathtakingly beautiful spectacle. Here, the varieties *R. sulphureum*, *R. trichocladum* and *R. adenogynum* are particularly worthy of mention.

'Deeper into Tibet, these varieties give way to *R. hippophaeoides* (usually in the vicinity of mountain streams) and to the hardy *R. beesianum*, which is frequently found on moist mountain slopes.

'*R. adenogynum*, on the other hand, seems to be a very widely distributed variety which occurs in the Hsifan Mountains as well as in the more humid Tibetan regions. The further we progress along the caravan routes through Tatsienlu, Litang and Batang towards Tibet, and into the less rainy areas, the more frequent become the thickets of bush rhododendrons on the dry slopes, always exposed to the strong sun. Here the strange fact is reinforced that the floral characteristics of the dry slopes of valleys are quite different from the shady wet slopes on which only rhododendrons grow. At the edges of the forests are frequently to be found the glorious bushy growths of *R. rubiginosum*.

'The third type of alpine rose native to western China and eastern Tibet is the dwarf variety which occurs only rarely in the rainy Hsifan Mountains, but which gradually becomes dominant in the arid regions of Tibet, above and north of the tree-line. The dryness of the atmosphere and the pronounced lack of rainfall seems to favour the small xerophilous varieties. These varieties, which have red, yellow and purple blooms and flower from June until August, can be distinguished by their small leaves and thick branches. *R. flavidum* and *R. impeditum* can be named here as typical dwarf varieties.

'When combined with dwarf willows in dense, often only knee-high masses, these rhododendron bushes sometimes spread out over a distance of hundreds of kilometres until they eventually merge (somewhere in the region of Jukundo in the upper Yangtze Kiang) with the undulating high steppes of the Tibetan central plateau which supports every type of bush.'

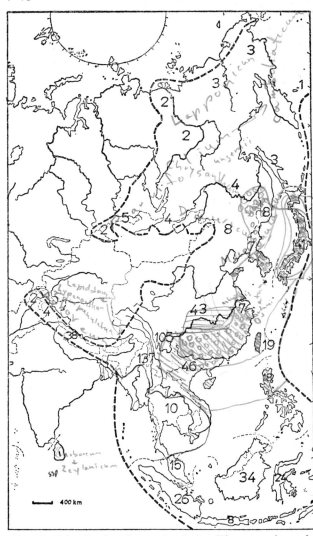

Fig. 2. Rhododendrons in Asia. The numbers in the diagram indicate how many varieties occur in each area. In the mountains of New Guinea (see Fig. 1) 157 varieties exist, the largest selection in the world; Australia has only one variety. The figures for China and the Himalayas have still to be confirmed. (After E. Jäger.)

The rest of Asia

Although no other region can compete with south-west China in richness of varieties of rhododendrons, and this despite the total lack of deciduous types, their number tails off rapidly towards the north. Northern China has a markedly cooler climate, which means that only a few evergreen varieties are to be found there. But, if we include Japan here, no less than fifty or sixty deciduous types grow in this part of the world. Taken on its own, Japan has ten evergreen varieties, of which the following are worthy of mention: *R. makinoi*, *R. metternichii* and particularly that variety so much under discussion at present, *R. yakusimamum*, which comes from Yakusima, the southernmost island of Japan. Among interesting azaleas which have long since become established in Europe are *R. albrechtii*, *R. reticulatum*, *R. pentaphyllum* and others, not forgetting *R. obtusum*, together with the innumerable garden varieties.

In Korea there are only three azaleas and four evergreen varieties. In Siberia we find *R. dauricum*, which during mild winters flowers in Britain as early as January. The two northernmost Asiatic varieties, *R. camtschaticum* and *R. parvifolium*, overstep their boundaries and reach right into Alaska.

Europe–Caucasus–Asia Minor

With regard to richness of variety, we should really place New Guinea and Malaysia next on the list. Despite the great interest of the plants to be found here, this area is so far removed from the scope of the ordinary rhododendron grower that we are leaving it until last.

In the far North *R. lapponicum* is very much at home. It is a tiny plant hardly bigger than 10 cm./4 in. in height. Strangely enough, it is found in two widely separated areas of Scandinavia: in southern Norway, on the highest peaks of the Dovrefjell and the Johinheimen, and in northern Norway, in an area reaching from about the 66th degree of latitude towards West Finnmark on the Norwegian and Swedish borders. This variety also occurs in Iceland, Spitzbergen, Novaya Zemlya, Greenland and in the north-eastern corner of North America. Botanically, the variety is very important, for the series *R. lapponicus*, to which many of the most beautiful low-growing types belong, is based on this modest little plant which, unfortunately, lives only a short while and presents the gardener with nothing but problems (Fig. 28).

R. ferrugineum, the rust-red alpine rose, known as 'almenrausche' to the Swiss mountain dwellers, and *R. hirsutum*, known colloquially as 'steinrose', are the two Alpine varieties. The first named occurs on the primitive rock of the maritime Alps and across to Carinthia and Lower Austria, and deeper in the Pyrenees in the Jura, the Appenines and in Illyria, particularly in altitudes around 1,500–2,000 m./4,500–6,000 ft. The second type lives on weathered limestone ground, together with *Erica carnea* and dwarf pines in the middle and eastern Alps of Tara and Illyria. Isolated growths in other districts can be ignored here (Figs. 19 and 22).

Between these two areas, which overlap to a certain extent, there is also found a natural hybrid, *R. intermedium*; this either resembles one or other 'parent' or is a balance between the two.

In the Carpathians, the Transsylvanian Alps and in north Bulgaria grow the variety *R. kotschyi* at altitudes of between 2,000–2,300 m./6,000–6,900 ft. It is similar to *R. ferrugineum* (Fig. 26).

R. ponticum, a large-leafed, evergreen strain which can grow as high as 5 m./15 ft. and which is already very much at home in our gardens —in England it is so prolific it is very nearly a weed—is in fact Asiatic rather than European. It originates from the south slopes of the Caucasus, on the shores of the Black Sea. On the Iberian peninsula it is replaced by a variety differing from it only in relatively minor respects. This is *R. ponticum* var. *baeticum* which grows in a few parts of Portugal and in southern Spain, usually in places over 700 m./2,100 ft. high (Fig. 3).

In the mountains of the Caucasus, chiefly on the Asiatic side at a height of about 3,000 m./9,000 ft. occur the white- or pink-flowered *R. caucasicum* and also *R. smirnowii* with its thick white downy shoots (Fig. 4).

Fig. 3. Distribution area of Rhododendron ponticum (wide lines and black dots) and R. ungernii (fine lines); among R. ungernii are found R. smirnowii (not marked here). Varieties of R. ponticum in Spain and Portugal are often listed as a separate type R. baeticum (Boiss. & Reut.); the same applies to the variety found in the Lebanon, var. brachycarpum Boiss. (After E. Jäger.)

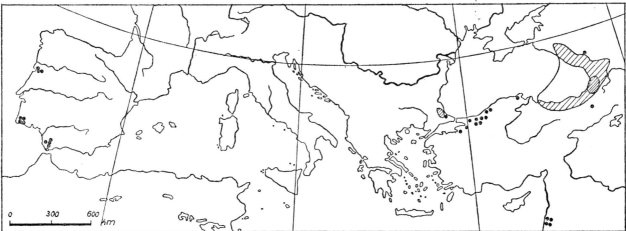

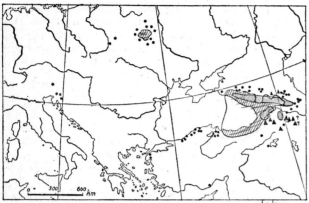

Fig. 4. Distribution area of Rhododendron luteum *(wide lines and dots) and* R. caucasicum *(fine line and triangles). (After E. Jäger.)*

Fig. 5. Distribution of the rhododendron in North America. Figures refer to the number of varieties to be found. Only in the Allegheny Mountains do giant groups occur, but these are relatively few in number. (After E. Jäger.)

The last European variety to be mentioned is an azalea, *R. luteum*, better known under the now no longer valid name *Azalea pontica*. This comes from Eastern Europe, particularly from the northern slopes of the Caucasus, where it follows the Georgian highway to a height of 100 m./300 ft. and then ends. There, too, the watershed marks the boundary between the two continents. (The Russians have set up boundary stones here which are marked 'Europe' on the north side and 'Asia' on the south.) Examples of *R. luteum* are found here either individually or in large groups, particularly in woods, which on warm days are filled with their scent and colour.

North America

We have already seen that the United States boast hardly twenty wild varieties of rhododendrons and only four deciduous strains. In South America there are none at all! There, the rhododendron family is supplanted by around thirty types of 'Andean roses'—*Bejaria* (formerly *Befaria*). Its northernmost equivalent, *Bejaria racemosa*, forms a link between the pine groves of Georgia and Florida and the other examples of this genus (Fig. 5).

It would be a very great mistake to assume a scarcity of rhododendrons in America merely because there are not many different varieties. On the contrary. As usual, Rhododendrons grow in the mountains, but also on the coastal plains. They stretch right across the wooded chain of Appalachian Mountains which reach from the state of Alabama right up to Newfoundland in the north, comprising a territory almost 2,600 m./7,800 ft. long and 300–400 m./900–1,200 ft. wide. National parks have been made out of the most scenically beautiful areas, among which is Great Smoky Mountains National Park. Here the evergreen *R. catawbiense* and *R. maximum* grow in gigantic clumps on the moist gorges and the hilltops or along the river banks.

Far more impressive than these evergreen varieties, however, are the deciduous azaleas, of which there are about fifteen varieties growing in the woods along this mountain range—which incidentally is twice as long as the European Alps. These are particularly splendid in the Shenandoah National Park in West Virginia. What's more, the two parks I have named are joined by a motorway 700 km./420 mls. long. The chief varieties found here are *R. roseum*, *R. nudiflorum*, *R. arborescens* and *R. viscosum*. Further to the south, in the states of Georgia, Tennessee and Alabama, we find *R. atlanticum*, *R. speciosum* and *R. prunifolium*, while the southern part of the continent—from Florida to Texas—is the domain of *R. canescens*, and also of *R. autumnum* and *R. serrulatum*.

In the Pacific area of North America there is one further type of azalea, *R. occidentale*, stretching from Oregon to Southern California. In this area too are huge impenetrable masses of *R. albiflorum* (Fig. 14) occurring as undergrowth in the coniferous forests of the northern mountain slopes from British Columbia to Oregon. Finally, we must not forget *R. canadiense*, the northernmost variety, which thrives on cold marshes and moors.

Malaysia and Australia

In the rain forests of southern China there are already several types of rhododendrons growing epiphytally. They have adapted themselves so that they can survive on the small amount of humus available

COLOUR PLATE 2

Rhododendron hybrids

1 'Concinn' R
2 'Pink Pearl'
3 'Elizabeth'
4 'Seville' DAZ
5 'Honeysuckle' DAZ
6 'Tangerine'

1

2

3

4

5

6

in the fork of a tree, and they are able to draw the greatest possible quantity of moisture from the air.

The further we travel south towards Malaysia, the moister and warmer the climate becomes. It is only since the last world war that various botanical expeditions have explored this and brought back living plants which are now growing in nurseries in Holland, Britain and North America, and which will one day be more widely cultivated. Although we cannot here describe the many shapes and colours which they show in their natural state, do not forget that one of our favourite varieties, R. 'Pink Pearl' (Colour Plate 2, 2), has Javanese forefathers.

Among the 300 or so varieties natural to Malaysia there is R. *leucogigas*, the variety with the largest flowers of the whole family.

Australia has only one variety, R. *lochae*.

Summary

We have seen that rhododendrons occur everywhere in areas with plenty of rain or of moisture in the atmosphere during their flowering span. This means either mountains, hills or coastal plains. When growing rhododendrons in the garden we must take care to preserve their natural conditions as far as possible. With the tropical varieties this is possible only by greenhouse cultivation.

Most of the Japanese varieties are hardy; of the Chinese varieties, only those from the high mountain regions last through European winters.

Today, Britain is the country furthest advanced in the raising of wild garden varieties of rhododendrons. Even if we cannot all travel to China—to Setschuan or Yunnan—we can at least see the great number of interesting specimens to be found in our own country, and derive pleasure from them. (See list of show gardens, page 49.)

CULTURAL HISTORY

The story of the cultivation of rhododendrons is already very old. Around fifty million years have elapsed since the first emergence of the plant. Although the range of shape and of colour is particularly rich in rhododendrons, it does not satisfy mankind. So he has taken it upon himself to make everything just that little bit better. When you think that in the space of less than 150 years about 200 gardeners and enthusiasts, particularly in Britain, Holland, Belgium, Germany, the United States and Japan, have put about 10,000 new varieties—the results of their work of hybridization—into circulation, the mind boggles at the tremendous amount of work involved. What's more, their work is just the beginning: far more is yet to come.

Many readers will ask why all this work of cultivation is necessary when there are already something like 1,000 wild varieties, which must surely supply every demand. But the fact is that they do not. We must not forget that of these 1,000 varieties only a small proportion satisfies our aesthetic sense, or, in other words, look really good in our gardens. This accounts for perhaps 200 varieties. But even this number dwindles rapidly when we take away all those that will not grow in our climate without being improved in some way.

It would be useless trying to achieve the same breathtaking effects with the rhododendrons in our gardens as we see among the wild mountain varieties. British botanists and enthusiast-collectors first acquired a taste for rhododendrons when the glorious, large-flowered east Asian varieties were brought home—that was at the beginning of the nineteenth century—and when, almost fifty years later, *R. catawbiense* (Plate 3, *1*) reached Europe from North America. But this hardy American variety, which survived even European winters, unfortunately had lilac-coloured, rather small flowers, while the east Asiatic plants possessed much more beautiful gleaming red blooms.

None the less, one of the most beautiful varieties, *R. arboreum* (Colour Plate 1, *1*), was completely hardy when grown in the milder districts of Britain, and on the mild southern coast grew all the glorious, strongly scented varieties which Sir Joseph D. Hooker had brought back from Sikkim in the Himalayas between 1799 and 1851. So the early gardeners began to cross the hardy American varieties with the better colours and shapes of the east Asiatic varieties.

The history of the cultivation of rhododendrons can be traced back to its earliest origins without too much difficulty. But in view of the amount of literature on the subject, we will here limit ourselves to those growers and discoveries which are still important today.

The first hybrids

Until the year 1800 only about a dozen varieties were known. The first crossing took place in Britain in 1817. Dean William Herbert, in Spofforth, Yorkshire, crossed *R. maximum* with *R. viscosum* and produced an 'azaleodendron' which he named *R. hybridum*. The flowers were pink-edged and flecked with yellow, and scented. Exactly 100 years ago this variety was still being grown in the Methuen Nurseries in Edinburgh. The Rhododendron Register (1958) considers it doubtful whether this variety is identical to 'Odoratum', which appeared from the Thompson Nurseries before 1875 and was a cross between *R. nudiflorum* and *R. ponticum* and was also an azaleodendron. The story of the first crossing does not seem to be too clear, for F. Street (*Rhododendrons*, pages 8–11) is of another opinion. However, his views do not altogether tally with the Rhododendron Register.

Cultivation begins

During the first third of the nineteenth century around twenty further wild varieties of rhododendrons were introduced into Britain, among which were (1809) *R. catawbiense* from North America, *R. arboreum* from the Himalayas, *R. caucasicum* from the Caucasus and many others. Growers were now attempting to unite the great hardiness of *R. catawbiense* with the glorious colours of *R. arboreum*, and the results were thoroughly satisfactory.

J. R. Gowen, who is often erroneously listed as the Head Gardener of the first Earl of Caernarvon at Highclere in Hampshire, crossed *R. arboreum* with *R. catawbiense* and named the hybrid 'Altaclarense', which is a free translation of Highclere into Latin. This hybrid, which was named in 1831, distinguished itself by its strong growth, good foliage and dark red blooms; it remained in general cultivation for well over a hundred years, and is still to be found today in many parks and gardens. Incidentally, Dean William Herbert, whom we encountered earlier as the first rhododendron grower, was the second son of the Earl of Caernarvon, so he, too, presumably encouraged the work being done in his father's gardens.

Next I should like to mention those cultivators whose work did much to encourage the spread of rhododendrons in Europe. Interesting as it would be to trace the cultured history of both the natural

varieties and the work done on hybrids in each country, as well as discussing all the growers, it is impossible to deal adequately with the subject in a book this size. Therefore, only the most important gardeners will be listed. Anyone wishing to study the subject in greater depth should consult the relevant books already written on the subject.

The rhododendron growers

ARENDS, GEORG, Wuppertal-Ronsdorf, Germany

G. Arends was in the front line of shrub growers. He also improved many pot plants, for example, *Primula obconica*. From 1910 on he also crossed rhododendrons, particularly with *R. mucronatum*. He put several varieties on the market in 1926, under the name *Azalea arendsii*, and identifiable by numbers. Shortly afterwards the numbers were replaced by names—for which the names of the dams of southern Westphalia were chosen. He also crossed *R. oreodoxa* with hardy hybrids and produced 'Ronsdorfer' early flowering varieties which he later sold to the Böhlje nursery, with all rights. Two further groups of small-flowered Japanese azaleas, 'Aronensis' and 'Multiflora', were produced after the last war. Finally, *R. radistrotum* and improvements on *R. racemosum* are worth a mention.

CUNNINGHAM, JAMES, 1784–1850, Scotland

Crossed *R. arboreum*, *R. ponticum* and *R. maximum*; his most important hybrid is 'Cunningham's White', which came on to the market the year he died. He always kept the parent plants of his hybrids a secret, so that they can only be guessed at.

DAVIES, ISAAC, Nurseryman, Ormskirk, Lancs.

Mentioned only because he produced two hybrids still important today, namely *R. praecox* and, in 1879, the *Daviesii* range.

DE CONINCK, FRED, Ghent, Belgium

He was the first to cross *R. japonicum* with *R. molle* (horticulturally *Azalea mollis* × *sinensis*), but in 1890 he sold all his seedlings to M. Koster & Zonen of Boskoop in Holland. In 1892 they named the first eight seedlings and put them on the market. All these are still in general cultivation today: 'Hortulanus H. Witte', 'Hugo Koster', 'T. J. Seidel', 'Anthony Koster', 'Dr. Reichenbach', 'Frans van der Bom', 'Emil Liebig' and 'Nicolaas Beets'.

DEN OUDEN, H. & Zonen★, Boskoop, Holland

This firm occupied itself as much with the cultivation of new azaleas as with producing hardy red-flowered hybrids by crossing *R. catawbiense* hybrids with *R. arboreum* hybrids—particularly with 'Atrosanguineum'. Some of their best known crossings are: 'Dr. H. C. Dresselhuys' (1920), 'Prof. F. Bettex' and 'Mrs. P. den Ouden' (both 1925) and 'Dr. H. J. Lovink' (1929) as well as 'Dr. V. H. Rutgers'.

ENDTZ, L. J. & Co., Boskoop, Holland

This was one of the best-known nurseries to have been functioning since 1910. Their main achievement was their improvement of the colour of 'Pink Pearl'; moreover, this plant's hardiness was increased in order to make possible exports to the eastern states of America. For this, 'Pink Pearl' was crossed with 'Stanley Davies', 'John Walter', 'Doncaster', 'Charlie Waterer', 'Prometheus' and others. The following successes are worth mentioning; 'Prof. Hugo de

★ Zonen = Sons

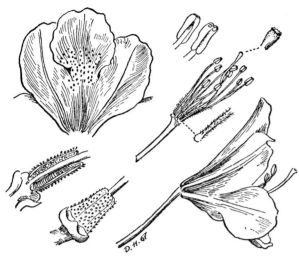

Fig. 6. Rhododendron catawbiense, *from North America. This variety is often used in crossing because of its great hardiness.*

Vries' (1913), 'Louis Pasteur' (1923), 'Souvenir de Dr. S. Endtz' (1927), 'Dr. Arnold W. Endtz' (1927), 'Annie E. Endtz' (1939); also 'Prof. H. Zaayer' and 'Antoon van Welie'. The variety 'G. Stresemann' was somewhat unnecessarily altered in 1946 to 'Hollandia'; 'Jan Dekens' was put on the market by Blaauw in 1940.

FLEISCHMANN, C., Wiesmoor, Germany

Crossed wild Japanese varieties with Kurume types and achieved cushion-shaped, particularly hardy, garden varieties of varying colours, which came on to the market in 1969. Was also concerned with the further development of the Exbury azaleas.

GABLE, Joseph B., Stewartstown, Penn., U.S.A.

A visit to the Hillier nurseries in Winchester (England) in 1918 spurred him on to his own research. He achieved many azaleas and evergreen hybrids which are extremely hardy, but which are as yet hardly known in Europe.

HOBBIE, Dietrich, Linswege, Germany

In 1937 he began crossing dwarf rhododendrons, in particular *R. williamsianum* and *R. forrestii* var. *repens*, with hardy garden hybrids (Plate 7, 4). In the meantime he achieved a large number of dwarf or medium-sized hybrids. Carried out further crossings with *R. yakusimanum, R. metternianum, R. wardii, R. puralbum*, and of wild varieties with garden hybrids. He sold some of his crossing to the Lefeber nurseries in Boskoop, who later put them on the market. Among his most successful rearings are: 'Elisabeth Hobbie' (1958), 'Baden-Baden' (1956), 'Scarlet Wonder' (1960), 'Gertrud Schäle' (1951), 'Jewel' (1960) (Colour Plate 5).

KOSTER, M., & Zonen, Boskoop, Holland

This firm has been crossing rhododendrons regularly since around 1880. At about this time were crossed *R. japonicum × molle* (then known as *A. mollis × sinensis*), resulting in what is now known as *R. kosterianum*. A series of plants was taken over from de Coninck (see entry under that name). From 1900 onwards hybrids were

achieved from *R. occidentale*; in 1930 came hybrids from *R. catawbiense × griersonianum*. Further work was done with hybrids derived from *R. caucasicum* and *R. griffithianum* as well as with 'George Hardy' and 'Combe Royal'. Among the most important hybrids worthy of mention are: 'Mme de Bruin' (1904), 'America' (1904), 'Nova Zembla' (1904), 'Peter Koster' (1909), 'Mrs. Charles E. Pearson' (1909), 'Mrs. Lindsay Smith' (1910), 'Hugh Koster' (1909), 'Attraction' (1915), 'Burgemeester Aarts' (1915), 'Mrs. G. W. Leak' (1916), 'Mrs. Helen Koster' (1916), 'Adriaan Koster' (1920), 'Betty Wormald' (1922), 'Marinus Koster' (1937), 'Harvest Moon' (1948) and many others.

LEE & KENNEDY, Nurserymen, Hammersmith, London

This nursery was the first to bring *R. luteum* on to the British market. They were rearing the *R. catawbiense*-hybrid 'Lee's Dark Purple' as early as 1851.

LIEBIG, Ludwig Leopald, Dresden, Germany, 1801–72

None of his evergreen hybrids is cultivated today. The best known was his *R. campanulatum*-hybrid 'Viola'.

MANGLES, H. J., Valewood, Haslemere, Surrey, 1832–82

After his death his sister Clara carried on his work for a time. He crossed *R. griffithianum* with *R. ponticum* (not, as is often wrongly maintained, with 'Album Elegans'); also *R. catawbiense × griffithianum* (='Manglesii'). His finest achievement is 'Loder's White', said to be from *R. arboreum* var. *album × griffithianum* (1911).

MORTIER, P., a baker from Ghent, Belgium

An amateur who crossed *R. luteum* with *R. arborescens, R. calendulaceum, R. nudiflorum, R. speciosum* and *R. viscosum* between the

Fig. 7. Rhododendron williamsianum, *when used as a crossing partner has resulted in many half-size, almost round-shaped descendants, which are especially suitable for the small garden.*

years 1804 and 1834. His results formed the basis of what was later known as the 'hardy Ghent hybrids'. In 1834 he sold all his seedlings to LOUIS VERSCHAFFELT, who assiduously carried the work further.

MÜLLER, BASTID, Stuttgart, Germany

The rearer of the so called 'Wilhelma-Rhododendron', which he derived from 'Alstroemerioides' (Standish & Noble, before 1860), together with around forty varieties in the years 1874–80. These were not all hardy. Most were a fine colour pink and heavily spotted. Presumably none are in cultivation now.

PARSONS, SAMUEL B., Flushing, Long Island, U.S.A.

The first American grower, he began in 1870. Today it is not known for certain whether his results were achieved by accidental crossing. Further, it would appear that in many cases he merely introduced varieties produced by Waterer into the States. One or two of his hybrids are still cultivated today, for example, 'Parsons Grandiflorum' and 'Parsons Gloriosum'.

PAUL, GEORGE & SONS, Cheshunt, Herts.

The first to cultivate *R. fortunei*. Two of his most important hybrids are 'Duke of York' (1894, *fortunei* × 'Scipio') and 'Essex Scarlet' (1899, *fortunei* × *catawbiense*).

ROTHSCHILD, LIONEL DE, d. 1942, followed by his son, Edmund, Exbury House, near Southampton

Occupied from 1923 onwards with cultivation of *R. arboreum*, *R. calophytum* and many other species not hardy in the colder parts of Europe. Thus, most of his evergreen hybrids have never been introduced on to the Continent. Took over from WATERER (see entry) a number of Knap Hill azaleas, which he further improved and put on to the market as 'Exbury' azaleas. The register of all his plants and a detailed account of his life's work by P. Barber was published in 1967.

SCHULTZ, OTTO, Berlin, Germany

Head gardener of the State Porcelain Works, he grew rhododendrons in greenhouses, and the plants served as models for the porcelain designs. He obtained *R. griffithianum* plants from Sir Joseph Hooker at Kew, and crossed these with hardy hybrids (for example, 'Prince Camille de Rohan' and others). In 1896 he sold 23 seedlings, most of which had already bloomed, to C. B. van Nes in Boskoop. There it was discovered that the seedlings were not hardy. Of these, only twelve were later named and put on the market, but many of these survive only in the milder parts of Europe. The best of them was the one named 'Mrs. A. M. Williams' in 1896. As recently as 1954 this variety received a horticultural award in Britain.

SEIDEL, JACOB, Dresden, Germany, 1789–1860

Began cultivation in 1822 with *R. arboreum*.—SEIDEL, T. J. H., 1833–1896.—SEIDEL, T. J. RUDOLF, 1861–1918.—SEIDEL, T. J. HERMANN. In this nursery's catalogue for 1859 were to be found over 200 English hybrid varieties, but they soon began their own work of rearing. In 1888 the first varieties hardy enough to stand up to a German winter became available, among which were: 'Cunningham's White', 'Everestianum', 'Jewess', 'Jacob Seidel', 'Gabriele Liebig', 'Hélène Schiffner', 'Queen Carola', 'Karl Mette' and others. As a grower, RUDOLF SEIDEL is the most important member of this family: he named over 600 individual hybrids. In particular, he crossed species with descendants of *R. catawbiense* × *arboreum* and *R. catawbiense* × *caucasicum*, and later also with *R. smirnowii*. His

Fig. 8. Rhododendron griersonianum *blooms a glorious red, but is very sensitive to frost. Passes on its lovely colour when crossed.*

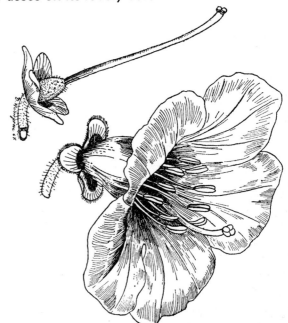

Fig. 9. Rhododendron edgeworthii *is also very useful for crossing. Its white flowers are strongly scented, but unfortunately it is not hardy.*

aims were: great profusion of blooms and of buds, large, dense clusters of flowers, clear, lasting colours, and a long, late flowering period. Further, he also tried to achieve: good growth, strong roots, dark, firm foliage and short-stemmed leaves, and absolute hardiness in winter. From 1899 onwards he began prefixing new species with a different letter of the alphabet each year: 1902 'Daisy', 'Darius', 'Delila', 'Dietrich', 'Donar'; 1903 'Ella', 'Erna', and so on. Very few of the Seidel varieties are still being grown today.

SHAMMARELLO, A. M. Euclid, Ohio, U.S.A.

Began cultivating in 1940. Aim: dwarf, hardy plants in pink and in red. To achieve this he crossed 'Cunningham's White' and 'Jacksonii', among others, with red hybrids. His results are hardly known in Europe.

SLOCOCK, W. C., Ltd, Nurseries in Woking, Surrey

Work of cultivation did not begin until after 1920, with the production of beautiful wild varieties, such as *R. campylocarpum*, *R. dichroanthum*, *R. discolor*, *R. fortunei*, *R. wightii* and so on. Although these varieties survive in a temperate climate, they are more or less susceptible to the frosts in European countries. The most important varieties are: 'Goldsworth Yellow' (1925), 'Mrs. W. C. Slocock' (1929), 'Dairymaid' (1930), 'Faggetter's Favourite' (1933), 'Blue Ensign' (1934), 'Unique' (1934), 'Souvenir of W. C. Slocock' (1935), 'China' (1936), 'Goldsworth Orange' (1938), 'Butterfly' (1940), 'Lavender Girl' (1950) and so on.

STANDISH, JOHN & NOBLE, CHARLES; 1847–57 Windlesham, Surrey (now The Sunningdale Nurseries); in 1854 they split up and Standish began a new firm in Ascot

Both crossed plants with *R. catawbiense*, *R. arboreum* and *R. maximum*. Only a few of the resulting plants are still available today: 'The Bride' (St. & N. before 1850), 'Ascot Brilliant' (St. before 1861), 'Cynthia (St. & N. before 1870), 'The Queen' (N. before 1871) and 'Prometheus' (N.).

VAN HOUTTE, LOUIS, Ghent, Belgium

Particularly concerned with the development of the Ghent azaleas.

VAN NES, C. B., & ZONEN (now J. Blaauw & Co) in Boskoop, Holland

In 1910 he brought back from the garden of the Emperor's Palace in Kyoto, Japan, the two Kurume varieties, 'Hinomayo' and 'Benigiri'. At that time 'Wilson's Fifty' were completely unknown in Europe, and they were not introduced into the United States until 1919. The greatest success of this firm was the plant 'Britannia' (1912); later there followed the *R. griffithianum*-hybrids 'Queen Wilhelmina' (1896), 'Graf Zeppelin', 'C. B. van Nes', 'Mrs. W. H. Gaze' (before 1922), 'Unknown Warrior' (1922), 'Douglas McEwan' (before 1922), 'Countess of Athlone' (1923), 'Armistice Day' (1930), 'Earl of Athlone' (1933), 'Jean Marie Montague'. This firm also crossed the *R. fortunei*-hybrid 'Sir Charles Butler' with 'White Pearl', and produced three new specimens in 1925 under the names: 'Admiral Piet Hein', 'Van Nes Sensation' and 'Mrs. A. T. de la Mare'.

VAN NES, VUYK, Boskoop, Holland

Began his work of cultivation while still employed by the firm Koster & Co, around 1921. Was particularly concerned with improving Japanese azaleas. His aims were thick growth, large blooms, good weather resistance. In 1939 he put his first nine varieties on to the market; among which were: 'Johann Sebastian Bach', 'Beethoven', 'Mozart' and 'Palestrina'. He named his plants 'Vuykiana' types. Other widely grown types are 'Chopin' (1954), 'Purple Triumph' (1951), 'Sibelius' (1931), and above all the two types 'Vuyk's Rosyred' and 'Vuyk's Scarlet', both put out in 1954.

VERSCHAFFELT, JEAN, 1811–84, Ghent

Reared the *R. caucasicum*-hybrid 'Prince Camille de Rohan' and first put it on the market in 1865.

VERSCHAFFELT, LOUIS, Royghem, near Ghent, Belgium

Purchased the Ghent azaleas from MORTIER and continued working on them after 1834.

VUYLSTEKE, CHARLES, Ghent

Went to Loochristi in 1882, where he reared Indian azaleas, orchids and *R. mollis*-azaleas; did a roaring trade in Britain. In 1888 he placed his entire range of double hardy azaleas on the market, under the name 'Rustica' types (=*R. mixtum*). In fact, he was only responsible for distributing these, for the grower was LOUIS DE SMET from St. Amandsberg, who had achieved these plants by crossing double Ghent azaleas with *R. japonicum*. Many of these are still being grown today, for example, 'Aida', 'Norma', 'Freya' and so on.

WATERER

Many plants carry the name WATERER, with the christian names Anthony, Michael and Gomer. The explanation is somewhat complicated. The firm of Waterer had two branches, of which one was in Knap Hill—the original branch—and the other was in Bagshot. Complications arise from the fact that in Knap Hill there were two Michaels, and in Bagshot there were two Johns. There then followed two Anthonys in Knap Hill, and after the Johns in Bagshot came a Gomer, who eventually returned to Knap Hill. The two firms still exist today, under the names of J. Waterer, Sons and Crisp, in Twyford, Berks. and Bagshot, Surrey, and The Knap Hill Nursery Ltd., Knap Hill, Woking, Surrey.

The WATERERS appear to have begun their work of crossing in 1830 or thereabouts. They worked chiefly with *R. arboreum*, *R. caucasicum*, *R. catawbiense*, *R. fortunei*, *R. griffithianum*, *R. metternichii*, *R. maximum*, *R. smirnowii* and *R. ponticum*. Many of the plants they produced are still being grown today, and are as important and as competitive as they ever were: 'Nobleanum' (1835), 'Mme Carvalho' (1866), 'Mrs. R. S. Holford' (1866), 'Sappho' (before 1867), 'James Marshall Brooks' (before 1870), 'Mrs. Charles S. Sargent' (1888), 'Michael Waterer' (before 1894), 'Pink Pearl' (1897), 'Gomer Waterer' (before 1900), 'Mrs. E. C. Stirling' (1906), 'Alice' (1910), 'Mother of Pearl' (1925).

These few alone would be sufficient to ensure for the Waterers a lasting fame as rhododendron growers, but the name of one of their nurseries is firmly linked with what are now called the Knap Hill azaleas. Work on these has continued without interruption for very nearly 100 years. It would take up too much room to describe the entire cultivation history of these plants at this stage. Briefly, the story began with a desire to produce large-bloomed, strongly growing azaleas, preferably multiflowered, scented and showing new colours. This was achieved through controlled crossing of *R. viscosepalum*, *R. viscosum*, *R. molle*, *R. calendulaceum*, *R. japonicum*, *R. arborescens* and *R. occidentale*. The seedlings were carefully selected

Cultural history

and crossed again, until a whole array of suitable rootstocks were available. In 1925 these were announced and very well received. As a result of this, vegetative propagation was begun in order to sell the resulting plants. A selection of seedlings was sold to the Goldsworth Nursery (W. C. Slocock) and were later put on the market by this firm. But the development of these azaleas was also carried further by Lionel de Rothschild (see entry).

Hybrids from *R. catawbiense* and *R. caucasicum*

Finally, here is a list, in chronological order, of the hybrids derived from *R. catawbiense* and *R. caucasicum*.

The last column is based on information contained in the *Rhododendron Handoook II*, which is known as the Stud Book. In this are found the most important crossings only. These two particular wild varieties have been selected as an example because they are extraordinarily hardy and in most cases (though unfortunately not in all cases) they have passed on their weather resistance to the strains derived from them.

Anyone browsing through *Rhododendron Handoook II* would be forgiven for thinking that the variety *R. catawbiense*, which is so important to us today, was of little use to the growers, for there are only eight entries under *R. catawbiense* in the book. Yet nothing would be further from the truth. If we just leaf through the *International Rhododendron Register* for a moment we find that *R. catawbiense* is mentioned almost 100 times as a 'crossing partner'. This tells us that either the wild variety itself or else one of its descendants, 'Grandiflorum' or 'Boursault', was employed. And if you added to

List of varieties most often used for crossing purposes

The number immediately following the name of the variety refers to the known different sorts available in 1964.

H = hardy in central Europe.

Name		Series/subseries	Home	Colour	Hardiness
R. griersonianum	152	Grierson	Yunnan, North Burma	Scarlet	∧∧∧
R. griffithianum	92	Fortunei/Griffithianum	Sikkim, Bhutan	White	∧∧∧
R. thomsonii	72	Thomsonii	Sikkim, Bhutan	Red	∧∧∧
R. fortunei	67	Fortunei	Chekiang	Pinkish white	∧–∧∧
R. discolor	67	Fortunei	Setschuan, Hupeh	White-pink	H–∧
R. arboreum	59	Arboreum	Himalaya, Ceylon	Red	∧∧∧
R. campylocarpum	58	Thomsonii/Campylocarpum	Nepal, Tibet	Clear yellow	∧∧
R. dichroanthum	55	Neriiflorum/Sanguineum	Yunnan	Salmon pink	∧–∧∧
R. williamsianum	48	Thomsonii/Williamsianum	Setschuan	Pale pink	H–∧
R. haematodes	41	Neriiflorum/Haematodes	Yunnan	Carmine pink	∧
R. forrestii repens	41	Neriiflorum/Forrestii	Tibet	Scarlet	H
R. elliottii	40	Irroratum/Parishii	Nabuoyr (Nagaland)	Scarlet	∧∧∧
R. wardii	39	Thomsonii/Souliei	Yunnan, Setschuan, Tibet	Yellow	H–∧
R. eriogynum	37	Irroratum/Parishii	Yunnan	Scarlet	∧∧∧
R. cinnabarinum roylei R	30	Cinnabarinum	Tibet	Carmine	∧∧∧
R. souliei	29	Thomsoni/Souliei	Setschuan, Tibet	White-pink	H–∧
R. neriiflorum	26	Neriiflorum	Yunnan, Tibet	Scarlet	∧∧∧
R. calophytum	24	Fortunei/Calophytum	Setschuan	Pinkish white	H–∧∧
R. auriculatum	23	Auriculatum	Hupeh	White	∧∧∧
R. augustinii R	23	Triflorum/Augustinii	Hupeh, Setschuan, Tibet	Blue to lilac	H–∧∧∧
R. decorum	22	Fortunei	Yunnan, Setschuan	Light pink	H–∧∧
R. barbatum	19	Barbatum	Himalayas	Scarlet	∧∧∧
R. ciliatum R	19	Maddenii/Ciliicalyx	Himalayas	White-pink	∧∧∧
R. moupinense R	15	Moupinense	Setschuan	White-pink	∧
R. racemosum R	14	Scabrifolium	Yunnan, Setschuan	White-pink	∧∧∧
R. sutchuenense	13	Fortunei/Davidii	Setschuan–Hupeh	Pinkish white	H–∧∧
R. venator	13	Irroratum/Parishii	Tibet	Scarlet	∧∧∧
R. lutescens R	12	Triflorum	Setschuan, Yunnan	Pale yellow	H–∧∧
R. concatenans R	11	Cinnabarinum	Tibet	Orange-copper	∧∧–∧∧∧
R. Orbiculare	11	Fortunei/Orbiculare	Setschuan	Carmine pink	∧–∧∧
R. scyphocalyx	10	Neriiflorum/Sanguineum	North Burma	Orange-copper	∧∧–∧∧∧
R. smirnowii	13	Ponticum/Caucasicum	Caucasus	Pink	H
R. ponticum	7	Ponticum	Near East	Lilac	H–∧
R. yakusimanum	4	Ponticum/Caucasicum	Japan	White	H

this the crossings carried out with *R. catawbiense*-hybrids the number would grow considerably.

Period	Types	Grower
1831	1	RUSSELL, Windlesham, Britain (Russellianum.)
Around 1846	1	FRANCOISI, Ghent, Belgium ('Fastuosum')
1850–51	4	H. WATERER, England ('Atrosanguineum', etc).
1849	1	BERTIN, France
	1	LOUIS VAN HOUTTE, Belgium
1850–70	3	STANDISH & NOBEL, England
1850–1909	29	A. WATERER, Britain
1860–1900	6	J. WATERER, Britain
1870–80	15	PARSONS, U.S.A. ('Parsons Grandiflorum', etc).
1903–29	25	SEIDEL, Germany
1925–30	8	H. DEN OUDEN, Boskoop
Around 1930	5	W. E. STOKES, Butler, U.S.A.
1930–55	5	J. B. GABLE, U.S.A.
Since 1940	8	A. M. A. SHAMMARELLO, U.S.A.
?	2	L. J. ENDTZ & Co., Boskoop, Holland
1922	1	Miss Clara Mangles, Britain

This adds up to almost 100 different types, of which many are of particular importance to Europe, including the northern and east European countries.

A glance at the most important R. caucasicum hybrids

Crossed with	Result	Grower and year
R. arboreum	'Nobleanum'	A. Waterer, 1835
'Nobleanum'	'Jacksonii'	Herbert, 1835
R. arboreum	'Pulcherrimum'	J. Waterer, 1835
R. arboreum	'Venustum'	W. Smith, 1850 (?)
R. arboreum album (Mutation?)	'Cunningham's White'	Cunningham, 1850
	'Cunningham's Sulphur'	Cunningham, 1850 (?)
Unknown	'Prince Camille de Rohan'	Verschaffelt, 1865
Hardy hybrid	'Chevalier Felix de Sauvage'	Sauvage, 1870
R. caucasicum album (back crossing)	'The Bride'	Standish & Noble, 1871
Unknown	'Rosamundi'	Standish & Noble
R. griffithianum	'Dr. Stocker'	North, 1900
R. fortunei	'Caubut'	Magor, 1916
R. catawbiense	'Stanwellianum'	Methven, 1917
'Dr. Stocker' × *R. campylocarpum*	'Damaris'	Magor, 1918
R. campylocarpum	'Goldsworth Yellow'	Slocock, 1925
R. arboreum	'Nobleanum Lamellen'	Magor, 1921
'Dr. Stocker' × *R. lacteum*	'Mariloo'	Rothschild, 1941
'Kewense'	'Mrs. Arthur Fawcus'	Knap Hill, 1946
Unknown	'Melpomene'	Unknown
R. smirnowii	'Elisabetae'	Unknown

Despite the profusion of glorious varieties available, there is no getting away from the fact that still—and probably for many years to come, in Europe as well as in North America—the market is completely governed by hardy hybrids, even in areas where they are not essential. Luckily, the varieties 'Pink Pearl', 'Britannia', etc., belong to these hardy types. In Germany, thanks to the untiring efforts of Dietrich Hobbie, the dwarf *R. repens* and *R. williamsianum* hybrids can be added to these. To a large extent, German nurseries base their selection work on advice given by the Deutsche Rhododendron Gesellschaft. Not all the 'hardy' varieties grown in Germany survive in the colder northern States of America. For this reason, Dutch and German nurseries, who export to North America as well as to the colder parts of middle and northern Europe, are forced to cultivate hardy hybrids which will survive all weathers. This is the main reason why certain varieties are not grown in Germany. Continentals determined to obtain different varieties must travel to Britain to obtain them.

GROWING
RHODODENDRONS

Perhaps the foregoing account of success in the growing of rhododendrons has inspired the reader to try his hand himself. And why shouldn't he? The number of active rhododendron growers in the world is very small. Most of them live in Britain, and these are mainly amateurs. They do their work of crossing for the pleasure of it, without expecting any great financial rewards. This aspect must not be confused with the aims which professional growers set themselves. These people have to lay out a large amount of money in order to try out all possible combinations, and they must have a definite idea of the sort of plant they wish to achieve. This obviously entails a detailed study of all the characteristics of the plants to be crossed.

Here are a few tips, so that your decision to grow your own rhododendrons will not be reversed by a few small snags:

Good results are more likely to be obtained by crossing plants of related types.

Bad results are obtained when extremely different plants are crossed together, so don't try crossing tree rhododendrons with dwarf varieties, small-flowered plants with large-flowered ones, etc., just to find out what happens.

Don't cross long-pistilled varieties with short-pistilled types, because the pollen tube (utricle) of the short-pistilled varieties is not capable of growing through longer pistils than those occurring in its own variety.

If you have a greenhouse at your disposal it is advisable to carry our crossings there in order to avoid any damage or disturbance by the weather.

If you have to work in the open, choose a sheltered corner and surround it with wire netting in order to keep intruders out.

Now we can begin to describe the work of crossing. We have already decided what it is we want to achieve, and all we now have to do is wait until the partners are ready for the 'marriage'. The crossing is done in the following way:

Before the flower buds on the mother plants are open, say one or two days earlier, they are 'castrated'. This sounds horrific, but in fact it doesn't hurt the plants at all. It merely means that, using a pair of pincers, you removed the closed stamens, making sure the stigma is not damaged. Then, take a sufficiently large polythene bag, and fasten it over the stem so as to protect the stigma from pollination.

As soon as the stigma has secreted a special fluid, which makes it shiny and sticky—this is easily visible through the polythene bag—the great moment has come. We now take newly grown stamens from the father plant and rub them several times up and down with a hair grip, so that the pollen sticks to the pin. Then transfer the pollen on to the stigma of the mother plant. And that's all there is to it.

All these steps must be carried out very carefully, preferably on a sunny morning; careless work leads to failure, and you then have to wait until the following year. Or else, the bad work does not become apparent until the resulting seedlings bloom. In this case the whole thing was just a waste of time. Remember that care, thought and great patience are necessary for this type of work.

The pollinated bloom is then given a tag bearing a number, and this, of course, is supplemented by detailed notes in your crossings notebook, including date, name of mother plant, pollen donor, etc.

As soon as the flower has gone over, and the pistil begins to go brown at the tips, the plastic bag can be removed. The calyx now begins to develop. Its size depends on the variety and type, and can vary considerably, as can the tiny seeds, which are mostly brown. The calyx capsule can hold several thousand fertile seeds, and these ripen approximately six months after pollination. In the greenhouse the process is slightly quicker.

When the capsules are dry and just about to burst open, pick them off, store them in individual containers (glasses will do) and let them open without allowing their tiny seeds to escape. For best results, shake gently and separate the seeds from the capsule; you then immediately have individual seeds which will need no more attention. They should now be stored in a dry place.

March–April is the time to sow the seeds, and this is done in exactly the same way as any other rhododendron seeds are sown. However, since there will be only a very small quantity of seeds, these are planted in normal pots, and not in seed trays, where they will tend to dry out much too quickly. A sandy, peaty soil which has not dried out is best for the seeds. If this is not available, sandy loamy leaf-mould will do instead. Fill the pots up to within 1 cm./ ⅜ in. of the top and press the earth well down with the bottom of another pot so that the seed bed is nice and smooth. Then sprinkle the seeds in, not too close together. Now sieve a very fine layer of sand over the seeds and water the pots gently. Germination takes place after three or four weeks, although it can take twice as long, since the time taken varies considerably from one type to another. After a time prick out the seedlings into larger pots. It is not possible to say exactly when this will be necessary, but in any case it will be when the seedlings have hardened leaves and a minute bud at the tip of the stem.

Then you just have to wait patiently for about six years to see whether your efforts have been successful.

An expert in grafting techniques, and one who, moreover, owns a hothouse, can shorten the time of waiting by up to two years.

This is how a graft is carried out: young, strong-growing seedlings of the same species are needed. As soon as the young wild seedlings are large enough to handle (when they have four leaves) cut them at a height of about 2 cm./¾ in. from the ground. Then cut a long thin piece out of the stock, and cut a piece from the scion of the plant on to which it is to be grafted. Lay the two parts together so that the cambium of each comes into contact with the other. Then fasten the joint with one or two plastic clips (they look like tiny washing pegs) and transfer the plant to the propagating bed in the greenhouse. If the bed is covered, development should be fast and active.

Anyone who has not done the work of grafting before, or who does not have the necessary equipment available, is advised not to try these experiments, as he will probably lose the seedlings.

Rhododendrons in the garden

Although this book is dedicated to rhododendron enthusiasts, I should like to state here and now that anybody can grow these plants. The following section is intended to make clear any details which were not fully explained in previous pages.

The rhododendron family is so large and so full of variety that it is understandable if some enthusiasts, particularly those with small gardens, wish to grow nothing else but. This is all very well for the specialist, who looks upon his garden as an area of study, but it will not do for the man who sees his garden as a source of lasting joy and creativity.

After all, you must realize that a garden planted with nothing but rhododendrons will eventually become monotonous, even when plenty of azaleas are added, to bring their glorious autumn colours to view. The differences in growth, in the shape and the colour of leaves and of flowers do not seem nearly so pronounced when seen in large numbers. In any case, it is quite impossible for us to reproduce the vast landscapes in which the wild varieties of rhododendrons occur. Our best bet is to create a well-lit grove in which the rhododrendrons are distributed, accompanied by the sort of plants which suit them. Of course, it is not essential to select only those plants which grow naturally alongside rhododendrons. The final choice should also be an aesthetic one. After all, this is your garden we are discussing, and you are the one to whom it should give pleasure.

There are, however, a few useful hints to ponder over before the work of planting begins. First of all, prop the rhododendron up temporarily while you stand well back and consider its suitability for that particular site. And make sure it is not immediately underneath the crown of a tree. Do not plant the rhododendron until you are absolutely certain you have the right site for it.

Large rhododendron bushes, those which grow to a considerable height or a considerable width, must be positioned where they will look good. The best and most beautiful sites are those which slope towards the south or south-west, preferably not towards the north.

Don't forget to plant particularly beautiful individual specimens on the lawn if possible, but make sure that their growth in ten years' time will not block access to other parts of the garden. For this reason, when planting out, it is very important to consider how high, deep and wide the plant will be in a decade's time. Of course, individual plants can be transplanted when they become too large for a particular site, but this involves a great deal of trouble, since the larger plants are usually very heavy.

In particular, beware of those hollows which always seem to

catch the frost. This happens in depressions and valleys into which cold air from the surrounding slopes descends on frosty days. Since this cold air is then trapped, it forms a lake of freezing air in which the plants nearly always freeze to death. Here, too, the ground remains icy for far too long. This means that the rhododendrons are unable to obtain any water, and as a result, they die.

There is, of course, no way of avoiding frost altogether. We must think of other ways of overcoming the problems it poses. This we can do in two ways: either we can select 'ice-hard', extremely tough varieties or we can give the plants ample protection in winter. Advice on these two points can be found under the sections on the correct choice of plants (page 27) and in the section on tending (page 37).

For this reason it is particularly important to protect rhododendrons from the wind. On no account must rhododendron bushes be planted as a windbreak. Even the hardiest hybrids do not like the icy east winds one bit. Thus, it is a good idea to plant a row of firs or pines within whose shelter the rhododendrons can grow. Neither are the moist west winds ideal, particularly when they are blowing strongly, but they are none the less far less dangerous than the east or north winds.

The high point of the rhododendron's flowering period lasts at best for one month, and varies from May until the beginning or end of June. However, when you add the early flowering varieties and the stragglers the flowering period is extended to about four months, from the middle of February until the end of June (see the calendar, page 33). And we can, of course, add the azaleas to this number, which gives us in late autumn (in October) a further crop of flowers. Unfortunately, however, a garden devoted exclusively to rhododendrons will be devoid of flowers (and fruit) throughout both summer and winter. It therefore makes sense to limit the number of rhododendrons you have. The longer one thinks about it, the more one comes to the conclusion that other types of plants must be added.

Plants to grow with rhododendrons

Many trees, bushes, shrubs and ground-covering plants can be grown in association with rhododendrons. At this point we will confine ourselves to the generalities only, for more detailed hints the reader is recommended to refer to a special study of trees and shrubs.

We shall deal with trees first, remembering to choose rather those trees with dense, compact crowns and decorative foliage which will shield the rhododendrons from the sun as well as affording some protection from the frost.

Above all, choose the type of trees that get on well with rhododendrons, e.g. larches, oaks, sorbus, pines, firs, Pseudolarix, perhaps also a few Prunus varieties (although these grow mainly on chalky soil). Zelkova, Ginkgo trees and others. Further conifers with good thick foliage are the Tsuga varieties, Cryptomeria, all firs and pseudo-cypresses and also Thuja. This gives us a good selection of trees suitable for inclusion in our rhododendron garden. Just one word of warning about hornbeams, however. Their roots tend to deprive rhododendrons of all nourishment, and their roof of leaves is so thick that hardly any sun penetrates through.

The chief points to look for here are leaves of a different shape from our rhododendrons, graceful growing habits and blooms and flowering periods which do not coincide with that of the rhododendrons. The following are a few useful varieties: various kinds of forsythia, autumn-flowering Encianthus, autumn-flowering *Cornus kousa*, also *Photinia villosa*, Cotoneaster varieties with orange berries, evergreen Elaeagnus with gold-green foliage, Hippophaë with silver foliage and orange berries, dwarf varieties of sorbus in the spring, Hamamelis to flower in winter, *Halesia carolina* and varieties of *Ilex* to carry on after the rhododendron flowering period.

Of the smaller bushes I should like to name Cotoneaster varieties Gaultheria, Erica, Corylopsis, *Ilex glabra*, Comptonia, varieties of Berberis (deciduous and evergreen types) and *Pinus pumila*, Ginster and Cytisus, etc.

Among the ground-covering plants there are evergreen dwarf cotoneaster, varieties of erica of different colours (not too few of each sort) *Pachysandra terminalis*, *Hypericum calcymum*. To these can also be added *Waldsteinia geoides*, Tiarella, Lamium 'Florentinum'. Make sure, however, that you plant the latter under strong-growing shrubs, and not between two Japanese azaleas, then *Claytonia sibirica* (a plant which grows to a height of 18–25 cm./7–10 in. and flowers for many weeks in spring and summer, covering the ground with a carpet of pale pink starlike flowers), ferns, varieties of *Phlox setacea* and *Asarum europaeum*.

Lilies may be planted between the rhododendrons, but only when the shrubs are placed far enough apart. Blue or yellow Meconopsis are suitable here; Peltiphyllum grows well in wet patches (Beware! This one spreads very quickly) and produces porcelain-white flowers in spring and red leaves in the autumn. I would also mention *Aruncus silvester* for wooded areas. And finally, a tip for a really breathtaking display. Plant a few sheaths of pampas grass (*Cortaderia selloana*) near a clump of rhododendrons, if possible somewhere where both are mirrored in the water. The result is astonishing. Evergreen grasses and firs are described on pages 35–7.

Choosing your rhododendrons

Careful thought must be given to the matter of choosing rhododendrons. Above all, do not make the mistake of ordering only one of each variety. It is far better to choose fewer different types and more of each one. Beginners should choose only the simplest and most hardy varieties; there is a wide range of shapes and colours to suit every taste. The best to begin with are the standard types which are recommended by the *Deutsche Rhododendron Gesellschaft* and various experts. Lists of these will be found on pages 27–32. Later, when you have acquired more experience, you can start risking the wild varieties (also known as 'species'), and the more sensitive hybrids.

You can make the choice somewhat easier by considering very carefully what the possibilities are with regard to the size, soil and climate of your garden.

If you have a chalky soil, with a reading of *pH* 7 or over, you would be well advised not to grow any rhododendrons at all, for they will give you very little pleasure. A heavy clay soil or very sandy ground with a reading of *pH* 5 is recommended, for here you can plant whatever you like and it will grow. You may perhaps have a small area of wooded ground at your disposal, preferably mixed forest—oaks and conifers, but not beeches or hornbeams. If this land faces south you have the best possible site for planting rhododendrons.

The next point to consider is the size of your garden. If you have land measuring about 1 hectare (10,000 sq. m., or 2·471 acres) you will have to lay out considerable capital if you want to find the rhododendron again once you have planted it. Of course, you can start

off by planting young specimens, in which case you need to be both young and patient, two qualities very rarely found in the same person. Within ten years young plants will grow to a considerable size. Finally, you can also grow the plants yourself, in which case you need even more patience, and you must be able to bear with numerous setbacks and disappointments.

The smaller your garden is, the more difficult it is to choose, for only a few plants thrive in a small space. These must therefore be chosen with extra care, and it is a good idea to buy them when they are already fairly large, so that you immediately have something to show for your money. If the amount of space available is very small a rock garden is a useful answer, for, after all, many rhododendrons grow high up in the mountains and acclimatize very readily to this sort of garden. To these can be added low-growing wild varieties and hybrids, but always bear in mind the size of your garden. The high-growing varieties should be planted only in larger gardens.

A few more words about dwarf rhododendrons. Do not imagine that these are anything like the popular Japanese bonsai trees, which have been cunningly twisted and carefully stunted. Dwarf rhododendrons are small by nature, and they remain so. They either grow as mats over the ground or they form small round pillows, and the shape and colour of both leaves and flowers are easily distinguishable. They all need a very sunny spot, but do not like dryness. Shade displeases them considerably, and even a partly shaded location is unsuitable.

To their disappointment, British rhododendron enthusiasts have frequently learned that wild varieties of rhododendrons, which are described by discoverers or collectors as only 30–50 cm./ 12–20 in. high, often grow to twice that height when cultivated in Britain.

The exact opposite happens with the tree varieties. These usually grow to only half the height they reach in their native home.

At the other end of the scale from the dwarf varieties are large-leafed types. If you look at the pictures on Plate 8 you will probably be tempted to acquire some of these yourself. Unfortunately, none of the large-leafed varieties are really hardy in Europe. Those you may have seen in botanical gardens are nearly always 'dwarf' giant varieties.

At this stage I should like to mention that even *R. arboreum*, the ancestor of so many glorious hybrids, and itself such a majestic specimen when seen in its natural setting covered with red flowers, is not completely hardy, and this brings us to another factor which plays an important role in our choice of plants.

Half-hardy rhododendrons are like children who grow better and better every year but who, when put to the test, fail to make the grade. So it is with rhododendrons. You care for them for years and years, laughing off all prophecies of doom from gardening experts, and then, at the height of its career, along comes a severe winter and kills your favourite rhododendron stone dead—and you then have to start all over again. This can be a bitter blow.

What is to be done? Plant only hardy types? This is certainly one way around the problem. But a real enthusiast would remain satisfied with this solution only until he went elsewhere and saw some of the glorious half-hardy rhododendrons there are. At this stage the sportsman's pride begins to function. He would be no true enthusiast if he did not wish to try his luck with them, and it is possible that his efforts and untiring care would be crowned with success.

Late frosts can have no effect upon our choice, since there is nothing we can do about them. Late frosts occur unexpectedly in May, often after glorious spring days, when the thermometer sinks to below zero during the night. The next morning, the sight that greets the gardener who goes to see what effect the frost has had is enough to make him weak at the knees, for it is possible that every single flower on both azaleas and rhododendrons has succumbed. Sometimes, however, a number of buds do survive. As we have already said, this is one factor we cannot take into consideration, for it is impossible to produce varieties to flower just after the May frosts (if any). This is one risk we just have to take.

Once you know exactly how large your garden will be—perhaps you will wish to divide it up into sections—and when you have decided how much money you wish to spend the business of choosing can begin. If you are undecided, or if you would prefer to obtain more plants more cheaply, specialist nurseries usually offer a good selection of hardy specimens. A firm of this sort will certainly have a range large enough to cater for the beginner, and they usually carry large stocks.

How to distribute rhododendrons

The budding enthusiast will no doubt have formed some sort of plan, and will not be intending to plant his rhododendrons haphazardly. Waiting until the plants are delivered before deciding where to put them is far too late, as the plants themselves will later show.

But whether you have a plan or not, the following points should be borne in mind. Always remember to plant rhododendrons, whether trees or bushes, far enough apart for them to develop properly. On planting, take a glance towards the sky, not to see whether divine providence is assisting you but to ensure that there is sufficient room for the rhododendrons to grow upwards and that their growth will not be hindered by the low-lying branches of a tree. This operation can be very important on land where rhododendrons are to be planted among a number of trees.

It is important to make sure that rhododendrons are not planted within the area of the tree crown or too near the trunk. The thicker an old tree is, the further from it the rhododendron should be planted, in order not to harm the roots. Rhododendrons planted here suffer from lack of moisture, for the tree roots take much of the water, and the tree's leaves drink up most of the rest.

Spaced out planting looks more natural than setting one plant immediately next to the other, in the hope of creating the illusion of a plantation of long standing. By planting rhododendrons too close to each other you will deprive yourself of watching your garden grow. After one or two years you will have to start lifting out the earlier plants and replanting them further apart. When pressed too close together they tend to be very bare at the sides.

The larger your garden is, the more azaleas of the type *R. luteum* you should plant, although these are among the simplest and cheapest plants. (This way you should save yourself considerable outgoings, and at least recoup the price of this book!) Admittedly, the flowers are not particularly large, but they are golden yellow in colour and very strongly scented. You can smell their scent from several yards away, and these azaleas tend to fill the garden with veritable clouds of scent. Naturally, it is an advantage to group these scented azaleas in the vicinity of paths or benches, so that the plants will not emit their scent for their own pleasure alone. Many American azaleas are scented, but none so strongly as the pontic azalea. If you mingle with these, hybrid azaleas with larger flowers but no scent the result should be very much a matter for personal consideration. Personally, I would not do this. Pontic azaleas grow to a height and a breadth

of about 2m./6 ft. and provide us with renewed pleasure in autumn when their foliage turns a glorious red colour.

Generally speaking, I would advise you to plant all flowers (rhododendrons included) in fairly loose groups, and to leave plenty of space between the groups. The spaces in between can be filled with either ground-covering plants, particularly Erica, or with grass. In wooded areas it is not normally necessary to plant anything at all. There are in fact endless possibilities, and as long as the above advice is taken into consideration, it is unlikely that you will fail.

The groups of rhododendrons should not be too mixed, and the individual types should have flowering periods and colours that complement each other. It is preferable to have all the flowers in one group blooming together, rather than each one coming out at different times. Further, always try to put pale- or even white-flowered varieties as near as possible to the pathways, and put the dark blue or dark red ones in the background. In this way they look further away, and you create the illusion of a larger garden.

Is it also possible to plant rhododendrons as hedges? Why not? But there is no point in attacking your rhododendron hedge with shears, or you will undoubtedly chop all the flower buds off. Many English parks are surrounded by walls of rhododendrons. These grow to a height of 5–8 m./15–24 ft. and are quite impenetrable. Perhaps it should be added that a wall of this sort takes fifty years to grow, and only a few varieties of rhododendrons, the most hardy, are really suitable: *R. catawbiense* 'Grandiflorum', 'Boursault', 'Roseum Elegans' and others, for example.

Garden paths

Obviously, you will occasionally want to go for walks in your garden, and you will also wish to show it off to your visitors. Normally, you walk along pathways, but is it really necessary to construct proper paths? This is certainly worth thinking about. Proper paths, which will be between 1 and 2 m./3 and 6 ft. in width, depending on the size of your garden, necessitate a considerable amount of expenditure on their installation and constant upkeep. A path which slopes should really have a solid base beneath it, and adequate drainage must be provided. All this costs money which would be better spent on other things.

But what can we do instead? If your rhododendron garden is very big and you wish to keep it looking as natural as possible paths can be cleared through the plantations. In a few years' time these will look as natural as animals' tracks do in the open. Paths of this sort are not easily planned on paper. The only way to plan a path is to go out into the garden and do your measuring there. Interesting effects can be created by taking the path between tree stumps which you do not wish to remove altogether, or by dividing particularly beautiful clumps of bushes to let the path through. This also, of course, has the advantage of taking us to our favourite bushes by the quickest and most convenient route.

These paths should only be wide enough for one person to pass through, so friends will have to follow in a long file. Benches can be placed at varying intervals. However, their sites should not be decided until later, and you should choose areas with a particularly fine view, or a place from which the house can be seen in the distance, or somewhere very peaceful.

A smaller garden can be arranged with the rhododendrons arranged round the edges, and the middle left as a clearing or lawn. The grass on such a lawn should be cut once a week so that it is always as short and thick as a carpet. Here no paths will be needed, since you will be able to reach comfortably any plant you like from the lawn. As long as the lawn is well looked after, it should not suffer from being constantly walked upon.

Finally, it is also possible to lay short paved areas through our plants, either made from real stone or from concrete slabs. Artificial stone is just as long lasting as natural stone, and is, slab for slab, far less heavy and difficult to handle. Natural stone tends to crack in the frost; in shady spots they collect green and slippery algae—particularly red sandstone. Whether you lay the slabs edge to edge or leave spaces in between is a purely personal matter. But if you do leave spaces in between, make sure the gap is not too large for people to step over comfortably; you should be able to step from the centre of one slab on to the next, and not have to jump.

To get back to our simple, self-trodden paths. Even these can be given distinctive characteristics. Perhaps you know of a sawmill or woodyard where you can obtain wood bark from trees that have recently been felled. Generally, these are left lying about in the forest, or they are even taken away and burned. At the same time, ask for the chippings which come from poles or posts which have been sharpened with an axe. Pieces cut off by saw are not suitable for our purposes, however. Lay the chippings and the pieces of bark evenly on your path to a depth of about 5 cm./2 in. and you will be amazed at how attractive the result is. Both the bark and the wood last a considerable number of years until they have to be renewed, by which time you will probably have discovered a new path-covering material anyway. You are probably wondering why our own garden planners never employ this method of making paths. I'm afraid I don't know. I first saw one of these paths in the United States in a rhododendron park.

So much for paths and sites.

Lawns and rhododendrons

A meadow consists *mainly* of grasses, a lawn should consist only of grasses, and weeds do not belong in it. So although a meadow looks just as green as a lawn, they are both very different things. The general opinion that beautiful lawns exist only in Britain is not strictly true—there are some in other parts of the world, too. However, even in Britain some landscape gardeners do not know how to select the right grasses for the right lawn.

Instructions on how to obtain a good surface on which to plant your lawn do not really belong to this book, but I would like to give some advice about the choice of grasses, in order to save the reader considerable expense on his lawn.

The best time to sow grass is in the spring, but you can sow at any other time of the year when conditions are suitable. I have at various times been forced to sow grass in November or early in February, and the results have always been satisfactory. Many gardeners recommend their own blend of grass for your garden, but be wary of them. It is far better for you to mix your own, and, preferably, to include only two different sorts, namely

80% *Festuca rubra*
20% *Agrostis tenuis*.

Of this mixture, which is the one generally used on golf courses, you should sow at the rate of 15 g. per sq. m./$2\frac{1}{4}$ oz. per sq. yd. On particularly exposed, dry or shady areas you would be advised

to seek the advice of reliable seedsmen, but make sure that no ryegrass, *Lolium perenne*, is included in the mixture.

On particularly sandy ground silver grass, *Corynephorus canescens*, can be used, of the sort that is often found on moorland or on sand dunes. This grass does not produce a lawn surface. Instead it grows in single shoots 5–10 cm./2–5 in. in height, and can easily be planted in free spaces among Calluna heather, but remember that it does not like a limestone soil and that it must have plenty of sunshine.

Heathers and rhododendrons

There will certainly be those among the readers of this book who would prefer to lay a large expanse of heather in their gardens rather than an all-grass lawn. Perhaps some of you will want both. In either case this is work which, with care, you can do yourself.

To begin with, it is important that the space which you wish to fill with heather is large enough (it should be at least 50 m./150 ft. square) and that the materials necessary are easily available. Unless you live fairly close to a heath, you will find the cost of transporting a lorry-load of heather prohibitive. If you are able to meet these two requirements you should begin work in November, during rainy weather.

Natural heather (*Calluna vulgaris*) is sown in the following way. The area to be sown, which as we have said must not be chalky, must be thoroughly cleared of all weeds, particularly of couch-grass. If this does not please you there is no point in reading any further. Otherwise, particularly if you use one of the many proprietary weedkillers now available, you will after a few months find yourself with a completely weed-free surface. Read the instructions on the bottle or packet of weedkiller very carefully, for it is almost impossible to right any damage this may cause by being wrongly applied. If you are in any doubt, write to the chemical factory where your weedkiller was made, and they will almost certainly give you, free, the advice you need. Most firms do this willingly—indeed, many are even pleased to be of assistance. However, you must utilize the product exactly as specified, and not switch over to a different (and perhaps cheaper) product halfway through the job, whose action may be completely different.

Let us assume that we have now got rid of all our weeds, including couch-grasses. The ground has now been chemically cleansed. Unless you have a particularly sandy, meagre soil (i.e. if you live on or very near a heath), in which case no further preparation is necessary, you will have to get the soil ready for sowing. The first essential is sand (sand such as builders use when plastering walls, and not coarse seashore sand) and spread it 2–3 cm./$\frac{3}{4}$–$1\frac{3}{16}$ in. deep over the entire area. Over this place a layer 4–5 cm./$1\frac{1}{2}$–$1\frac{5}{8}$ in. deep of leaf-mould. The surface is now cultivated to a depth of around 10 cm./5 in., but no deeper. The result is that sand, leaf-mould and earth are thoroughly mixed, providing a surface too loose to work on. After this it is necessary to firm down the surface with a garden roller. With a small surface it is possible to tread down the surface by means of boards. This work is best done in October. During the winter the land will automatically become more compact, at the same time as receiving the required amount of moisture from the rain and frost.

A wet rainy day in November is the right time for you to take your cart, go to the heath and collect (with the permission of the owner or the Forestry Commission, of course) however much heather you need. The best way to gather it is by cutting it with a scythe. The heather must be moist; otherwise, either the disturbance caused by mowing or the journey by car will cause all the tiny seeds to be lost.

Once back in the garden, lay the heather immediately in a fairly thin layer all over the area to be covered, so that there is no ground visible. Make sure you lay only one single layer, and that they do not overlap too much. Over this lay birch twigs, or something similar, so that the heather will not be blown away in stormy weather. Once you have done this—and it must be done in November, and not earlier or later—you can celebrate Christmas and Easter without further worrying about the heather. At Whitsun, when there is still nothing to be seen, and even your best friends are beginning to make fun of you, ignore them, for your hour has very nearly come. In June under the heather you gathered in November, which is now looking very unhealthy, you will notice a green layer, very much like minute mosses. (In fact, there always is some moss present.) Now you can rejoice, for these are your young heather plants.

Leave them undisturbed until a rainy day in July—there are always plenty—and then take away all the dry twigs. There you will find a very natural-looking area of heathland, very sparse and thin to begin with, but it soon grows. The small plants grow very quickly, and in two to three years you will have created a glorious, flowering heath. It really is very simple when you know how to go about it.

Whether it is as easy to obtain a heath consisting of *Erica carnea* I'm afraid I don't know, for I have never tried it out. Neither am I ever going to, for it would mean fetching the heather down from the mountains. What's more, the mountain varieties do not have such a long flowering period as the garden varieties. They are therefore best left alone.

We now know all that we have to do, and how we ought to do it. On pages 28 and 29 you will find a planting plan which you can check to see if you have understood what has been said so far (Figs. 10, 11, 12).

Selection for the amateur gardener

The following list is intended mainly as a guide for the beginner; the more experienced enthusiast will probably not be very satisfied with it, and will seek different, better types which are also not too difficult to obtain.

See also the list of more important rhododendrons beginning on page 83.

Usefulness in the garden is shown by stars, which are designed to make the choice easier for the beginner. The stars have in the main been awarded by British, American, Dutch and German nurserymen, and in some cases have been added to by the author.

The more stars, the more valuable is the plant in question.

   *Good
   **Very good
   ***Excellent

Hardiness: the degree of a plant's sensitivity to frost is marked with this sign: ∧. The more of these circumflexes, the more sensitive the plant is. Plants with ∧∧∧ after them are suitable only for the very mildest temperate regions. They are listed here because these mild areas are in fact the very places where so many keen gardeners live.

Entries followed by ∧∧ mean that these plants are generally hardy in milder parts of temperate regions, but they should be covered with twigs during particularly severe weather. In the colder parts these should always be protected in the winter.

One ∧ is given to those plants which will survive even in the colder parts provided they are given some protection in winter.

No ∧ at all indicates that the plant in question will normally survive the winter in any part without protection. Naturally, all indications of winter protection are intended only to serve as a guide.

Evergreen plants are marked with the sign #.

1. STANDARD RANGE OF THE DEUTSCHE RHODODENDRON GESELLSCHAFT
(German Rhododendron Society) (all #)

Drawn up in 1954 by various German nurseries, etc. The following twenty varieties are hardy and able to bear periods of frost. They are all easily obtainable.

'Album Novum', white, light purple on opening *
'Catawbiense Album', white, pale pink on opening **
'Catawbiense Boursault', pale purple-violet ***
'Catawbiense Grandiflorum', pale purple-violet ***
'Catharine van Tol', ruby red *
'Charles Dickens', ruby red *
'Cunningham's White', white, very early **
'Direcktör E. Hjelm', purple-pink **
'Dr. H. C. Dresselhuys', dark ruby red ***
'Dr. V. H. Rutgers', Ruby red **
'Edward S. Rand', ruby red **
'Everestianum', pale purple-violet *
'Gomer Waterer', white, pink on opening **
'Lee's Dark Purple', dark purple-violet **
'Madame Carvalho', white with pale purple **
'Parsons Gloriosum', lilac pink *
'Purpureum Elegans', purple violet *
'Roseum Elegans', purple pink **
'Van der Hoop', dark ruby red **
'Van Weerden Poelman', dark ruby red **

2. THE SEIDEL RANGE (all #)

Particularly hardy specimens, selected by the Deutsche Rhododendron Gesellschaft; however, these are not frequently sold by nurseries.

'Alfred', lilac with green-yellow marks
'Allah', pale purple-pink
'Bibber', ruby red
'Bismarck', white, clear purple-pink on opening
'Dietrich', pale purple-red
'Eidam', white with pink
'Genoveva', white with yellow marks
'Gudrun', white with purple marks
'Hero', white with olive green marks
'Holbein', ruby red
'Hassan', carmine, large flowered ***
'Holger', pale purple-violet with green marks
'Homer', ruby red **
'Humboldt', pale purple-violet, dark marks
'Hymen', pale violet
'Leopold', dark violet
'Mexico', ruby red with dark fleck
'Oldewig', pale carmine pink
'Omega', pale ruby red
'Raphael', dark ruby red
'Scharnhorst', dark ruby red with darker marks
'Von Oheimb Woislowitz', pale purple pink

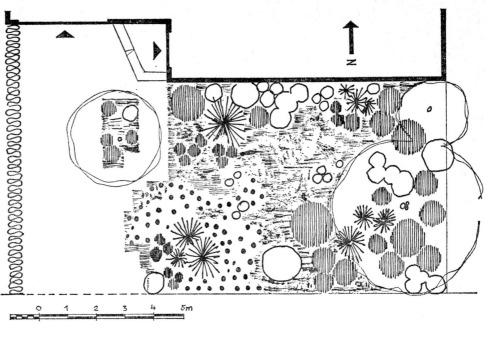

Fig. 10. Front garden of a terraced house. A third of the space is taken up with the drive to the garage and access to the house. The remaining planting space measures about 70 square yards. Near the front door is a small flower-bed beneath a flowering cherry. A graceful birch tree affords sufficient shadow for the azaleas and rhododendrons. A group of conifers alternates with the shrubs.

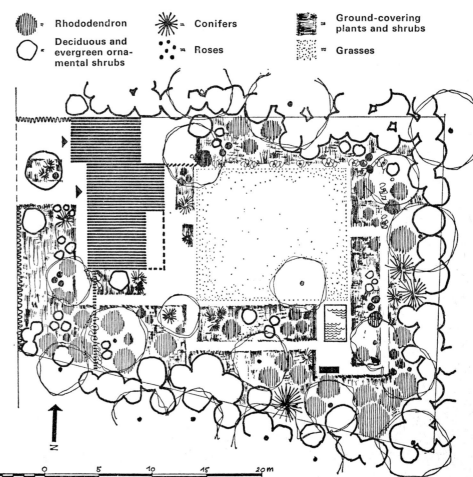

Fig. 11. A typical rhododendron lover's garden of about 1,000 square yards. From the terrace can be seen a small plantation of rhododendrons, particularly azaleas. The effect is enhanced by suitable shrubs and deciduous trees. To get the best from such a garden the paths must be carefully planned.

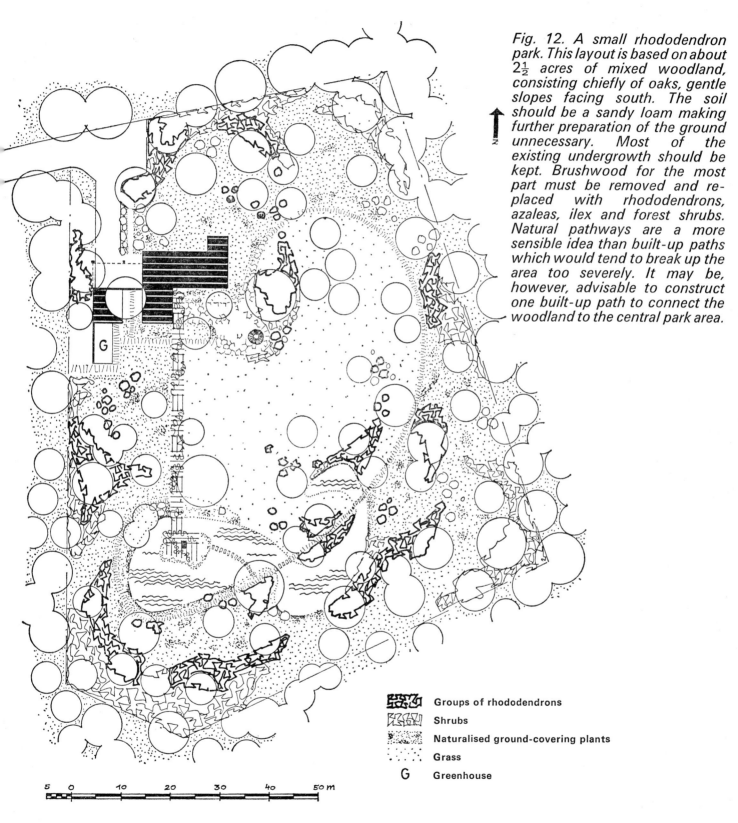

Fig. 12. A small rhododendron park. This layout is based on about 2½ acres of mixed woodland, consisting chiefly of oaks, gentle slopes facing south. The soil should be a sandy loam making further preparation of the ground unnecessary. Most of the existing undergrowth should be kept. Brushwood for the most part must be removed and replaced with rhododendrons, azaleas, ilex and forest shrubs. Natural pathways are a more sensible idea than built-up paths which would tend to break up the area too severely. It may be, however, advisable to construct one built-up path to connect the woodland to the central park area.

Groups of rhododendrons

Shrubs

Naturalised ground-covering plants

Grass

G Greenhouse

5 0 10 20 30 40 50 m

Growing rhododendrons

3. THE ENTHUSIAST'S COLLECTION, CHOSEN BY THE DEUTSCHE RHODODENDRON GESELLSCHAFT (all #)

These were also selected in 1954. They are for the most part large flowered, but less hardy than the two previous ranges. They will therefore be more suitable for enthusiasts living in milder areas. During a normal winter no protection is generally needed, but in particularly cold weather, e.g. below −15° C., and particularly when the sun is shining, bushes should be covered with twigs or with straw until the weather warms up a little.

'Adriaan Koster', pale yellow *
'America', dark ruby-red, late ***
'Antoon van Welie', pink with red-brown fleck *
'Britannia', dark scarlet, bell-shaped ***
'E. D. Godman', dark ruby-red *
'Goldworth Yellow', pale yellow, darker tones *
'Hugh Koster', dark red with darker fleck *
'Jacksonii', white, pink on opening, very early
'James Marshall Brooks', dark ruby-red, brown fleck
'Kate Waterer', pink with yellow-green fleck *
'Lady Annette de Trafford', pale pink, brown fleck, very late *
'Leopardi', white with brown fleck
'Louis Pasteur', white with pink rim *
'Madame Masson', white with yellow fleck *
'Mrs. P. den Ouden', dark ruby-red *
'Mrs. R. S. Holford', carmine red
'Pink Pearl', pale pink with purple tint ***
'Prof. Hugo de Vries', pale pink, red-brown marks *
'Purple Splendour', dark purple-violet **
'Van den Broeke', dark ruby red
'William Austin', dark ruby red with darker fleck *
'Zuiderzee', pale yellow with darker fleck

4. SELECTION CHOSEN BY THE AUTHOR AND GROWN IN DORTMUND (all #)

White
'Mrs. Lindsay Smith', white, large-flowered, small red fleck ∧∧∧–∧∧
'Mother of Pearl', pale pink on opening, then white *∧
'Sappho', white with large black fleck *

Yellow
'Diane', creamy yellow, red brown fleck *∧

Pink
'Betty Wormald', dark pink with lighter tones *∧∧
'Cynthia', carmine pink, very hardy *
'N. N. Sherwood', pale pink, yellow marks *

Lilac
'Blue Peter', lavender with purple fleck **
'Fastuosum Plenum', lilac, half-filled *
'Lavender Girl', pale lilac, very large-flowered **∧
'Susan', blue-lilac, very large-flowered **∧

Violet-purple
'Old Port', dark violet red *

Red
'Kluis Sensation', scarlet red, dark fleck ***

'Lord Roberts', dark red, black fleck *
'Moser's Maroon', dark red, black fleck, very late *

5. LARGE-FLOWERED HARDY AZALEAS WORTHY OF RECOMMENDATION
A. 'Mollis' types

Yellow to orange-yellow
'Adriaan Koster', best pure yellow variety ***
'Sunburst', dark yellow, large-flowered ***
'Bataaf Felix', dark yellow *
'Directeur Moerlands', dark yellow *
'Christopher Wren', orange yellow, large clusters of flowers ***
'General Eisenhower', orange-yellow, large-flowered **
'Hortulanus H. Witte', pale orange-yellow **
'Dr. A. Plesman', golden yellow, orange fleck, large-flowered **

Orange-yellow-salmon
'Salmon Queen', apricot yellow with salmon pink ***
'Lemonora', apricot yellow with pink, orange fleck **
'Frans van der Bom', salmon **
'Hugo Koster', dark salmon *
'Alice de Stuers', salmon, dark orange fleck **
'Apple Blossom', pure pink ***
'Samuel T. Coleridge', pale pink *
'Queen Emma', dark orange with salmon ***
'Spinoza', orange with pink tint **

Orange-red
'Polly Claessens', pure orange, large-flowered ***
'Spek's Orange', orange, late, wide growth, short **
'Winston Churchill', orange with red ***
'Orange Glow', orange with red **
'Hamlet', dark salmon with dark orange *
'W. F. Raiffeisen', pale orange-red *
'Dr. M. Oosthoek', dark orange-red ***
'Koster's Brilliant Red', orange-red *** (not always first class in colour)
'Saturnus', dark orange-red with red tint **
'Benelux', dark orange-red with red tint **
'Spek's Brilliant', orange-red **
'Franklin D. Roosevelt', orange-red, large-flowered **

Red
'Willem Hardijzer', dark-red with some orange ***
'Catharina Rinke', red, orange tint, dark red marks, very large-flowered, late ***
'Radiant', best dark red variety ***
'Dr. Jacobi', dark red with orange, smallish growth **
'Mrs. Peter Koster', dark red, smallish growth **
'Prominent', pale orange-red, large-flowered, strong growth **

Pink
'Suzanne Loef', dark reddish pink ** (noticeable improvement on the old variety 'Mathilde' *)

B. Ghent or pontic azaleas
Yellow
'Nancy Waterer', golden yellow ***
'Narcissiflora', sulphur yellow **
'Hollandia', orange yellow, very early *

Pink
'Corneille', pale pink, rosette-formed **
'Bouquet de Flore', pale pink, white striped, yellow fleck, late *
'Fanny' (= 'Pucella'), dark purple pink, small brown marks, very early and dense blooming **

Red
'Sang de Gentbrugge' is no longer recommended; Knap Hill varieties of 'Satan' are recommended instead
'Pallas', geranium red with orange fleck, early *
'Ignaea Nova', carmine red with yellow fleck, very late *

Orange
'Coccinea Speciosa', bright orange, richly flowering ***

White
'Daviesi', creamy white, yellow marks, blue-green foliage *

C. *'Rustica' varieties, double-flowered, low-growing*
'Aida', pale pink with lilac tones, double *
'Freya', salmon with yellow tint, double **
'Norma', pink with salmon, double **
'Phebe', sulphur yellow, double **
'Velasquez', creamy white with pale pink tint *
   All Rustica varieties are particularly suitable for growing in the greenhouse.

D. *Occidentalis varieties; scented and fairly late*
'Exquisita', pale pink, orange-yellow fleck, scented, late **
'Irene Koster', pale pink with small yellow fleck *
'Magnifica', creamy yellow, pale pink later, with orange fleck **
'Pink Cloud', pink, large-flowered (better than 'Irene Koster') **

6. RECOMMENDED JAPANESE AZALEAS
(For an explanation of the abbreviations see page 27)

White
'Adonis' (Kur.) *** fairly early, wide
'Annamaria' (Malv.) ** fairly late, dense
'Noordtiana' (mucr.) ** fairly early, wide, upright
'Palestrina' (Vuyk.) ** fairly early, upright

Pink
'Betty' (Malv.) pink, darker in the centre, early, upright **
'Blaauw's Pink' (Kur.) pale salmon, very early, upright **
'Chopin' (Vuyk), salmon, early, dense **
'Esmeralda' (Kur.), pink, early low growing *
'Favorite' (Kaempferi) deep pink, fringed, early, upright **
'Fedora' (Malv.), dark pink, fairly early, upright ***
'Helena' (Kur.), pink, early, low growing **
'Hinomayo' (Kur.), pale pink, early, wide *
'Johann Strauss' (Vuyk.), salmon darker in the centre, fairly early, wide *
'Kathleen' (Malv.), pink-red, fairly early, upright ***
'Little Beauty' (Amoena), pink, fringed, fairly early, wide **
'Matador' (Kur.), pink, fairly early, wide *
'Multiflorum' (Arends), dark pink, fairly early, wide **
'Sakata Red' (Kur.), pink, early, dense *
'Schubert' (Vuyk.) pale pink, fairly early, wide *
'Vuyk's Rosyred' (Vuyk.) 1 pink-red, late dense **

'Willy' (Malv.), pale pink, early, wide *

Salmon to orange
'Alive' (Malv.), salmon, fairly early, upright **
'Anny' (Malv.), orange-red, fairly early, upright **
'Kerspe' (Arendsii) pale salmon, fairly early, wide *
'Mikado' (Kaempferi) pale salmon, very late
'Orange Beauty' (Kaempferi) pale orange, very early, wide *
'Orange King' (Malv.), orange-red, fairly early, dense **
'Princess Juliana' (Vuyk.), orange, fairly early, wide **
'Salmon King' (Malv.), salmon, fairly early, wide **
'Sibelius' (Vuyk.), orange, fairly early, dense **
'Zampa' (Malv.), pale orange, fairly early, upright *

Red to carmine
'Addy Wery' (Kur.), dark vermilion with orange, fairly early, dense ***
'Aladdin' (Kur.), geranium red, early, upright ***
'Benigiri' (Kur.), red, very early, dense
'Christmas Cheer' (Kur.), dark red, early, low growing **
'Hinodegiri' (Kur.), red, early, wide **
'Hino-scarlet (Kur.), scarlet, early, upright ***
'John Cairns' (Malv.), deep red, fairly early, dense ***
'Maxwelli' (pulchrum) carmine, fairly early, wide
'Prince Bernhard' (Vuyk), vermilion, fairly early, wide *
'Sunrise' (Kur.), dark red, early, upright *
'Vuyk's Scarlet' (Vuyk.), carmine, fairly early, dense ***

Purple to lilac
'Agger' (Arendsii), lilac, fairly early, wide *
'Amoena' (Amoena) purple-red, early, wide *
'Beethoven' (Vuyk.), lilac, wavy edges, fairly early, wide **
'Bigge' (Arendsii), purple-lilac, fairly early, upright *
'Gretchen' (Malv.), dark lilac, early, upright *
'Hatsugiri' (Amoena), purple, early, wide *
'Johann Sebastian Bach' (Vuyk.), purple-violet, fairly early upright *
'Lilac Time' (Malv.), lilac, fairly early, dense ***
'Mahler' (Vuyk.), dark lilac, late, wide and low-growing **
'Malvatica' (Malv.), lilac, early, dense *
'Mozart' (Malv.), rose lilac, early, dense *
'Purple Triumph' (Vuyk.), violet, fairly early, wide ***
R. yedoensis (= 'Yodogawa'), lilac, double, very early, upright **

7. RECOMMENDED WILD VARIETIES OF RHODODENDRON
   The following choice has been made taking into account the varieties likely to be available.

Dwarf varieties, to a height of 50 cm./20 in. max.

Evergreen varieties
R. calostrotum, violet, April, 30 cm./12 in. ***
R. campylogynum var. myrtilloides, pink, cushion shaped, May **
R. forrestii var. repens, carmine red, cushion shaped, April–May ***
R. impeditum, purple-violet, April–May, semi-circular, 40 cm./ 16 in. ***
R. keleticum, purple-red, June, carpetlike ***
R. kotschyi, pink, May, seldom higher than 50 cm./20 in. **
R. protratum, purple to carmine, April–May, 30 cm./12 in. **
R. racemosum, whitish pink, March–April, hardly 50 cm./20 in. ***∧∧
R. radicans, purple violet, May, carpetlike ***

Growing rhododendrons

R. *saluernense*, purple-red, April–May, 40–50 cm./16–20 in. ***
R. *scintillans*, lilac blue, April–May, 50 cm./20 in. ***
R. *williamsianum*, pink, April, semi-circular, seldom over 50 cm./
20 in. *

Deciduous varieties
R. *camtschaticum*, purple-violet, May, grasslike **

Low-growing varieties, 50–100 cm./20–40 in. high

Evergreen varieties
R. *andenogynum*, whitish pink, April, up to 1 m./3 ft. *
R. *adenophorum*, pink, April–May, up to 1 m./3 ft. *
R. *campanulatum*, lilac, April–May, up to 1 m./3 ft. **
R. *camp.* var. *aeruginosum*, as previously, but with blue-green foliage **
R. *chryseum*, yellow, April–May, up to 70 cm./28 in. **∧
R. *detronianum*, pale pink, middle of April, up to 1 m./3 ft. *
R. *ferrugineum*, pink, May, 60–80 cm./24–32 in.
R. *ferrugineum*, var. *album*, white, May, 60–80 cm./24–32 in.
R. *fulgens*, blood red, March–April, up to 1 m./3 ft. ***∧∧∧
R. *glaucophyllum*, pink, May, up to 1 m./3 ft. **∧
R. *haemaleum*, carmine, May, up to 1 m./3 ft. ***∧∧
R. *haematodes*, dark red, May, to about 1 m./3 ft. ***∧∧
R. *hippophaeoides*, lilac pink, April, to about 1 m./3 ft., erect ***
R. *hirsutum*, pink, June, to 1 m./3 ft.
R. *heliolepis*, purple-pink, June, to about 1 m./3 ft. **∧∧
R. *hirtipes*, pinkish red, April, to 1 m./3 ft. *∧
R. *insigne*, pale pink, May–June, to 1 m./3 ft. ***∧∧
R. *lutescens*, primula yellow, March–April ***∧∧
R. *micranthum*, white, May–June, to about 1 m./3 ft.
R. *metternichii*, pink, April–May, to about 1 m./3 ft. **
R. *mucronatum*, pure white, May, to about 1 m./3 ft. high and
wide ***
R. *orbiculare*, carmine, April, to about 1 m./3 ft. ***
R. *oreotrephes*, lilac, May, to 1 m./3 ft. or higher ***∧∧
R. *orthocladum*, lilac, end of April, about 1 m./3 ft. *
R. *przewalskii*, pale pink, April–May, semi-circular, 1 m./3 ft.
R. *russatum*, violet, April–May, to 80 cm./32 in. ***
R. *souliei*, pinkish white, May, about 1 m./3 ft. ***∧
R. *yakusimanum*, carmine and white, May, to 1 m./3 ft. ***

Deciduous varieties
R. *atlanticum*, pinkish white, scented, May, to 60 cm./24 in. ***
R. *bakeri*, orange, June–July, to 1 m./3 ft. or more **
R. *calendulaceum*, orange-red, not scented, June, to 1 m./3 ft. ***
R. *canadense*, purple-lilac, April, 30–70 cm./12–28 in. high *
R. *dauricum*, lilac, January–March, about 1 m./3 ft. ***
R. *kaempferi*, red, middle May, 1 m./3 ft. or higher ***
R. *obtusum*, bright red, May, hardly over 70 cm./28 in. ***

Medium height, 100–200 cm./40–80 in. high

Evergreen varieties
R. *ambiguum*, yellow with green, April–May, to 1·5 m./4½ ft. **
R. *beesianum*, pinkish white, April–May, to 2 m./6 ft. large leaved ***
R. *brachycarpum*, whitish, June–July, to 2 m./6 ft. **
R. *carolinianum*, pale pink, small-flowered, May–June, to 1·5 m./
4½ ft.
R. *dauricum* var. *sempervirens*, purple, February–March, 1·5 m./
4½ ft. **
R. *floribundum*, lilac pink, April, to 2 m./6 ft. *∧∧
R. *litiense*, pale yellow, May, to 2 m./6 ft. ***∧∧

R. *makinoi*, pale pink, June, small leaved, 1–2 m./3–6 ft. **∧
R. *minus*, purplish pink, May–June, small leaved, 1–2 m./3–6 ft. **
R. *oreodoxa*, pale pink, March, 2–2·5 m./6–7½ ft. ***∧∧
R. *peregrinum*, white and pink, March–May, large leaved, 2 m./6 ft.
***∧∧∧
R. *puralbum*, pure white, May, to 2 m./6 ft. or even higher ***∧∧
R. *rex*, pink, April–May, large leaved, to 2 m./6 ft. ***∧∧
R. *smirnowii*, lilac pink, May–June, silver foliage, to 2 m./6 ft. *
R. *taliense*, creamy white with pink, May, to 1·5 m./4½ ft.
R. *traillianum*, white to pink, April–May, about 1 m./3 ft.
R. *ungernii*, pale pink, not till July, to 2 m./6 ft.
R. *williamsianum*-hybrids, white to red, April–May, 1–2 m./3–6 ft.
*–**

Deciduous varieties
R. *arborescens*, white with pink, scented, May–June, 2 m./6 ft. or
more ***
R. *linearifolium* var. *macrosepalum*, pink, April–May, to 2 m./6 ft. **
R. *mucronulatum*, purple pink, January–March, to 1·5 m./4½ ft. ***∧∧
R. *nudiflorum*, pale pink, scented, May, to 1 m./3 ft. **
R. *luteum*, golden yellow, strongly scented, to 2 m./6 ft. **
R. *occidentale*, white to pale pink, May–June, scented, to 2 m./6 ft.
***
R. *oblongifolium*, white, July, to 2 m./6 ft. *
R. *pentaphyllum*, purple pink, April–May, to 2 m./6 ft. ***∧
R. *roseum*, pink, May, strongly scented, to 2 m./6 ft. ***
R. *schlippenbachii*, white with pink, April–May, 2 m./6 ft. ***∧∧
R. *vaseyi*, pale pink, April–May, to 2 m./6 ft. ***
R. *viscosum*, white, not until July, very strongly scented, 1·5 m./
4½ ft. **

High, over 2 m./6 ft.

Evergreen varieties
R. *argyrophyllum*, pinkish red, April, 2–3 m./6–9 ft. ***
R. *augustinii*, purple to blue, April–May, to 3 m./9 ft. *–***∧–∧∧∧
R. *calophytum*, whitish pink, March–April, to 3 m./9 ft. **∧–∧∧
R. *catawbiense* (although not in cultivation the forms 'Grandiflorum'
and 'Boursault' are available) lilac blue, May, to 5 m./15 ft. ***
R. *decorum*, whitish pink, scented, March–May, 2–3 m./6–9 ft. ***∧∧
R. *discolor*, pale pink, June–beginning July, scented, 2–3 m./6–9 ft.
***∧∧
R. *fortunei*, pale pinkish white, scented, May, 2–3 m./6–9 ft. high and
wide ***
R. *ponticum*, lilac blue, July, almost star-shaped, 3–5 m./9–15 ft. *
R. *rubiginosum*, lilac pink, April–May, to 3 m./9 ft. ***
R. *sutchuenense*, pink, February–March, to 3 m./9 ft. ***∧∧
R. *thomsonii*, blood red, April, to 3 m./9 ft. (or more?) ***∧∧∧
R. *triflorum*, pale yellow with green, May–June, to 2 m./6 ft. **
R. *vellereum*, white to pink, April, to 2 m./6 ft. high and wide *∧∧
R. *vernicosum*, white to pink, May, to 2 m./6 ft. high and wide ***∧∧
R. *wallichii*, lilac, April, 2–3 m./6–9 ft. *∧∧∧
R. *wardii*, yellow, May, 2–3 m./6–9 ft. high and wide ***∧–∧∧∧
R. *wightii*, pale yellow, April–May, to 3 m./9 ft. *∧∧∧
R. *yunnanense*, pink to white, May, to 3 m./9 ft. high ***∧∧

Deciduous varieties
R. *albrechtii*, purple red, April–May, 2 m./6 ft. or higher ***∧∧
R. *reticulatum*, purple pink, April–May, to 2 m./6 ft. ***

PLATE 1

Rhododendron rufum on home ground in Kansu, China. The peak in the background is the highest point of Koangkei Shan. Photographed by J. F. Rock, 1925. (*Photo Arnold Arboretum.*)

Rhododendron reticulatum, photograph taken by E. H. Wilson at Miyanoshita, Hondo, Japan. The specimen is 9 feet high and the shrub behind it is an ornamental cherry. (*Photo Arnold Arboretum.*)

PLATE 2

Rhododendron macrophyllum in its natural habitat in the Great Smoky Mountains, North Carolina. (*Photo U.S. National Park Service.*)

Rhododendron luteum in its natural habitat in the Caucasus. Picture taken by Dr. M. Shalatlina. (*By courtesy of Dr. Lapin, Botanical Gardens, Moscow.*)

Rhododendron vaseyi in its natural habitat in the eastern States of North America. Picture taken by E. H. Wilson, 1925. (*Photo Arnold Arboretum.*)

PLATE 3

American varieties of rhododendron in their natural habitat.

1 200-year-old *R. catawbiense* in the Craggy Gardens on the Blue Ridge motorway near Ashville, North Carolina, U.S.A.
2 *R. roseum*.
3 *R. calendulaceum*.
4 *R. occidentale*.

1

2

3

4

PLATE 4

Rhododendron gardens.

1 Edinburgh: alpine plants with many varieties of dwarf rhododendrons.

2 Bremen Rhododendron Park: group of Arendsii azaleas.

3 Essen: rhododendron plantation in the botanical gardens.

PLATE 5 1 and 2: two views of the plantation of rhododendrons and conifers in Dortmund, Germany. 3 and 4: two views of the rhododendrons displayed at the Spring Flower Show, Dortmund. Some 3,000 varieties are shown. 5 and 6: rhododendrons in the botanical gardens, Dortmund.

PLATE 6

Wild varieties of rhododendrons.

1 *R. insigne.*
2 *R. bureavii.*
3 *R. roxieanum* var. *oreonastes.*
4 *R. arboreum* hybrid 'Russellianum'.
5 *R. thomsonii* with pale brown, often lilac coloured, peeling bark.

PLATE 7

Rhododendrons.

1 *R. metternichii.*
2 *R. sutchuenense* (flowers in March).
3 *R. fortunei.*
4 *R. forrestii* var*. repens* (hybrid).
5 *R. maximum* (flowers end of May).

1

3

PLATE 8

Large-leaved varieties of rhododendron.

1 *R. macabeanum.*
2 *R. calophytum.*
3 *R. basilicum.*
4 *R. sinograade.*
5 *R. rex.*

4

2

5

PLATE 9

Early-flowering rhododendrons.

1 *R. praecox* (April).
2 *R. dauricum* (April: photograph
  taken in Botanical Gardens, Leningrad).
3 *R. mucronulatum* (January to March).
4 *R. williamsianum* hybrid (April).

PLATE 10

Rhododendrons.

1 *R. degronianum.*
2 *R. wallichii.*
3 *R. dalhousiae.*
4 *R. rude.*
5 *R. discolor.*
6 *R. wightii.*
7 *R. crinigerum.*

PLATE 11 Rhododendron leaves emerging. 1 *R. lepidostylum* (blue green), 2 *R. traillianum* (silver grey), 3 *R. sherriffii* (brown), 4 *R. campanulatum* var. *aeruginosum* (verdigris), 5 *R. clementinae* (white), 6 *R. discolor* (bluish white).

PLATE 12

Wild varieties of
rhododendrons.

1 *R. rubiginosum.*
2 *R. orbiculare.*
3 *R. oreodoxa.*
4 *R. cinnabarinum.* var.
  roylei.
5 *R. dichroanthum* var.
  scyphocalyx.
6 *R. callimorphum.*

PLATE 13

Wild varieties of
rhododendrons.

1 *R. dichroanthum.*
2 *R. aberconwayi.*
3 *R. arizelum.*
4 *R. wiltonii.*
5 *R. edgeworthii.*
6 *R. habrotrichum.*

PLATE 14

Wild varieties of rhododendrons.

1 *R. argyrophyllum.*
2 *R. ferrugineum.*
3 *R. hanceanum.*
4 *R. minus.* -SE US.
5 *R. haematodes.*

1

3

4

2

5

PLATE 15

Wild varieties of rhododendrons.

1 *R. argyrophyllum* var. *cupulare.*
2 *R. keiskei.*
3 *R. hormophorum.*
4 *R. ambiguum.*
5 *R. scintillans.*

1
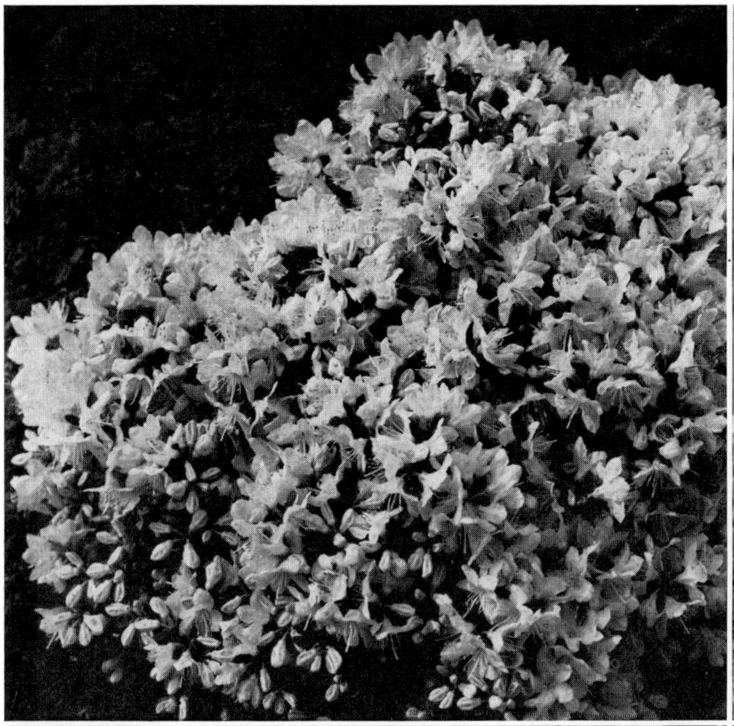

4
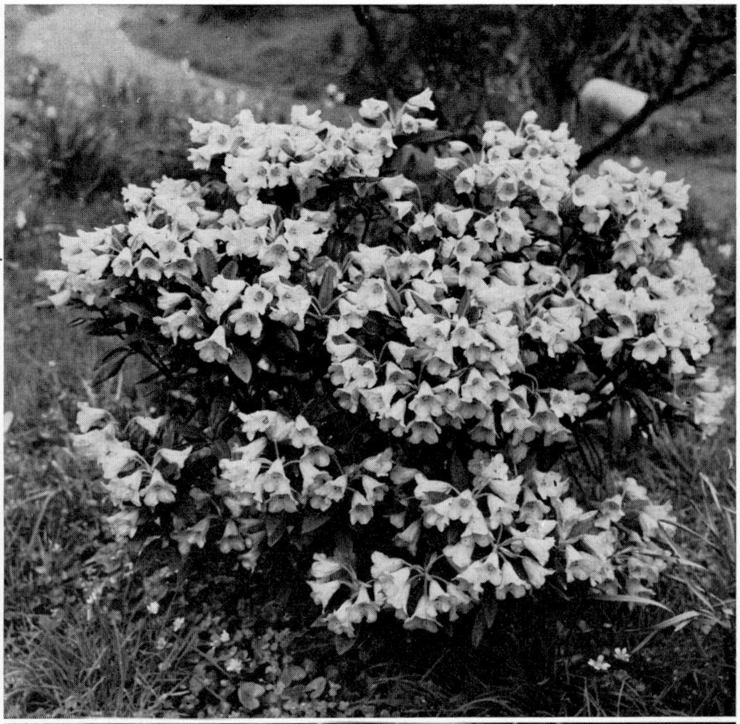

2
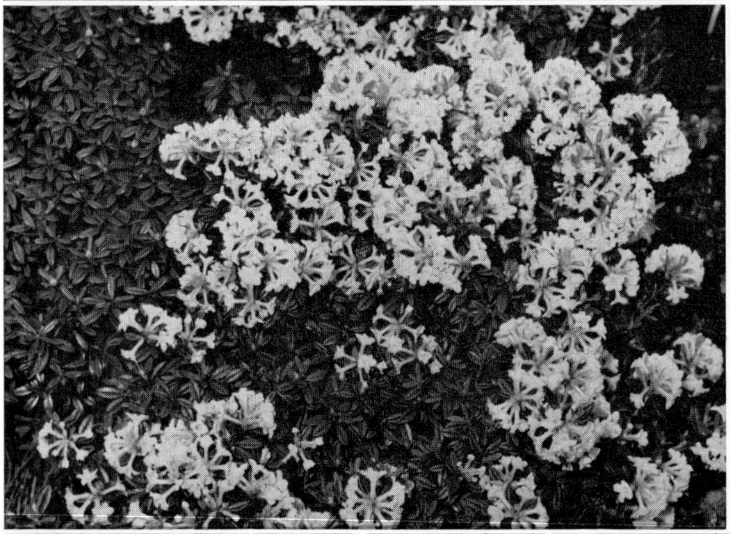

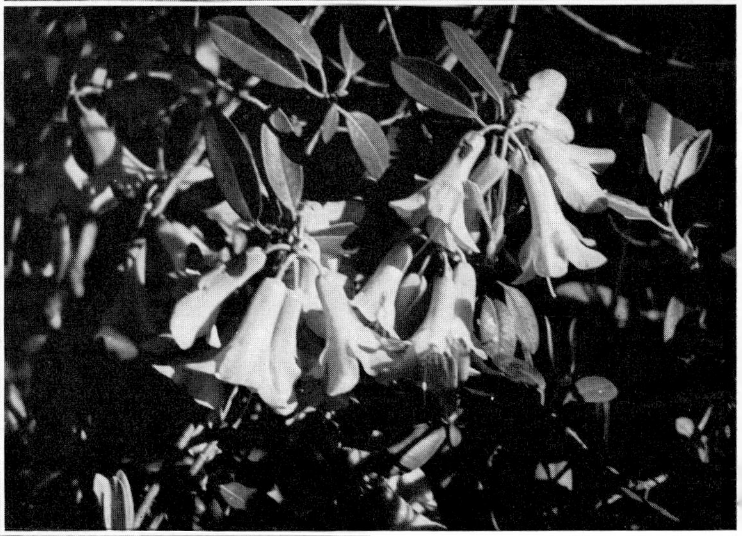
5

3
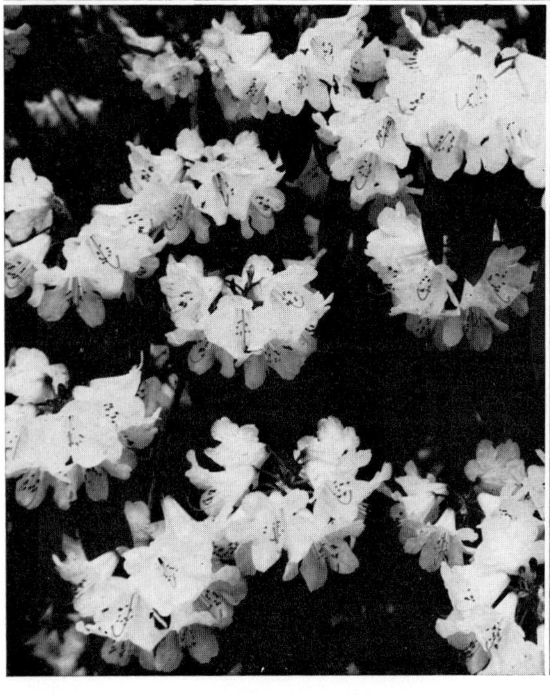

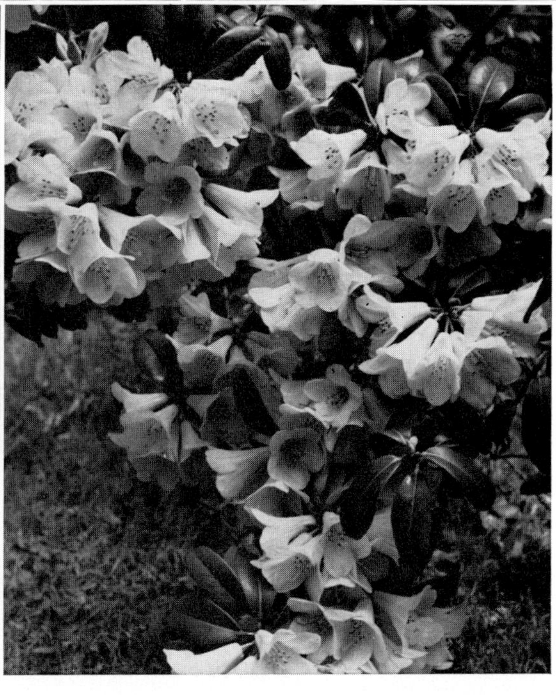
6

PLATE 16

Garden hybrids.

1 *R.* 'Pink Drift'. calostrum x scintillans
2 *R.* 'Sarled'.
3 *R.* 'Rombergpark'.
4 *R.* 'Winsome'. griersonianum x
5 *R.* 'Lady Chamberlain'.
6 *R.* 'Bodnant Yellow'.

3/4 cinnabarinum
1/4 maddenii

Rhododendron hybrids

1 *R. obtusum*
  'Amoenum'
2 'Schubert' Kaempferi × ×
3 'Multiflora' Kurume type
  (Arends)
4 'Agger' 'Macron' × ?
5 *R. pulchrum*
  'Maxwellii'
6 *R. yedoense*
  'Yodogawa'

Time	Blue to violet	Lilac to lilac-pink	Red tones	Pink	White or pale tones	Yellow tones
Very early (before 1 May)		praecox	Nobleanum Unknown Warrior Giganteum	Prince Camille de Rohan Ronsdorfer Early-flowering	Jacksonii	Canary Diane
Early (1st–10th May)	Blue Peter Old Port Susan	Progrès	Rubescens Chev. Félix de Sauvage Cynthia	Mrs. G. W. Leak N. N. Sherwood	Boule de Neige Cunningham's White	Adriaan Koster Zuiderzee Harvest Moon
Average (10th–25th May)	Lavender Girl Purple Splendour Purpureum Grandiflorum	*catawb.* Boursault *catawb.* Grandiflorum Everestianum Roseum Elegans	America Britannia C. B. van Nes Charles Dickens Dr. H. C. Dresselhuys Dr. V. H. Rutgers Edward S. Rand F. D. Godman Hugh Koster Mrs. P. den Ouden Mme de Bruin William Austin	Betty Wormald Catharine van Tol Direktör E. Hjelm Marinus Koster Mrs. E. C. Stirling Pink Pearl Prof. Hugo de Vries	Album Novum Mrs. A. T. de la Mare Mrs. Lindsay Mother of Pearl	China Goldsworth Yellow Koster's Cream Souvenir of W.C. Slocock
Late (25th May–5th June)	Lees Dark Purple Purpureum Elegans Blue Ensign Fastuosum Plenum Marchioness of Lansdowne	Caractacus Roseum Superbum	James Marshall Brooks Louis Pasteur van den Broeke van der Hoop van Weerden Poelman John Walter Kluis Sensation Lord Roberts Nova Zembla El Alamein Prometheus General Eisenhower	Antoon van Welie Duke of York Chintz Duchess of Teck Kate Waterer	Catawbiense Album Delicatissimum Gomer Waterer Mme Carvalho Mme Masson Sappho	Goldsworth Orange
Very late (after 5th June)		Parsons Gloriosum	Moser's Maroon Essex Scarlet	Ponticum Roseum Lady Annette de Trafford		Naomi

It is neither necessary nor possible to list all the wild and garden varieties of rhododendrons mentioned in this book in the order in which they flower. Instead, we are confining ourselves to the most important among them; these are listed according to their colour and flowering period.

The chief flowering period in Europe is the month of May. Anything blooming in April or even earlier is therefore regarded as early; anything blooming after 20th May and up to July is listed as late-flowering.

9. RHODODENDRONS WITH SCENTED LEAVES AND FLOWERS

Chief among these are the series Anthopogon, Cinnabarinum, Glaucophyllum, Heliolepis, Lapponicum, Saluenense and Triflorum, whose leaves, when touched, emit a strong, pleasantly aromatic smell which is discernible on the hands several hours after touching the plant. Indoors their scent is perhaps too oppressive, and for this reason it is best not to cut the flowers for indoor use.

(a) *Wild varieties with strongly aromatic foliage*

R. ambiguum	R. radicans
R. augustinii	R. rigidum
R. calostrotum	R. rubiginosum
R. chryseum	R. russatum
R. glaucophyllum	R. saluenense
R. heliolepis	R. scintillans
R. hippophaeoides	R. taliense
R. impeditum	R. traillianum
R. keleticum	R. triflorum

(b) *A few low-growing garden varieties with aromatic leaves*

'Bluebird' (*R. augustinii* × *R. intricatum*) violet
'Blue Diamond' (*R. augustinii* × 'Intifrast') blue
'Blue Tit' (*R. augustinii* × *R. impeditum*) blue
'Pink Drift' (*R. calostrotum* × *R. scintillans*) magenta
'Sapphire' ('Blue Tit' × *R. impeditum*) pale blue

C

Growing rhododendrons

(c) Hardy evergreen varieties with scented flowers

The most strongly scented varieties of rhododendron are not hardy enough to live out in the open in our climate, since they originate for the most part in the milder areas of the Himalayas. On the other hand, they offer a marvellous spectacle in the greenhouse (see page 44). The only varieties which are really 'successfully scented' in this country are those in the Fortunei series, namely:

R. calophytum	R. fortunei
R. decorum	R. vernicosum
R. discolor	

To these can also be added the hybrids: 'Sir Charles Butler', pale pinkish-white; 'Mrs. A. T. de la Mare', white; 'Naomi', yellowish white with pink tint.

Further, the 'Azaleodendrons' can be included here: 'Fragrans' (catawbiense × viscosum), lilac with white, 'Govenianum' [(catawb. × pont.) × azalea] lilac-pink.

(d) Hardy deciduous varieties with scented flowers

With the exception of R. luteum, all the following mentioned varieties stem from North America. The flowers are for the most part small, but appear in great profusion. Except for the golden yellow European variety, all scented azaleas are either white or pink in colour, never brilliant red or orange.

R. arborescens, white	R. oblongifolium, white
R. atlanticum, whitish-pink	R. occidentale, white
R. luteum, golden yellow	R. roseum, pink
R. nudiflorum, pink	R. viscosum, white

10. RHODODENDRONS WITH ORNAMENTAL FOLIAGE

R. arizelum, leaves 25 cm./10 in. long, downy brown underleaves

R. beanianum, leaves 10 cm./4 in., downy brown underleaves

R. calophytum, leaves over 30 cm./12 in. long

R. campanulatum, small leaves, deep reddish brown underneath

R. campanulatum var. aeruginosum, young leaves verdigris coloured (see Plate 11, 4)

R. cinnabarinum, young and fully grown leaves strikingly blue-green to grey-green

R. concatenans, young leaves blue-green, purple underneath

R. falconeri, leaves 30 cm./12 in. long and 10 cm./4 in. wide, rust brown underneath

R. fictolacteum, variable leaf size, up to 30 cm./12 in. long and 10 cm./4 in. wide, rust brown underneath

R. fulvum, young leaves downy grey on opening

R. giganteum, leaves to 40 cm./16 in., with scarlet top leaves (see Colour Plate 5, 3)

R. grande, leaves 25–30 cm./10–12 in. long and to 10 cm./4 in. wide, shining dark green above, silvery white beneath

R. insigne, medium-sized leaves, pointed, silver underneath (see Plate 6, 1)

R. lepidostylum, young leaves remain a glorious blue-green colour for some time

R. macabeanum, leaves 30 cm./12 in. long and 12 cm./5 in. wide, deep green above, downy silver beneath

R. nuttallii, young leaves reddish violet (see Colour Plate 5, 5)

R. orbiculare, leaves regularly heart-shaped

R. oreotrephes, young shoots reddish

R. lutescens, young leaves bronze coloured

R. rex, leaves almost 30 cm./12 in. long and 10 cm./4 in. wide, deep green and shining above, downy silver-green beneath (see Plate 8, 5)

R. sinogrande, leaves 70–80 cm./28–32 in. long, the largest of the entire family, extremely shiny and veined on top, silvery grey beneath (see Plate 8, 4)

R. smirnowii, young leaves and shoots silvery white

R. thomsonii, young leaves blue-green; stems with smooth rolls of bark (see Plate 6, 5)

R. williamsianum, young shoots copper red. (Some of Hobbie's R. williamsianum hybrids have orange, salmon or brown shoots) (see Colour Plate 5, 2)

R. yakusimanum, young shoots dense, downy silver coloured

11. HARDY VARIETIES FOR PARTICULARLY COLD AREAS

'America', dark red, strong growth, fairly late ***

R. catawbiense 'Boursault', lilac, fairly late ***

R. catawbiense 'Grandiflorum', fairly late, lilac ***

'Dr. H. C. Dresselhuys', red, late high growing ***

'Hassan', carmine, large flowered, early ***

'Nova Zembla', red, late ***

'Van Weerden Peelman', red, fairly late ***

'Caractacus', lilac red, late **

R. catawbiense 'Album' white with lilac tint, late **

'Cunningham's White', white, yellow brown mark, very early **

'Dr. V. H. Rutgers', dark red, fringed, average **

'Duke of York', pink, brown fleck, late **

'Edward S. Rand', red, dense growth **

'Gomer Waterer', white with lilac tint **

'Mme Carvalho', white yellow-green marks **

'Parsons Gloriosum', pale lilac pink, late **

'Van der Hoop', dark carmine pink, late **

'Album Elegans', pale lilac white, small growth, late *

'Album Novum', white with lilac tint, average *

'Burgemeester Aarts', red, early, high growth *

'Catharine van Tol', carmine pink, fairly late, dense *

'Charles Dickens', red, fairly early *

'Everestianum', lilac pink, bronze fleck, fringed, average *

'F. D. Godman', dark magenta, average *

'Giganteum', bright red, particularly early *

'Ignatius Sargent', pale red, late *

'Mrs. P. den Ouden', dark red, late, very dense *

'Parsons Grandiflorum', dark dilac pink, average *

'Purpureum Elegans', dark violet, late *

'Roseum Elegans', pinkish lilac, average *

The 'Mollis' azaleas, the Ghent azaleas, together with all the other garden varieties excluding the Japanese azaleas, will not survive hard frosts without some form of protection.

12. RHODODENDRONS FOR COOL AND MOIST AREAS

It is worth remembering that by far the greatest number of rhododendrons come from mountainous areas; in other words, they come from places with a very high average rainfall over the course of the year, but being on sloping ground, they never become waterlogged. From this we learn that rhododendrons appreciate a large quantity of water in the form of rain, but they certainly do not like to be planted in a swamp. Only a very few rhododendrons are swamp-dwellers, and these include R. canadense, which lives in the cold northern moors. R. calendulaceum, R. vaseyi and R. viscosum, all deciduous varieties, can take a good deal of moisture in the ground.

13. RHODODENDRONS FOR CHALKY SOIL

Before deciding to plant rhododendrons on chalky soil you are advised to read the remarks on this subject on pages 24 and 38. Random planting of rhododendrons in chalky soil can lead to very unsatisfactory results. The following varieties (which incidentally all grow far better in an acid soil) have acclimatized themselves more or less successfully to chalky soil:

R. andenogynum	*R. fargesii*
R. ambiguum	*R. fictolacteum*
R. augustinii	*R. haematodes*
R. brachyanthum	*R. hanceanum*
R. campylogynum	*R. hirsutum* !!
R. cephalanthum	*R. insigne*
R. clementinae	*R. kotschyi* !!
R. davidsonianum	*R. lutescens*
R. decorum	*R. micranthum*
R. oleifolium !	*R. taliense*
R. oreodoxa	*R. traillianum*
R. rubiginosum !!	*R. trichostomum* var. *ledoides*
R. sutchuenense	*R. vernicosum*

14. RHODODENDRONS WHICH PREFER OR WILL STAND SHADE

There are, of course, various degrees of shade. For example, the shadow cast by the wall of a house is much more dense than that cast by the crown of a tree. The size of the leaves of rhododendrons give us a good indication of the amount of shade that plant will tolerate. Small-leaved, low-growing varieties are those that originated high on the mountain slopes, and these are the sun-loving types. They should therefore always be planted in open ground. Those with large thin leaves prefer woodland, and plenty of moisture both in the air and in the soil.

This rough rule makes it unnecessary to list in detail all the types and varieties which will live in the shade. Generally speaking, evergreen varieties like or tolerate more shade than deciduous varieties, which prefer a partly shaded or sunny area. All varieties tolerate more sunshine when they are planted in moist ground than when growing in very dry soil.

15. RHODODENDRONS WHICH CAN BE PLANTED INDIVIDUALLY

All varieties which naturally grow in regular, dense clumps, and bloom regularly and profusely, are suitable for planting on the lawn. However, this should not be done too often in one lawn space, or the grass will suffer. All the extra hardy hybrids mentioned above will grow on a lawn site, and they will flower better and better each year if the dead heads are picked off as soon as possible after flowering. The following varieties grow to an imposing height in our climate:

R. catawbiense 'Boursault', to 5 m./15 ft. high and wide
R. catawbiense 'Grandiflorum', to 5 m./15 ft. high and wide
R. ponticum and *ponticum* 'Roseum', to 4 m./12 ft. high and wide
R. calophytum, to 3 m./9 ft. high and wide

16. RHODODENDRONS FOR THE ROCK GARDEN

All the varieties listed under section 7 (page 31) are suitable here, as are all Japanese azaleas (but don't forget to protect the latter in winter); also recommended are other azaleas and evergreen hybrids which grow to a maximum height of 1 m./3 ft. For sunny locations, choose only small-leaved wild varieties, also 'Blue Tit', etc.

17. RHODODENDRONS AS HEDGES

For high hedges
R. catawbiense 'Grandiflorum', 4–5 m./12–15 ft.
R. ponticum, 3–4 m./9–12 ft.
R. ponticum 'Roseum' 3–4 m./9–12 ft.
R. yunnanense, 3 m./9 ft.
R. Cunningham's White, 3 m./9 ft.

Medium-sized hedges
R. minus, 2 m./6 ft.
R. praecox, 1·5 m./4½ ft.

It is certainly not this author's intention to recommend one nursery rather than any other as being the best place to obtain rhododendrons. I merely wish to list some of the better-known suppliers of rhododendrons.

The reader is warned not to let himself be persuaded to buy varieties other than those he had originally decided upon.

The best thing to do is to obtain first of all a catalogue from one of the larger nurseries, study it carefully, and, having decided which plants you wish to buy, find out who your nearest stockist is. Garden varieties may be obtained without too much difficulty in any of the countries listed below, but for unusual wild varieties and greenhouse plants, British nurseries provide the best range.

Germany

G. D. Böhlje, Nurseries, 291 Westerstede i. O.
Joh. Bruns, Export-Baumschule, 2903 Bad Zwischenahn
Herm. A. Hesse, 2952 Weener-Ems
Dietr. Hobbie, Rhododendron-Kulturen, 2911 Linswege bei Westerstede

Great Britain

John Waterer Sons & Crisp Ltd., The Floral Mile, Twyford, Berks.
Glendoick Gardens Ltd., Perth, Scotland
G. Reuthe Ltd., The Nurseries, Keston, Kent (400 species, 500 hybrids)
W. C. Slocock Ltd., Godsworth Nurseries, Woking, Surrey
Sunningdale Nurseries, Windlesham, Surrey
Hillier & Sons, Nurserymen and Seedsmen, Winchester (largest selection in Europe)
Knap Hill Nursery Ltd., Woking, Surrey

Holland

Most of the rhododendron nurseries are to be found in Boskoop, not far from The Hague. As far as I know, these firms do not deal with private orders; instead they supply to the various nurseries first. Among the most important of these Boskoop firms are J. Blaauw & Co., Vuyk van Nes, Felix & Dijkhuis, F.J. Grootendorst & Zonen, Lefeber & Co., N.V., H. den Ouden & Zonen.

Evergreen ferns and bamboos

Evergreen ferns. All the ferns mentioned here are perennials which are easily obtainable. They go very well with rhododendrons and evergreen trees, and prefer a semi-shady to shady position and humus soil.

Asplenium trichomanes. Rhizome short and upright, grasslike, leaves 4–20 cm./2–8 in. long, evergreen, slightly pinnate, blades round to oval, coarse, fairly thick, 5–12 mm./$\frac{1}{4}$–$\frac{1}{2}$ in. long, entire or serrated, about 2–30 pairs of pinnules, stem and sori wiry, dark reddish brown. Northern temperate zones; on carbonate and silicate rocky ground *

Blechnum spicant. Leaves simply pinnate, with 30–60 pairs of pinnules; sterile leaves evergreen, grouped in rosettes, 20–50 cm./8–20 in. long; fertile leaves deciduous, up to 75 cm./30 in. long. Northern hemisphere, wild at the edges of forests and in clearings on lime-free soil.

Ceterach officinarum. Small xerophyte, leaves evergreen, longish, 3–25 cm./1–10 in. long, with 9–12 lobes on each side, oval shaped with rounded tips, dark green layer on top side, underneath, pale brown overlapping scales. Western Europe to the Crimea; chiefly found in Balkans in dry crevices and growing on walls.

Phyllitis scolopendrium. Evergreen fern, 15–30 cm./6–12 in. high, upright, paleaceous stem; leaves occurring in small clumps, 10–40 cm./4–16 in. long, entire; petiole lanceolate, entire or slightly waved, shiny (= *Scolopendrium vulgare; Sc. officinarum*). Northern hemisphere; moist, shady cliffs in rocky forests. From the occasionally found garden varieties I should mention 'Undulatum', whose leaves are more strongly waved at the edges.

Polypedium vulgare. Sweet-tasting rhizome. Evergreen fern fronds no more than 10–25 cm./4–10 in. long, narrow, coarse, usually pinnate, pinnules entire, 15–35 cm./6–14 in. long, narrow, rounded at the tip, one or two bifurcations in the veins. Northern temperate zones, chalk-free forest and heath, on cliffs.

Polystichum aculeatum. Thick, woody rhizome, leaves 30–90 cm./1–3 ft. long, stiff, generally evergreen; top layer (?) 5–22 cm./2–9 in. wide, oblong, single or double pinnate, up to 50 blades on either side, serrated and steeply inclined; leaf stem paleaceous (= *P. lobatum; Aspidium lobatum*). In mountain forests all over the world.*

Polystichum setigerum. Rhizome thick and woody, leaves 30–120 cm./1–4 ft. long, soft, not necessarily always evergreen; occasionally green only in winter; top layer 10–26 cm./4–10 in. wide, oblong, double pinnate, up to 40 blades on either side; blades serrated, markedly pedunculate, (= *Aspidium aculeatum*) Western Europe, North Africa, Asia; in mixed deciduous forest, on volcanic soil. Of the numerous garden varieties, I should just like to mention 'Proliferum', small leaves, as also blades, loosely grouped, with many buds along the haft from which young plants can easily be detached, evergreen **

Bamboo varieties. Although very many types of bamboo will grow in our climate, I shall list only those which are relatively easily available in nurseries in this country.

Arundinaria simonii. Evergreen bamboo, grows to a height of up to 8 m./24 ft. in its homeland, but generally only reaches 2–3 m./6–9 ft. over here. Stems hollow, 2–3 cm./1–1$\frac{1}{4}$ in. thick, upright, leaves 10–30 cm./4–12 in. long, 1–3 cm./$\frac{1}{2}$–1$\frac{1}{4}$ in. wide, long and pointed, clear green on the upper side, often with narrow white stripes; blue-green on one side underneath; almost green on the other side, with 8–14 veins. Japan * Likes a partially shaded site.

Pseudosasa japonica. Evergreen bamboo with creeping rootstock, stems 2–3 m./6–9 ft. high, with pale brown divisions up the stem; leaves lanceolate, 10–24 cm./4–10 in. long, 2–4 cm./1–2 in. wide, long-pointed, smaller at the base, shining dark green above, blue-green beneath except for green stripe around the edge, rough edge (= *Arundinaria japonica*).

Arundinaria japonica. This is easily the best known bamboo grown over here.

Sasa palmata. Evergreen bamboo, rounded stems, which put out offshoots, up to 2m./6 ft., but usually only 1 m./3 ft. high, coated with waxy substance, particularly under the knots, hollow, with spaces 12–15 cm./5–6 in. long between nodes; leaves 12–32 cm./5–12 in. long, 7–8 cm./3–5 in. wide, long-pointed, gathered at the base, pale green and shiny on top, bluish green beneath and covered with fine hairs, finely checkered, with 7–13 pairs of veins (= *Sasa senanensis*). Japan * Hardy, and not very often grown in gardens.

Sasa pygmaea. Evergreen bamboo, stems set closely together, thin, only up to 50 cm./20 in. high, hollow, very twiggy, the twigs about 3 mm./$\frac{1}{8}$ in. thick; leaves in pairs, lanceolate, pointed, 5–12 cm./2–4$\frac{1}{2}$ in. long, round base, short-stemmed, 3–13 mm./$\frac{1}{16}$–$\frac{9}{16}$ in. wide, rough edge, ciliate, green on top, usually paler beneath, with 2–4 pairs of veins (= *Arundinaria Pygmaea*). Japan. Hardy.

Sinarundinaria murielae. Dainty evergreen bamboo, up to 3 m./9 ft. high, creeping rootstock, thick and grasslike, upright stems, about 10 mm./$\frac{3}{16}$ in. thick, several side shoots at each knot, stems yellow, coated when young; leaves lanceolate, 7–12 cm./2$\frac{1}{2}$–4$\frac{1}{2}$ in. long, 10–15 cm./4–6$\frac{1}{2}$ in. wide, with stems, pointed at the tip, setaceous (= *Arundinaria murielae*). Central China ***∧∧–∧∧∧

Sinarundinaria nitida. Very similar to the previously mentioned variety, but the stems here are blackish brown, upright during the first year and without leaves; during the second year twigs develop and the stems bow over. Leaves 5–8 cm./2–2$\frac{1}{2}$ in. long, 6–12 mm./$\frac{1}{4}$–$\frac{1}{2}$ in. wide, clear green above, blue-green below, curling up during frost, partly deciduous in autumn (*Arundinaria nitida*). China **∧–∧∧. Must have a partly shady site and sufficient moisture in the soil; it will die in full sun and in dry soil.

Evergreen grasses

Avena sempervirens. Evergreen oat, grasslike, long lasting, leaves evergreen, rigidly upright, rolled up when young, rough; stems about 1 m./3 ft. high, leaf cluster 30–40 cm./12–16 in. high, June–July (= *A. candida*). Western Alps, north Italy on chalky heath.

Carex, sedge. Grasslike clumps, but easily distinguishable from the true grasses by its three-edged, solid (not hollow!) stems; leaves in three (not two) rows, with closed leaf sheaths. Over 2,000 varieties throughout the world, generally distributed in the temperate and cold zones.

Carex morrowii. Plants 40–50 cm./16–20 in. high, leaves evergreen, narrow, long, pointed, 4–8 mm./$\frac{3}{16}$–$\frac{3}{8}$ in. wide, pale green, rough (= *C. japonica*). Japan, in woodland. *– More commonly found in cultivation is its garden variety 'Variegata', with stiff evergreen leaves with a white line on the edge, and stem about 30 cm./12 in. high. It is occasionally known as 'Carex japonica variegata' and is fairly hardy in sheltered locations.

Carex pendula. Bushy clumps, without offshoots, stems 90–125 cm./3–4 ft. high, overhanging; leaves flat, about 15 mm./$\frac{5}{16}$ in. wide, overhanging; inflorescence 10–15 cm./4–6 in. long, cylindrical (= *C. maxima*). Europe, moist, swampy areas. Needs lime-free site and plenty of room.

Carex plantaginea. Evergreen grasslike clumps, stems 30–60 cm./1–2 ft. high, red at the base and at the divisions, leaves on sterile shoots 10–25 mm./$\frac{7}{16}$–1 in. wide, almost covering the stem; leaves on the stem very small, almost nothing but a sheath; inflorescence 2 cm./1 in. long. North America in wet forests.

Cortaderia selloana. Pampas grass. Imposing clumps, stems 2–3 m./6–9 ft. high, even higher in particularly favourable locations;

leaves seldom longer than 1 m./3 ft., overhanging; after a few years occurring in large clumps, blue-green, edges sharp as a knife; stems the thickness of a finger, with panicles about 50 cm./20 in. long, in autumn, silvery white and shining with a silky look, which remain on the plant during the entire winter (= *Gynerium argenteum*). Argentine, southern Brazil ∧∧

Festuca glauca. Long-lasting grass, 15–20 cm./6–8 in. high, heads thick and half-round; leaves very narrow, blue-green, coated, rigid, nodes and sheaths also coated; panicles set closely together. Europe; One of the most beautiful and most popular garden grasses, looks good during the entire year, but particularly so in spring.

Festuca scoparia. Evergreen, forming very thick cushions, about 10–15 cm./4–6 in. high, leaves almost cylindrical, very thin, pale green even in winter; stems very thin, almost like threads (= *F. crinumursi*). Pyrenees.

Luzula nivea. Evergreen, grasslike perennials, loose growth; leaves evergreen, straight edged, those below being up to 30 cm./12 in. long, flat, about 4 mm./$\frac{3}{16}$ in. wide; edges more or less thickly lined with white hairs; large white blooms in thick panicles, June–August, 30–40 cm./12–16 in. high, white. Southern Europe, woodland.

Luzula silvatica. Evergreen grasslike perennials, with short rootstock; leaves straight edged, flat, shiny, up to 30 cm./12 in. long and 11 mm./$\frac{7}{16}$ in. wide; stems upright, 30–70 cm./12–28 in. high, blooms brown, April–May (= *L. maxima*). Europe, Caucasus, Near East; on acid soil, in moors and on stony river banks.

THE PLANTING AND CARE OF RHODODENDRONS

When you have thoroughly read and studied the following pages —and it is something well worth doing if you wish to plant and care for rhododendrons—you will probably have the impression that these plants are particularly demanding. This is by no means the case, for many other plants (magnolias, all the ericas, etc.) require very similar treatment. Disregarding exceptions for the moment, you will need:

a climate with a cool summer, but a relatively warm, i.e. mild, winter;
ample rain during the growing period;
a humus soil with a *p*H reading of around 5·0 (acid) and good drainage.

Where all these conditions are not completely fulfilled, we shall have to try to discover whether there are possibilities for creating suitable conditions.

As far as the climate goes we just have to make do with what we have. We have not yet learned how to warm the air, so we must compensate for the cold in one of two ways: either we can choose particularly hardy varieties (see page 34) or we must select more sensitive plants and give them some protection in winter, particularly from the very damaging February sunshine. Too little rain can be compensated for by watering ourselves, and too sunny a site can be made shady if we plant fast-growing, shadowy trees such as pines, larches, birches, etc.

Our problems are unfortunately far more difficult to solve when we are faced with a lime-containing soil, for this must be altered if we are to grow rhododendrons satisfactorily. More will be said on this subject.

Climatic conditions and sites

The word 'conditions' sounds very restricting, but there are in fact many ways in which we can carry out the plans we have formed.

We have already seen that rhododendrons fare better in a cool climate than in a hot one; they do not like the burning midday sun one bit, yet they will do splendidly in a wet summer; the same goes for the sort of winter during which we get only rain and slush, and no snow and ice. However, if you have a very sunny garden, don't despair; this disadvantage can be overcome in the following ways.

Most varieties like a partly shaded site, but several evergreen varieties can tolerate a far greater degree of shade. Deciduous azaleas, on the other hand, prefer somewhat more sun. However, all rhododendrons should receive one or two hours' worth of sunshine during the morning and the evening. It is only possible to plant rhododendrons beneath trees when their branches are 5 m./15 ft. or more above the ground, and about 2 m./6 ft. in length from the trunk. Occasionally it will be found necessary to plant nearer to the tree-trunk, in which case care must be taken that the tree-roots do not rob the rhododendron of all its moisture.

Soils

Unless you are planting rhododendrons in a wood with a good layer of leaf-mould, your soil will almost certainly need some improvement. Light, sandy soil requires the addition of plenty of peat in order to retain sufficient moisture; a heavy clay soil, on the other hand, needs peat and also coarse sand mixed in with it to assist drainage.

Because peat is so necessary, and because it is also expensive—and particularly because large quantities will probably be necessary—it is important that you obtain your supplies from a peat dealer. Otherwise you are likely to obtain poor-quality peat which is not free from weeds. Make sure, too, that the lower-priced varieties of peat are genuinely cheaper, and that their price is not simply a reflection on the quantity contained within.

The chalky type of soil, which occurs in certain parts of Britain, will provide its owners with a considerable amount of trouble. There is a saying among gardeners that a rhododendron planted on chalky soil looks like a clergyman in prison. This is reason enough for us to ascertain how much chalk our soil contains. You can do this yourself by going to a firm of garden suppliers and obtaining a pH meter and carrying out the experiments yourself. However, I would not recommend this, for the apparatus is not completely reliable, and anyway it becomes redundant once you have tested your soil. It is better to take a soil sample to your nearest agricultural college and ask them to test it for you. If the reading is 5·0 or below you have an acid soil; the lower the reading, the more acid the soil is. For our purposes a reading of between 3 and 5 is the most successful.

Neutral soils give a reading of between 6·0 and 7·2. These can be improved without too much difficulty. Very chalky soils have a reading of 7·2–8·0 and higher. This soil will have to be replaced, to a considerable extent, and at this point enthusiasm for rhododendrons tends to become an expensive business. When you have your soil tested, ask what you should do in order to obtain the ideal reading of 5·0 or lower. (And you can also read what to do about it on page 41.)

Buying the plants

Long before getting round to correcting the soil in preparation for planting, you will presumably have been scouring the immediate neighbourhood, looking at the parks and cemeteries. If you see no trace of a rhododendron in any of these places the probability is that you live in a chalky area. If in May you see many rhododendrons flowering, but you notice that these are almost exclusively white or lilac or pinkish lilac, and that the flowers are all very small, you will deduce that this particular area is either too cold or that no one is adventurous enough to attempt some of the less well-established varieties. Many parts of England are mild enough to support varieties of rhododendron other than the extra hardy ones mentioned previously.

On page 16 of this book I gave a brief list of the best known suppliers of rhododendrons and azaleas. These firms will all supply catalogues on demand, and these, if used in conjunction with the lists of suitable plants given in this book, will enable you to make the right choice.

All firms naturally prefer to receive orders in good time, not only so that they can meet all orders but also because the business of dispatching plants can be controlled more carefully.

The best times are when growth is almost dormant. This means from the beginning of March until May, and again from the beginning of September until the beginning of December. If your order is fairly small it is usually possible to have the plants sent directly by train to your town. With large quantities it is usually preferable to have the plants delivered by van directly from the nurseries to your garden. The plants must be unpacked immediately, the string cut off and the roots well watered. If the plants arrive during frosty weather, leave them in a frost-free room (a shed will do) and plant them out at the earliest possible opportunity. Do not place them, even for a short while, in a heated cellar or garage. They are better off in a well-lit, unheated area.

When awaiting delivery of rhododendrons the difficulties posed by unexpected frost can be avoided if you cover the planting area with a thick layer of leaves or paper. This should keep the ground in good enough condition for you to plant out your rhododendrons when they arrive.

Preparing the soil

Immediately after placing your order (or before if possible) you must start preparing the ground in readiness. First dig the areas concerned (which have, of course, been freed of weeds) and let the soil lie in rough lumps (i.e. do not rake it smooth) so that the rain can penetrate thoroughly. If the soil is good and loose, and if it has not been compressed or damaged by having been built on at some stage, it is sufficient to dig to a depth of 20 cm./8 in. This will ensure that your fork picks up all the roots of weeds, particularly couch-grass, bindweed and thistles and so on. If these are not carefully removed at this stage they will cause a great deal of trouble later on. Do not put these weeds on to the compost heap—that would be tantamount to encouraging them!—but throw them instead on to your rubbish heap.

If you have just moved into a recently completed house, and you would like to plant rhododendrons and azaleas, it is imperative to remove all bits of chalk, plaster and cement—a very nasty job indeed. And don't forget to look for stones and plaster which have become buried in the earth. Limestone need not be carted straight off to the rubbish heap. Instead, it can be put in a corner of the compost heap, for you are sure to find a use for it at some later stage. We know that rhododendrons do not like limestone one bit, but other plants have different requirements. Fruit trees, and stone-fruit in particular, are grateful for a shovelful of such debris in their planting hole.

If the soil is naturally heavy in clay, and if it has been densely compressed, it will have to be thoroughly worked first. But this is not satisfactorily achieved by hand. The best way to deal with the soil is to loosen up the ground with a garden rotorvator machine; after this has been done, rake the surface smooth and then lay over the top a layer of peat about 5 cm./2 in. thick; over this put a good sprinkling of coarse sand and then work the soil over once more. If you find this work too difficult, see if there is anyone who would lend or hire machinery for the job, but it is important that all this is done if the rhododendrons are to thrive. This work should not be done during very wet weather, or in late autumn, for the ground tends to become very muddy as a result.

Planting

Before ordering your plants you will obviously have made a detailed plan and decided exactly where each specimen is to go. Above all, do not fall over yourself trying to get the plants into the ground in a hurry. Take your time and do the job properly if you want good results. On unpacking your rhododendrons and azaleas you will probably have noticed that they all have an almost circular ball of earth round their roots which, even without being tied by string, does not fall to pieces. (Compare this with the way in which conifers and other plants are packaged.) The reason for this solid ball of earth is that these plants have a very compact system of fine roots, all of which lie very near the surface of the earth. When the plants are dispatched from the nursery the diameter of the ball is about one-third the diameter of the plant.

Before planting set the rhododendron on the spot where it will later be planted. With the spade, dig out a few small holes so that the plant will remain upright, then step back and make sure that the effect is right. You may wish to alter the position of bushes, or to swap them around, if you have bought more than one. When you are satisfied dig out the planting hole, which should be only about one-third larger than the ball, place the bush in the ground, add a small quantity of moist peat and fill the hole in again. All you have to do now is tread the roots well in, making sure that the plant is perfectly vertical. Naturally, if you have already worked a considerable quantity of peat into the ground you do not need to add any more at this stage.

Planting and transplanting can be done at any time in spring or in autumn, but make sure you retain a good ball of earth around the roots. Plants which have previously not flowered quite frequently are so discomposed by being moved that they promptly produce flowers the following year. Why they do this I do not know, but it is a fact that plants quite often flower after being transplanted.

Many textbooks and catalogues will tell you that there are rhododendrons which like a limestone soil, or which will at least tolerate limestone. This in itself is true, but the varieties referred to are most certainly not those which the enthusiast had imagined for his garden. The whole question of toleration of limestone looks very different in

nature than it does in your garden. In mountainous areas there is always a layer of humus of varying thickness over the limestone itself, and the plants in fact root in the humus. This can hardly be compared with the circumstances of your garden in a low-lying area.

If your soil shows too high a proportion of alkali, and gives a reading of over pH 7·0, it will have to be made artificially more acid. This can be done by adding peat or heath or moorland and mixing it in to a depth of about 30 cm./12 in. However, if the reading is extremely high, say 8·0 or even higher, there is nothing for it but to change the soil altogether and replace it with one containing more acid. About one-third the quantity of original soil can be retained for mixing with the new earth, but all the rest will have to be carted off somewhere, and perhaps used to build up the ground elsewhere in the garden. If there is not adequate drainage where the new soil is to go, dig down a further 20 cm./8 in. or so and line the hole with wood, twigs, gravel and larger stones. Over this you can put in the new earth mixture.

In the *Rhododendren Jahrbuch* 1952: 14–20, H. Harms gives a detailed analysis of the reasons why rhododendrons will not grow in a limestone soil. In this helpful tract he states that 'it is not "lime" in itself which is so damaging to rhododendrons but a particular compound of lime, which is unfortunately also the most widespread and the most important, namely calcium carbonate, which is often advantageously used as a fertilizer for other plants. In other words, in calcium carbonate it is not the metallic component calcium which is harmful but the acid (carbonic acid in this case) which does the harm, chiefly because it is so weak. It must therefore be replaced by a stronger acid, preferably one which suits the plants.'

After considerable research and experimentation, Harms advises 'not merely to neutralize soil containing too much calcium carbonate by the addition of phosphoric acid, but to bear in mind also how best to improve the flowering ability of the plant at the same time. It is a good idea to water the sides of the hole as well as its base with a strong solution of phosphoric acid, and then to mix in the harmful calcium carbonate soil with the beneficial phosphoric acid-containing soil. This should also ensure that water is not drawn from below the new soil, thus eliminating the action of the acid.'

As you have seen, you have to go to a considerable amount of trouble if you wish to grow successful rhododendrons in a limestone soil. F. Penningsfeld, working near Munich in Germany, has shown that there is another way to overcome the problem. He points out that in many gardens the soil can be sufficiently improved by the addition of plenty of peat. On older-established sites the peat can be spread over the surface, but on new sites it is better worked into the soil. Or else a layer of peat can replace the top layer of existing soil. He recommends a thickness of about a foot (25–30 cm.) of suitable quality peat well mixed with other ingredients including manure and small amounts of copper sulphate and sodium molybdate.

He maintained that liming was necessary for the healthy growth of rhododendron buds, unpopular though this idea is. More on this subject will be found on page 41.

It quite often happens that people dig the planting hole too deep, with the result that the ball of earth is 10–20 cm./4–8 in. deeper than previously. What happens then? The plant does not grow any further. Instead, it sets to work growing a new network of roots, since the low-lying roots either no longer work at all or they do not work sufficiently hard. If after two to three years a plant which has been planted too deep is uprooted you will see all the new roots near the surface of the ground, and the old roots, still contained in a ball of earth, at the bottom, with a length of stem in between on which there are no roots at all. At this stage the ball of dead roots at the base can either be left where it is or removed. In the latter case, make sure you do not immediately plant the rhododendron too deep again.

Protection against winds

The thick foliage of bushes provides a large surface for the wind to batter against; what's more, newly planted shrubs are not very firmly held in place by their own roots. We must therefore ensure that the wind does not blow the plants over. You can, of course, drive a couple of stakes into the ground and fasten the stems to these, but it is very easy to injure the roots in this way. The better method is the one generally employed in this country, whereby two stakes are driven into the ground, one in front and one behind the rhododendron, in the direction in which the wind usually blows. The posts stick out of the ground to a height of about 50 cm./20 in. A strong lath is then nailed to the posts, passing straight through the middle of the bush, and to this one or more stems can be made fast.

Watering

After planting, the rhododendron should be well watered in so that any air spaces left in the planting hole will be filled and the roots encouraged to grow.

During the course of the year it will be necessary to water the plants a great many times, particularly when the leaves are all out. At these times the earth must be thoroughly moistened, preferably by the action of the rain, for rainwater penetrates more easily into the soil, and there is less danger of evaporation. If you occasionally dig a spadeful of earth from beneath a large rhododendron bush you are likely to find that it is bone dry.

In late autumn, October or November, give the plants a really good watering in preparation for the winter. Moisture evaporates from the leaves even in winter, and the plants must always be able to replenish their water supplies.

Care of rhododendrons

Luckily, growing rhododendrons does not involve too much work. Hoeing and digging between plants is not recommended, because the roots lie so close to the surface that they are liable to become damaged. If you take care to ensure that the ground has been freed from weeds before you plant the rhododendron it will be easy to pull out the few new weeds that do crop up, and hoeing will be unnecessary. Of course, some weed seeds will be blown by the wind into the spaces between rhododendrons, but this is unavoidable.

Chemical weedkillers are not recommended for these areas because they are likely to damage the fine hair-roots near the surface. In any case, the enthusiastic gardener should not let the weeds get thus far out of control.

Mulching is very important, for this feeds the soil, contains its moisture and also makes life more difficult for the weeds. For this reason, mulching—which is nothing more than covering the earth over with leaves, grass, peat, etc.—should become a regular habit with you. In any case, the ground between the plants should not be

planted with any of the ground-covering small trees or bushes so popular nowadays; the earth must be completely free.

It does not matter what you use as a mulch as long as it:

(1) is present in large quantities;
(2) lies firmly on the ground, and cannot easily be blown about by the wind;
(3) remains moist and fairly loose;
(4) does not decompose too rapidly.

These conditions are fulfilled by peat, leaves and leaf-mould, as also by finely chopped wood from trees, although the latter can be used only between the larger bushes. The looser and less well rotted the mulch is, the more thickly you can heap it on. In autumn put 10–20 cm./4–8 in. of mulch on the ground. During the course of the winter it will fall in on itself and decompose. There are, of course, other possibilities for mulching: you can, for example, use straw, or hay that is otherwise unusable, or clippings of heather, etc., or even peat, although this does, of course, tend to be more expensive.

Removing dead heads

Next to mulching, picking off dead heads is a time-consuming job. However, it is most important to do it, and, what is more, to do it at the right time. As soon as the flower has wilted and started to turn brown, the seedpods begin to develop, and this process considerably weakens the plant. At this time the new shoots which will develop into next year's buds are developing under the flower heads. On many varieties these shoots are already visible while the flowers are in their full glory; this is a regrettable characteristic which unfortunately cannot be altered. The withered flower heads are easily removed by sharp pressure of the thumb on the base of the stem. Occasionally, if there has not been any rain for a long time, the stems are soft and will not break easily. In this case, use cutters for the job. But do be careful that not a single leaf, or leaf bud, is cut by mistake. Dead flower heads can be added to the mulch round the base of the plants.

Incidentally, this job makes your fingers extremely sore, black and sticky, and the only way to get them really clean again is with petrol or some other resin solvent. Gardening gloves are unfortunately not very practicable for this job. With azaleas most of this work is not necessary, since many varieties are infertile, and in most other cases the full development of fruits and seeds does not appear to weaken the plant.

Pruning

The true gardening enthusiast always has something in his garden which he wants to prune: fruit trees, roses, hedges, the lawn and so on. But what about pruning his rhododendrons? Perhaps a particular branch or twig displeases you, in which case it is usually safe to prune it, and of course dead or unhealthy wood must be pruned and then burned; but otherwise rhododendrons should not be pruned. The one exception to this is wild shoots.

Imagine for a moment that you have a glorious rhododendron bush with beautiful red flowers; then, one day, you suddenly notice a branch with blue flowers growing out of the middle of it. Hardly have you got over your astonishment than you notice a branch of heavily scented golden yellow flowers in your red-flowering azaleas. You will no doubt first of all wonder whether these were growing in your garden originally, or whether your own efforts have brought this about. You will probably decide to consult an expert on the subject at the earliest opportunity. He will explain to you that, in the nurseries, rhododendrons are often improved by grafting on to a wild variety (usually *R. ponticum*), which has blue-lilac flowers, or that your azalea was grafted on to *R. luteum* (known to gardeners everywhere as *Azalea pontica*, in spite of the true facts), which is golden yellow in colour and heavily scented. He will also explain to you that both are the wild shoots of the improved varieties. If you do not immediately cut these shoots off below ground level—a job which is easiest done during the flowering period, since this is when they are most easily recognizable—the wild shoots will very soon smother the rest of the plant, and the improved red flowers will eventually die off altogether. So cut off the wild shoots—they can be used to decorate the living-room.

Feeding your plants

The word manure always tends to conjure up a picture of filth, and, quite understandably, proud owners of brand-new houses are not very keen on the idea of importing filth in to their homes. What is more, most people associate manure with the dreadful smell they remember from otherwise pleasant excursions into the countryside. Even the countryman does not find the job of manuring particularly pleasant, but he knows from experience that the results from the earth make the effort well worth while. The action of manuring is basically the action of feeding your plants.

But how should you feed your plants? On planting your rhododendrons give the plants a good start in life by throwing a couple of handfuls of leaf-mould into the planting hole. Or, of course, the leaf-mould can be forked into the ground. But the addition of leaf-mould is necessary only in March or April, and not in late autumn. It does not smell at all, yet it is most beneficial; the job can be repeated every year at the same time. If you do not do it the plant will not suffer too much, for it is so constructed that it will absorb its necessary foodstuffs from the earth. However, if you become aware that your rhododendrons have less flowers this year, or that the flowers are becoming smaller and smaller, this is the moment to wonder whether perhaps your plants are not feeling hungry.

Their hunger must be satisfied during the course of the second half of winter by the addition of potting compost (free from weeds!) and of cattle manure, which should be mixed with peat and spread evenly over the ground to a depth of about 3 cm./$1\frac{3}{16}$ in. Apart from that there is nothing you need do. After the flowering period is over, and when the new shoots are beginning to appear, give them a mineral dressing free of lime and chlorine. But this should not be done until the plant has been established in its present position for at least a year, and is well rooted in.

Normally, rhododendrons do not require the addition of manure, since they obtain their own foodstuffs from the earth. But it does sometimes happen that the soil is rather meagre, or that the plants do not appear to be faring very well, and in this case it is as well to give them a good feed.

The best sort of food is cow dung which has been diluted to the colour and consistency of weak tea. This can be fed to the rhododendrons from the middle of April until the end of June at fortnightly intervals. Make sure you do not spray the leaves, or they will scorch. Further, the earth must be thoroughly watered before application of the fertilizer or the roots will be scorched. After June

it is no longer necessary to feed the plants. Clearly, the plants need most additional strength just after the flowers have finished, for the plant is then exerting all its energy in producing new shoots.

Equally effective is the spreading of the ground with manure in spring—this then means you have no more bother for the rest of the year. You are probably asking where one obtains manure, and this is indeed the chief problem. Probably the most successful way is to come to some arrangement with a farmer who will let you cart away sufficient quantities of cattle dung. This is then left to lie for a while in a shady spot in the garden and later mixed with peat and spread in a thin layer over the ground.

If you do not like the thought of this for one reason or another, or if all the farmers in your neighbourhood use all available manure for their own purposes, you will have to fall back on artificial manure. There are many reliable brands of peat on the market which will serve our purpose, but make sure you order sufficient quantities in good time.

A last resort would be to spread ordinary peat—if you happen to have any lying around—and then to spread an organic manure over this. A suitable brand will probably be obtainable from the nursery which supplied you with your rhododendrons. An organic fertilizer should be applied at the beginning of May at the rate of about 30 g./$4\frac{1}{2}$ oz. per square metre/yard, and then again at the beginning of June in the same quantities. 30 g./$4\frac{1}{2}$ oz. is not very much—about 1 tablespoonful—but the plants really do not need more.

Finally, I should like to list a few foods which will set your plant on the quickest route back into the ground, and which should therefore not be used: No lime; no calcium nitrate. (Lime is the rhododendron's worst enemy.) No horse manure; no pig manure. No potash.

As promised on a previous page, I should here like to say a few words about F. Penningsfeld's experiments with differing types of manure. He, as you will remember, maintained that liming was necessary for the healthy development of the rhododendron buds. However, his experiments were conducted only on certain particular varieties of rhododendrons, including 'Cunningham's White', 'Roseum Elegans' and *R. catawbiense* 'Grandiflorum'. He gave three applications of lime (of 0.2–4 g./$\frac{3}{200}$–$\frac{3}{5}$ oz. CaCO$_3$/l.), combined with a complete fertilizer of 3 g./$\frac{3}{20}$ oz. The results vary considerably, and in my opinion they are not yet conclusive. At least, I certainly do not think they are sufficient to encourage gardeners to start using lime in their own gardens.

Sprinkling the ground with an inorganic fertilizer is not really necessary when the ground beneath the plants is covered with a good layer of mulch, for the components will only partly penetrate through rotted mulch. If the mulch is fairly fresh, move it to one side while applying an inorganic fertilizer and then replace it afterwards.

Beware of giving your plants too many 'calories'! If they are overfed they will concentrate on producing masses of leaves and forget about producing flowers. What is more, overfed plants are very frequently the victims of winter frosts. Which brings us to the subject of winter protection.

Winter protection

There is available to us a whole range of extra hardy rhododendrons and hybrids which will survive even our coldest winters without coming to any harm. Among the garden varieties, these are chiefly

Planting and care

the hybrids based on *R. catawbiense*. Admittedly, these are not the most beautiful sorts, but if you live in a really cold area you do not have much say in the matter.

Many rhododendrons protect themselves against the frost by rolling up their leaves, which then hang from the bush like so many cigars. If you walk through the garden in a temperature of minus 5° C. or lower, you will notice that each variety of rhododendron rolls its leaves in a different way. This is so different from one set of plants to another, and the method is so constant that even in nurseries this is an accepted way of distinguishing one variety from the next. Unfortunately, there is also a range of hybrids which do not roll up their leaves, or which only make half-hearted attempts to do so. Because their ancestors came from the frost-free region of the Himalayas, these species have never developed this particular habit. Unfortunately, one of the latter varieties is 'Pink Pearl', which must therefore be protected during the winter, as must Japanese azaleas. But how should we do this?

The time to start is around the beginning or the middle of December, but not earlier. Try to obtain branches from a fir tree, but do not take those more than about 1 m./3 ft. long. Make a tent of the branches over the plant, or fix pieces of wood first and then lay the pine branches over them, remembering always to put them far enough apart for the snow to get in. If the branches are too closely set together a really heavy fall of snow lying on top can severely damage the plant. If there is no snow before Christmas your Christmas tree will come in very handy for this job. Most sellers of Christmas trees find themselves with some left over once Christmas is past, and they are usually only too pleased to find someone who will take one or two off their hands. I have been doing this for several years now with highly successful results.

Another way in which to use your Christmas tree is to cut it up into small pieces, rather than merely burning it, and spread the pieces over the ground beneath your rhododendrons as protection for the roots.

If you are unable to obtain spruce-fir branches pine twigs will do, but unless you happen to know a forestry official or two you are unlikely to be able to obtain these.

If ever there is another Siberian winter, as there was in Europe in 1955, when for weeks on end the temperature did not rise above minus 20° C, the only thing you can do is to lay straw on top of the plants, so that the entire rhododendron is covered by a thin layer. This doesn't look at all pretty, but in the last resort this is all you can do, and it really does work. As soon as the really heavy frost is over, remove the straw immediately.

You will not find out whether anything has succumbed to the frost until the thaw sets in. The leaves that have died will not unroll themselves in the warmer air; they will begin to look limp and dull on the surface, and eventually they will dry up altogether. These branches should be removed, but this is a job which need not be done until May, shortly before the flowers come out. Cut the dead wood off immediately above the healthy shoots. Even when the entire bush looks as though it has died, new shoots frequently start to grow again, so don't be too quick with the cutters. It is far better to wait and see what happens.

And this is basically all that a good rhododendron grower should know. Of course, the longer you grow rhododendrons, the more problems arise, and it may even be that you decide to grow your own plants from seed or from cuttings.

Propagating rhododendrons

Unfortunately, this is not the sort of question I can answer with a simple 'yes'. In fact, I would strongly advise against propagating these plants. Not even professional gardeners, with all the equipment and hothouses at their disposal, will generally undertake the work of propagating rhododendrons. It is the sort of work that requires exceedingly green fingers. You must know exactly how it is done, when it must be done and how to treat the plant at all stages of its life. It takes gardeners years and years to learn how to propagate these plants successfully. However, I will willingly give a few tips to those of you who are absolutely determined to try your hand. I shall just warn you once more that this is difficult, unrewarding work, and often causes nothing but trouble.

The way in which seeds are sown has already been described in the section dealing with crossing one species with another. The same method applies to whatever type of seed you sow.

Explorers such as Kingdon Ward and many other Englishmen usually financed their expeditions by collecting seedlings in the plant's country of origin, and selling them to a circle of people who had guaranteed to buy in advance. If you ever get the chance to obtain seedlings of this sort should you take advantage of the opportunity? Kingdon Ward maintained that plants grown from seeds taken directly from plants growing in their own country are always far more hardy than seeds taken from plants grown in exile (i.e. outside their natural environment). Further, seeds gathered from the upper regions of a plant's area of distribution are more resistant to frost than those from the more low-lying areas.

This is generally applicable only to Japanese azaleas. Cuttings are taken in June and placed in the propagating bed in the greenhouse, where the soil is warmed and the windows opened. If you do not have a greenhouse it is possible to obtain portable propagating frames which can be kept indoors; or you can even build one yourself. The portable propagating frame is usually about 1 m./3 ft. long, 0.5 m./18 in. wide and 0.3 m./10 in. high. It is electrically heated. Frames of this sort are usually available from normal garden suppliers. Put the cuttings in a mixture of half sand and half peat, and with any luck they will produce roots after about three weeks. This does, of course, mean that you cannot go on holiday in June—azalea cuttings need a babysitter.

The rooted cuttings are then planted out into a hotbed consisting of a mixture of leaf-mould, compost, peat and sand in equal quantities. There they remain for one year under glass, until they have a good system of roots. After this time the glass covers can be removed. In November the windows must be replaced so that the plants will come through the winter successfully.

The following year, the by now fine-looking plants are pruned so that they will become more bushy. They are transplanted once more, but this time further apart, and are preferably left in a hotbed for a further year, until they are around two years of age. They can then be planted out in the open, either in a cold frame or in the spot for which they are eventually destined.

Evergreen hybrids can also be propagated from cuttings, but this really is far too complicated a subject for the amateur.

Nurserymen generally propagate evergreen hybrids and azaleas, with the exception of Japanese azaleas, by grafting. As a basis for the evergreen types, seedlings of *R. ponticum* are taken, and for azaleas *R. luteum* (= *Azalea pontica*) is used. The graft takes place in either summer or winter and is far too complicated for the amateur to undertake. This is not so much because of the process of grafting itself as because of the aftercare the plants require.

Naturally, rooted shoots can be cut from the main plant at the base of the rootstock and replanted without further ado. You can also take an individual shoot and partly cut through it just below the surface of the ground. The wound is then pegged open and left for a year or so, by which time a good root system will have formed. You can then remove the shoot and replant it elsewhere. This sort of propagation is easy to do and nearly always successful. It is therefore the one recommended to the amateur.

Rhododendron diseases and pests

This book is not long enough for me to discuss all the diseases which attack rhododendrons. I will simply list a few of the more common diseases and their remedies. On the left-hand side of the table below you will see the symptoms of disease; on the right-hand side will be found the causes and the remedies. It is possible that your rhododendrons will never contract any disease—I hope for your sake that this is so, but even if they do, don't despair. As with humans, rhododendrons generally recover from their ailments and become perfectly healthy once more. If you are in doubt it is possible that someone at your local nurseries will come and inspect your rhododendron for you and prescribe a cure. Or perhaps you could telephone him and describe the symptoms to him—he may be able to recognize the problem immediately from your description and recommend a cure.

Symptoms	Cause and remedy
Newly planted bushes: unsatisfactory growth, leaves of new shoots smaller than previous growth, unhealthy leaf-colour, shoots rather short.	Probably *errors in planting*: planted too high or too deep, ball of roots not opened out, not enough water, ground perhaps too heavy (drainage!!), site too sunny and dry.
Plants put out no shoots, leaves grey-green, dry.	Plants are *frostbitten* (you have chosen too sensitive a variety!)
Leaves wilt in high summer.	*Lack of water*; water thoroughly *immediately*, or the plant will die.
Leaves wilt, as do stems, or even the entire plant, although the soil is moist.	Root, stem or twig failure, a serious disease (*Phytophthora cinnamomi*). Cut off and burn affected parts, and eventually the whole plant.
Plant begins to die off; yellow fungus at the base of the bush.	Soil infection cause the roots to become diseased and stems eventually die back; remove these and burn them.

Symptoms	Cause and remedy
Individual leaves swollen into 'lobes' first pale green or pink, later covered with whitish powder; usually affects young plants.	Known as *Exobasidium rhododendri*. Pick off diseased leaves and spray plant repeatedly with Captan spray.
Evergreen, large-leaved varieties show half-moon shaped bites on the edges.	The weevil (*Otiorrhynchus sulcatus* is responsible for this. The larvae damage the roots and the bark. Dust and spray with DDT or Parathion as soon as the damage is seen.
Large yellow flecks appear on the leaves; on the undersides are found brown-black rough patches and 4-mm./$\frac{1}{6}$ in.-long insects with transparent wings; occurs on rhododendrons with downy undersides.	The dreaded rhododendron bug (*Stephanitis rhododendri*) and its larvae; dust or spray with DDT from the middle of May until the middle of July.
On hot summer days the leaves start going brown at the edges and begin to roll up to a greater or lesser degree.	*Sunburn*; plants are situated in too sunny a position and should be transplanted at the earliest opportunity.

RHODODENDRONS
UNDER GLASS

In this book whenever anything is referred to as being grown 'under glass', I am referring to the so-called Indian azaleas as well as to rhododendrons. Incidentally, Indian azaleas originate in Japan and not in India, and are usually to be found on sale in flower shops between Christmas and Easter. No doubt the enthusiast is hoping to read a few tips on how to care for these azaleas, but there is already so much literature available on the subject that I do not intend to deal with it in detail. A list of the most important varieties will be found on page 48.

I am certain that many rhododendron enthusiasts either have a greenhouse already or have sufficient garden space to install one, for they know that there are species (tropical and subtropical wild varieties or hybrids) which are best cared for in the greenhouse during the winter. The rewards of this type of attention are glorious flowers, generally far more beautiful than those grown in the open, often divinely scented and, what is more, not everyone has them. It is not possible to grow these indoors, however, for the temperature and climate that suits these flowers would not suit your furniture one bit. So they must stay in the greenhouse.

If all the predictions about our future life on this earth come true, rhododendron enthusiasts can look forward to a very pleasant life. We will work less, have more free time and be able to fly off to different continents for the length of the resulting longer weekends. Nature lovers will be able to collect plants from different parts of the world and bring them home. Who knows, we might all be able to visit China one day and see the place of origin of most of our rhododendrons.

Luckily, continental firms are beginning to build small greenhouses for enthusiasts, of the sort we have long been used to in England. Modern greenhouses are extremely easy to erect and need very little after care. They are well suited to the care of tropical or not completely hardy rhododendrons. I do not really need to say that it is advisable to begin with plants which are easily obtainable. By this I do not mean that you will be able to obtain what you want from your nearest nursery, but it is advisable to order from one of the better known specialist nurseries.

A simple way to force plants

Even among gardening circles it is not generally known that it is possible to bring on most rhododendrons and azaleas so that they flower several weeks earlier, by forcing them. By forcing is meant the action of encouraging faster growth and earlier flowering by increased warmth and atmospheric moisture. Very few specialists know how to go about forcing rhododendrons, and even fewer are able to guarantee successful flowers. The author of this book has worked in ten large flower shows in Dortmund, on up to 3,000 flowering rhododendrons, and part of the job has involved studying the forcing of the plants at all stages. Forcing is not a very difficult process, even for the layman, as long as you are not determined to have the flower bloom on a particular date. Why, then, force a plant at all? Simply because you want to have flowers in your garden when nothing else (including unforced rhododendrons) is in bloom.

Apart from a greenhouse which can be heated to 18° C., no special equipment is necessary. There must, of course, be ample ventilation, so that if the flower buds should begin to develop too quickly their growth can be slowed down by decreasing the temperature. This is done by opening as many windows as is necessary. Plants that are overforced often do not grow to their full size, much less to their full scent or colour. Pink-flowered varieties often end up very pale, sometimes even white.

Now to the method of forcing rhododendrons. The plants selected for forcing are chosen in autumn; they should have a good complement of buds on them. They are then heeled in very close to the greenhouse, with their ball of roots covered with just enough peat for the plants to be easily removable, even during frosty weather. This should be done towards the end of December or beginning of January. In March the plants are moved into the greenhouse, where they are planted very close together, i.e. with their foliage touching. Remember that greenhouse space is costly in winter, and it should be utilized as fully as possible. Make sure the ground never dries out, and several times a day, especially when the sun is shining, water the plants gently, thus providing them with the spring showers they would be getting outside. This will also keep the air moist. The buds should now be beginning to swell, but it will be eight to ten weeks before bushes treated in this manner are fully out. Evergreen rhododendrons do not generally develop any new shoots or leaves in the forcing bed, but only flowers; this also applies to most azaleas. Hardy outdoor azaleas therefore have no leaves at all when they burst into flower, and, if anything, look even more magnificent than when left to their own devices, for a part of their leaves have normally developed by the time the buds flower in May.

Within the greenhouse flowering rhododendrons and azaleas in all stages of development can be transplanted if you feel they are too close together, or if you do not like a particular grouping, or if you wish to make way for new plants.

As soon as the buds in the greenhouse begin to unfold, the temperature must be lowered to about 8°–10° C. (This is done by increasing ventilation.) Apart from the fact that this temperature is quite warm enough for the plants to develop satisfactorily, it has the advantage of keeping the flowers alive and healthy for around two weeks. At a higher temperature they normally die after one week.

Keep watering the plants regularly during the flowering period, for the rhododendrons will not have grown any new roots yet, and will to a large extent be depending upon their original ball of roots for their food. These must therefore be kept moist.

The corollas of outdoor-growing azaleas do not fall off the plant once the flower has died, but hang there for some time afterwards. This is because the pistil of these flowers has a large round stamen at its upper end, and the corolla has a narrow opening at its base, through which the stamen will not easily pass. Outdoors, the flowers all eventually fall off through being blown about by the wind. In the greenhouse, however, it is the gardener's job to remove them all. But once the flowers have all gone over, what do you do with the rhododendron bushes?

This is the sort of question you must ask yourself when you start forcing rhododendrons and azaleas, for you cannot simply put them back outdoors immediately after they have finished flowering. This is because frosts in early May are not unknown. The best thing to do is to leave the plants in the greenhouse a while longer, but to lower the temperature even further, so that all the new shoots will be gradually hardened off. By the middle of May it should be safe to plant the bushes outdoors once again.

If for one reason or another you cannot keep the plants in the greenhouse once they have finished flowering you can move them out during frost-free weather, under the following condition. The plants can be covered with netting, which should protect them from late frosts, and also from the sun, which young shoots take some time to get used to. But even if new shoots are harmed or destroyed altogether by frost the old wood should be strong enough to survive without further damage. During May new shoots will develop, but these will be so weak that they will generally not flower until the second year.

Flower heads must be detached from evergreen rhododendrons as soon as possible, so as to make way for the new shoots.

Suitable varieties for forcing

Anyone wishing to force rhododendrons regularly should preferably not experiment but use the already proven varieties. Not all varieties are equally suitable for this purpose. In Holland, where forcing is practised more frequently than anywhere else, the following sorts are recommended:

(a) *Evergreen hybrids*
'Blue Peter', lavender with dark fleck
'Britannia', clear scarlet
catawbiense 'Boursault', lilac with a little pink
catawbiense 'Grandiflorum', lilac
'Chevalier Felix de Sauvage', bright red, dark fleck, fringed
'Dr. Arnold W. Endtz', carmine, fringed
'El Alamein', dark red
'General Eisenhower', dark carmine
'Hollandia', carmine
'Jean Mary Montague', bright scarlet
'Kluis Sensation', scarlet with dark fleck

'Madame de Bruin', clear red
'Marinus Koster', dark pink with lighter patches
'Mrs. Lindsay Smith', white, very large flowers, red throat
'Nova Zembla', red
'Peter Koster', magenta
'Pink Pearl', bright pink
'Prof. J. H. Zaayer', bright red
'Purple Splendour', violet, dark fleck
'Queen Mary', dark pink
'Roseum Elegans', rosy lilac
'Sappho', white with black fleck
'Souvenir de D. A. Koster', dark scarlet
'Souvenir de Dr. S. Endtz', deep pink
'Wilgen's Ruby', dark red

(b) *Japanese azaleas*
'Adonis', white, fringed
'Aladdin', lacquer red
'Chopin', dark pink with large fleck
'Christmas Cheer', dark red
'Diana', salmon pink
'Esmeralda', pink
'Favorite', dark pink, fringed
'Helena', pink
'Kirin', pale pink
'Lilac Time', pale lilac
'Matador' bright red
'Palestrina', greenish white
'Princess Juliana', orange
'Purple Triumph', dark purple
'Salmon King', orange salmon
'Schubert', bright pink
'Vuyk's Rosyred', rosy red
'Vuyk's Scarlet', dark red

(c) *Ghent azaleas (previously known as pontica hybrids)*
'Coccinea Speciosa' bright orange
'Corneille', pink, double
'Daviesii', white with yellow fleck
'Fanny' (= 'Pucella') purple pink with brown fleck
'Grandeur Triomphante', dark violet pink
'Nancy Waterer', golden yellow
'Narcissiflora', sulphur yellow, double
'Pallas', red with orange
'Sang de Gentbrugge', carmine

(d) *Mollis hybrids*
'Alphonse Lavallée', orange with pink
'Anthony Koster', dark yellow
'Directeur Moerlands', golden yellow, darker inside
'Dr. M. Oosthoek', dark orange red
'Hortulanus H. Witte', clear orange yellow
'Queen Emma', dark orange with salmon
'Koster's Brilliant Red', orange red
'Oreana', dark orange red
'Spek's Brilliant', orange with yellow anthers
'Willem Hardijzer', dark red
'Winston Churchill', dark orange red

Under glass

(e) *Rustica azaleas* (*all double*)
'Aida', pink with pale lilac
'Freya', pale salmon with a little yellow
'Norma', rosy red with salmon
'Phébé', sulphur yellow

The 'Exbury Azaleas' can also be forced, but not many experiments have been conducted with them as yet.

Rhododendrons suitable for growing in the greenhouse; listed according to botanical family

According to the temperature, flowering period is generally between March and May.

Name	Series / Subseries	Colour of flower	Scent	Rating G.B.	Rating U.S.A.
(a) Up to 1 m./3 ft. high					
R. simsii	Azalea	White, pink, red, purple	—	All good	—
(Garden varieties)	Obtusum	Two toned	—	—	—
R. boothii	Boothii	Lemon yellow	—	**	—
R. leucaspis	Boothii Megeratum	Milky white	—	****	—
R. edgeworthii	Edgeworthii	White with pink	Strong	****	****
R. bullatum	Edgeworthii	White with pink	Strong	***	****
R. seinghkuense	Edgeworthii	Bright yellow	—	**	—
R. ciliatum	Maddenii Ciliicalyx	White, pink outside	Yes	****	***
R. ciliicalyx	Ciliicalyx	White with pink, yellow inside	Yes	****	**
R. cubittii	Ciliicalyx	Buds reddish and yellow, Flowers pure white	Yes	**	—
R. formosum	Ciliicalyx	White, pink striped outside	Usually strong	***	—
R. johnstoneanum	Ciliicalyx	Bright yellow or white	Yes	***	—
R. scottianum	Ciliicalyx	White, reddish outside	Yes	**	*
R. valentinianum	Ciliicalyx	Butter yellow	—	***	—
R. moupinense	Moupinense	White to pink	—	****	—
R. spinuliferum	Scabrifolium	Red	—	***	—
(b) Up to 2 m./6 ft. high					
R. xanthostephanum (= aureum)	Boothii Tephropeplum	Yellow to greenish yellow	—	**	—
R. maddenii	Maddenii	White	Yes	***	***
R. veitchianum	Maddneii Ciliicalyx	White, greenish inside	Yes	***	—
R. dalhousiae	Maddenii Megacalyx	White, lily shaped	Yes	****	****
R. rhabdotum	Megacalyx	Cream white and yellow	Yes	****	—
R. virgatum	virgatum	Purple to white	—	**	—
(c) Over 2 m./6 ft. high					
R. griffithianum	Fortunei Griffithianum	Pure white Very large	Very often	****	****
R. griersonianum	Griersonanum	Red	—	****	***
R. elliottii	Irroratum Parishii	Scarlet	—	****	****
R. taronense	Maddenii Ciliicalyx	White with yellow	Yes	***	—
R. lindleyi	Maddenii Megacalyx	White with yellow	Yes	****	****
R. megacalyx	Megacalyx	White, lily shaped	Yes	***	—
R. nuttallii	Megacalyx	Yellow to yellowish white	Yes	****	****
R. taggianum	Megacalyx	White with yellow	Yes	***	***

Handwritten annotations:
- Next to R. simsii: "Ts."
- R. ciliatum: "Nepal + Sikkim + adjacent Tibet 8,000 to 13,300 ft."
- R. formosum: "Meghalaya (Khasi Hills) 4,500 to 7,600 ft."
- R. maddenii: "Sikkim to N Assam 6,300–9,600 ft."
- R. veitchianum: "N. Burma, N. Laos, + W + NW Thailand 4,000 to 8,000 ft."
- R. megacalyx: "N Assam + SE Tibet to WNW Yunnan + NNN Burma 6,600 to 11,200 ft."
- Left margin symbols ("R" / crossed marks) beside many species.

Handwritten at bottom: burmanicum from Mt. Victoria in WC. Burma 9,000 to 9,730 ft

Name	Parents and year	Colour	Scent	Height group	Rating G.B.	Rating U.S.A.
(d) Hybrids						
R 'Countess of Haddington'	ciliatum × R. dalhousiae 1862	White	Yes	a	**	**
R 'Countess of Sefton'	R. edgeworthii × R. 'Multiflorum' 1877	White	Yes	b	*	**
R 'Forsterianum'	R. edgeworthii × R. veitchianum 1917	White	Yes	b	?	***
R 'Fragrantissimum'	R. edgeworthii × R. formosum 1868	White	Strong	c	***	***
R 'Lady Alice Fitzwilliam'	unknown before 1889	White	Strong	c	***	***
R 'Princess Alice'	R. ciliatum × R. edgeworthii before 1862	White	Strong	c	?	?
R 'Tyermannii'	R. formosum × R. nuttallii, before 1925	White	Strong	b	****	—

Rhododendrons for year-round greenhouse cultivation

As we have already seen, there are many particularly beautiful wild varieties as well as hybrids which cannot endure our cold winters and which must therefore be given a place in the greenhouse. I shall not deal here with the tropical varieties which come from Malaysia, since these are hardly available to the amateur, and in most cases are merely of scientific interest. However, even many of the glorious varieties from south-east Asia are not hardy in our climate; this fact has not prevented many rhododendron growers from crossing these with other plants and thereby achieving more or less hardy hybrids. More details about this subject can be found in the section on the development of new varieties (page 20).

Beginners are advised not to start with these sensitive varieties. Varieties to be grown in the greenhouse should be very carefully selected. They must have markedly more beautiful flowers than the outdoor varieties, and a better scent if the effort is to be worth while. First of all, small varieties growing to a height of about 1 m./3 ft. should be chosen, so that you can see them easily when they are in bloom. If you like, plants of this sort can be trained over a tree-trunk turned on its side, for many rhododendrons grow on trees in their natural state.

However beautiful you find the large-leaved varieties, and the tree-shaped ones, remember that there is simply not enough room in most greenhouses for them. The table on page 46 gives an indication as to suitable varieties.

Tropical varieties must be kept in the greenhouse the whole year round. As far as the wild varieties from New Guinea are concerned, the genus as a whole is not particularly highly rated for the garden, although very interesting; it includes among others R. leucogigas, which has the largest flowers of the entire family (leucogigas = white giant), a most impressive plant. On the other hand, the dwarf varieties from the mountains of this country are very pretty, but radically different from those from the Himalayas.

It is possible that some readers will be surprised to find anything at all in this book about growing rhododendrons in the greenhouse. About 100 years ago, at the beginning of the era of rhododendron enthusiasts, the only well-known varieties were the beautiful wild types found in botanical gardens, which J. D. Hooker had brought back from the Himalayas in the middle of the ninteenth century. Until the First World War there were many people with large mansions and equally imposing gardens where first-class gardeners were employed. It used to be a sign of class to have rare and exotic plants in your greenhouse, orchids in particular. Old gardening journals are full of details about experiments in cultivation. When rhododendrons appeared on the scene it is not surprising that they immediately found their way into the conservatories of the time.

A particularly unusual garden existed in those days in the grounds of the State Porcelain Factory in Berlin. Here rhododendrons were grown and crossed with the simple aim of providing new models for porcelain decorations. Otto Schulz, the gardener responsible for the garden, later became well known for his work, and eventually sold all his hybrids to Holland.

Care of 'Indian' azaleas

It is generally known, I think, that the so-called Indian azaleas (R. simsii) are not hardy in our climate; they cannot therefore be grown in the garden. Yet these very plants are sold in such vast quantities between Christmas and Mothering Sunday, and dispatched by the buyers to so many unsuspecting birthday children, confirmation candidates or merely plant lovers that a few words of advice about how to care for these plants would seem to be called for here.

Most azaleas are two to three years old when they are offered for sale, and they have behind them a carefully planned and well-nurtured childhood, somewhat similar (in terms of time devoted to them) to roasting chickens on a battery farm. From the beginning they have been used to optimal conditions for fast growth, early bud formation and timely production of flowers. When these plants leave the nursery they are like orphaned waifs whose stepmother doesn't know what to do with them. They therefore wait on the window-sill of an overheated living-room for their death. True they are given a daily ration of water at nine o'clock as long as the flowers are open, but once the flowers have died, love for the plant cools. It is then dispatched to the dustbin, or perhaps to the cellar in the hope that it will come in handy as a present for someone else next year.

The dustbin works fast and efficiently. The cellar-azaleas, however, put up a long fight before finally succumbing while the family is away on holiday. Attempts to revive them generally fail, since once the ball of roots is dry, water poured into the pot usually runs straight through and out of the hole at the bottom.

If plants in the nursery grow bigger and better (and more expensive) every year but die the moment a housewife gets her hands on them she is clearly doing something wrong. This is not really very surprising, since she is not a professional gardener and cannot be expected to keep up the programme of fertilizing, pruning, heating, etc., which the plant received in the nursery. But there are one or two things she can do:

Place the plant in a cool room, or else on a north-facing window-sill; there it will not die nearly so quickly as in a high temperature or in full sunlight. Regular watering is very important, but the amount to be administered must always depend upon the moistness of the plant pot. Weigh the pot once or twice in your hands, and if it seems extremely light immerse it in a bucket of lukewarm water up to the level of the top of the pot. Once the air bubbles have stopped rising, you may remove the pot. This is the only remedy for plants which have become completely dried out—and this applies to other pot plants too, not just to azaleas. However, if a plant is allowed to dry out completely several times in a row it will not survive.

If it is absolutely essential, azaleas may be placed in the cellar once they have flowered, but they should be given enough light, and they must be watered regularly. Turn the pot round slightly every two or three days so that the plant receives equal quantities of light from all sides. On warm spring days, and rainy days too, bring the plants, together with any fellow-sufferers from the window-sill, out into the fresh air and see how fast they recover. Finally, in May azaleas can be given a place in the garden. Sink the plant, pot and all, into the earth, so that the top of the pot is on the same level as the earth. The plant will then derive moisture straight from the soil, thus saving you the trouble of watering it, except on very dry days, when it will require extra water. Apply small quantities of fertilizer from time to time during the summer, and the plant should form a fair amount of flower buds. At the end of October azaleas should be brought back indoors and, if looked after correctly, they should delight you with more flowers during January and February.

Varieties of 'Indian azaleas'

It will probably come as a surprise to the enthusiast to learn that a century ago in Dresden, at that time the largest centre for the cultivation of azaleas in Germany, there were no less than 400 varieties. Instead of leaving it at that, the growers devoted themselves to improving the quality of their plants by continuous further cultivation. Today there are over 2,000 named varieties of 'Indian azaleas'. The most commonly obtained varieties are described below.

'Adventsglocke' (AMBROSIUS 1934). 'Paul Schäme' × 'Fritz Sander'; red, half filled.

'Albert-Elisabeth' (HAERENS & WILLE 1921). Half filled fringed, centre white flecked with green, edged with pink. Bud mutation of 'Vervaenina'.

'Ambrosiana' (AMBROSIUS 1948). Strong pink to red, strongly filled, waved, early.

'Coelestine' (old variety, origins unknown). Small leaved, delicate growth; numerous blooms, small, single, late.

'Dresden' (A. VOIGT 1936). Mutation of 'Paul Schäme'. Salmon with darker edges, tends to look darker than it is, early.

'Elsa Kärger' (AMBROSIUS 1940). Scarlet, well filled, glowing colour, fairly early.

'Eri' (AMBROSIUS 1928). Bud mutation of 'Paul Schäme', salmon, white round the edges, with a small rosette in the centre, 7 cm./ $2\frac{3}{4}$ in. across, early (E = 'Eric Schäme').

'Ernst Thiers' (RICHTER 1890). 'Hermann Seidel' × 'Liebigs Superba'; scarlet, average size, half filled, late.

'Hexe' (O. FORSTER 1888). *R. obtus.* 'Amoenum' × 'Herzog Adolf von Nassau'. Glowing red, small, late. Indestructible and very well-known variety.

'Knut Erwén' (ROGER DE MEYER 1929). Prés. Oswald de Kerckhove × 'Prof. Wolters' with 'Apollo' × 'Paul Schäme'. Strong pink, filled, waved, late, protruding anthers.

'Lentegroet' (HAERENS 1909) 'Camille Vervaene' × 'Hexe'; bright red, similar to 'Hexe' but with larger flowers and leaves.

'Leopold Astrid' (HAERENS 1933). Mutation of 'Armand Haerens', white, red edge, fringed, fairly late.

'Leuchtfeuer' (AMBROSIUS 1940). Bright red, fairly big, simple, late.

'Madame Collumbien' (J. COLLUMBIEN, 1944). 'Paul Schäme' × 'Rubis de Meirelbeke'. Deep red, darker in the centre, large, filled, fairly early. Important variety.

'Madame Cyrille van Gele' (VAN GELE 1936). Bud mutation of 'Madame J. Haerens'; orange, filled.

'Madame John Haerens' (GAERENS & WILLE 1907). Pink.

'Madame Petrick' (SIMON MARDNER 1880). 'Deutsche Perle' × 'Sigismund Rucker'; slightly filled, pink, early.

'Memoria Sander' (SANDER 1923). Clear red and purple, filled. #

'Olympia' (AMBROSIUS 1936). 'Fritz Sander' × 'Paul Schäme'; glowing red, fairly large, well filled.

'Oranje Boven' (HAERENS 1933). Improved 'Apollo', dark orange. #

'Paul Schäme' (SCHÄME 1890). 'Wilhelm Scheurer' × 'Deutsche Perle'; coloured, well filled, early.

'Princess Beatrix' (G. J. BIERT & ZONEN 1941). Mutation of 'Paul Schäme'. Salmon coloured but darker and more intense than the parent variety, well filled, early.

'Reinhold Ambrosius' (REINH. AMBROSIUS 1951). Seedling × 'Hexe'. Red, strongly filled, fairly early. The most important variety in Germany.

'Robert van Oost' (VAN OOST 1946). 'Dr. Bergmann' × ? Scarlet, medium sized, well filled early.

'Saturnus' (HAERENS 1934) Red, filled.

'Vervaeniana' (VERVAENE 1886). 'Comte Charles de Kerckhove de Denterghem' × 'Königin der Weissen'× *simsii vittatum*'; dark pink with white edge and broad purplish red fleck, well filled, always one of the more striking varieties.

'Violacea' (DE SCHVYNMAKER DE DORMAEL 1833), violet.

COLOUR PLATE 4

Rhododendron hybrids

1 'Fénélon'
2 'Coccinea Speciosa'
3 'Klondyke'
4 'Directeur Moerlands'
5 'Irene Koster'
6 'Willem Hardijzer'

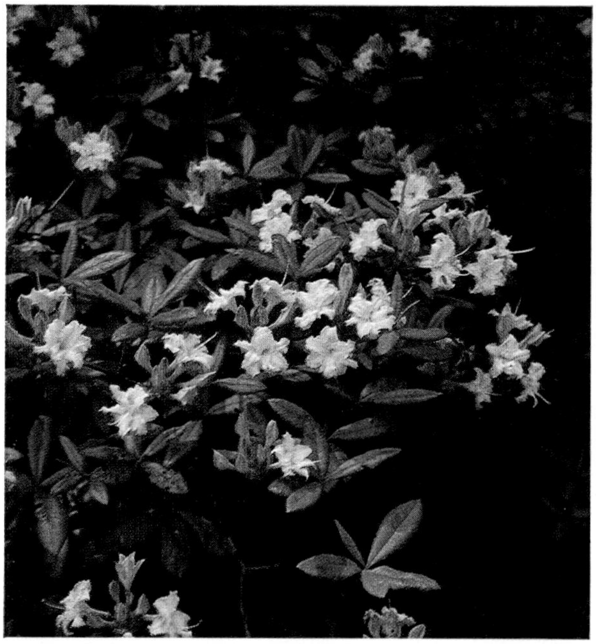

1

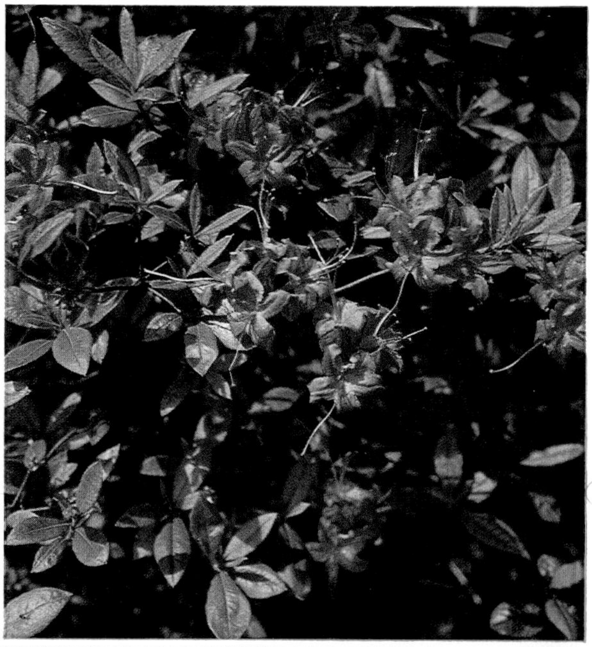

2

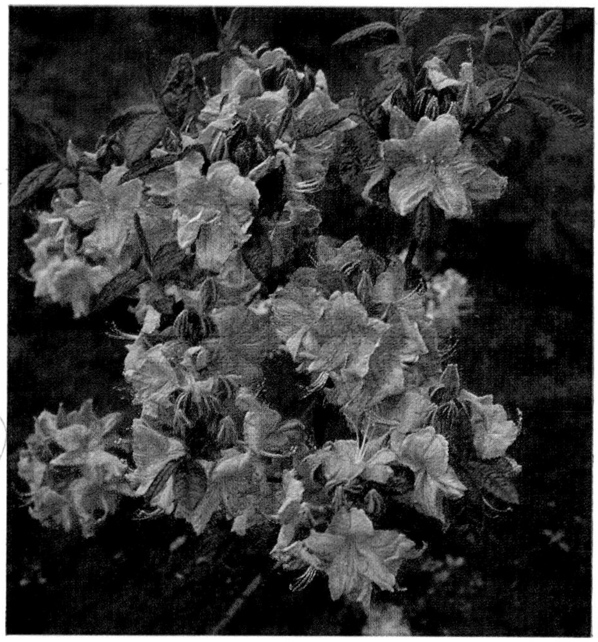

3

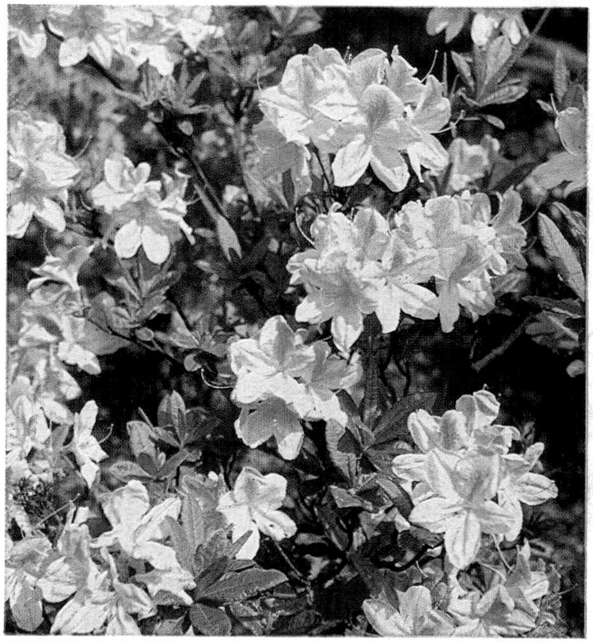

4

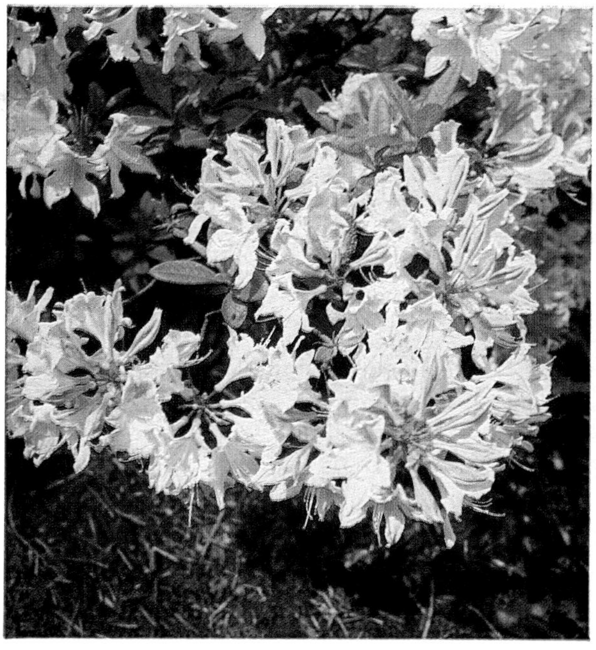

5

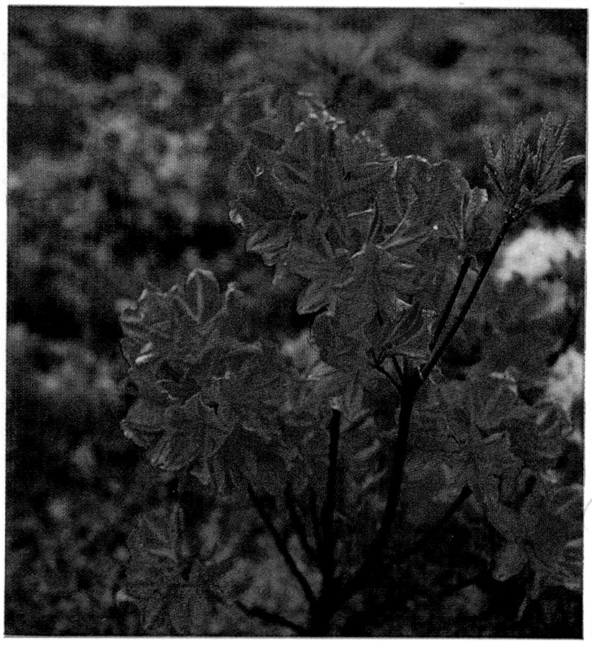

6

NOTABLE RHODODENDRON COLLECTIONS AND GARDENS

The true rhododendron enthusiast, whether he is a beginner or an experienced gardener, will surely be interested in visiting other gardens and seeing how his favourite plants are faring in other parts of the country—and abroad too for that matter. On the following pages are lists of gardens which are open to the public. With the exception of Sofiero in Sweden, the author has visited them all.

The best time to visit all these gardens is the month of May; English and Italian gardens can be visited at the beginning of the month, Scottish and Swedish ones from about 20th May. Unless anything untoward has happened, the plants should all be in full bloom. Most gardens charge admission, incidentally.

Gardens in England and Wales

Tal-y-Cafn, near Conway. On the south coast of Liverpool Bay, in Denbighshire (Wales). Access via A496; here are the famous Bodnant gardens, 24 hectares/60 acres in size, which are among the richest and most beautiful in Britain; open from April to October.

Caerhays. Caerhays Castle Gardens in Cornwall, 20 km./12½ m. as the crow flies from Falmouth; Owner, Mr. Julian Williams. This enormous park is so beautiful that it well deserves its name of 'Queen of Cornish gardens'. The largest, most beautiful and rarest rhododendrons and evergreens are to be found here.

Kew Gardens. (Royal Botanical Gardens, Kew), Richmond, Surrey, founded in 1759. 120 hectares/500 acres in size, easily reached from the centre of London. Europe's largest and most important botanical gardens; great range of all plants, including rhododendrons (visit the 'Rhododendron Dell'), but not so rich in this respect as Edinburgh.

Wisley Gardens. (R.H.S. Gardens in Wisley), Ripley, Woking, Surrey. Belongs to the Royal Horticultural Society, founded in 1804, 122–4 hectares/310 acres in size; unbelievably beautiful during May when the rhododendrons and azaleas are in flower. Easily reached by Green Coach Line from Oxford Circus to Guildford (takes about one hour).

Windsor Great Park. Property of the Crown, and includes the 'Savill Garden', 8 hectares/20 acres in size, open from March to October, 10 a.m.–6 p.m. Rather awkward to reach by public transport; wonderful park with widely varied collection of hybrid rhododendrons and azaleas.

Uckfield. Sheffield Park Gardens, Sussex. Property of the National Trust, 75 hectares/186 acres, dating since 1909 in its present form; very picturesque park, ancient groups of rhododendrons, many rare conifers; can be reached by train from London (journey takes 1 hour). Best seen in May or at the end of October.

Gardens in Scotland

Edinburgh. Royal Botanic Gardens, founded 1670, 32 hectares/

80 acres. 1 hour's flying time from London or 6 hours by train; in the author's opinion the finest rhododendron garden in Europe, with easily the largest selection, although not many hybrids. To study this garden in the depth it deserves you really need two to three full days (Plate 4).

Benmore near Dunoon. Loch Long. Younger Botanical Gardens, state owned since 1928, 6,000 hectares/15,000 acres, with woods, meadows, a rich variety of conifers and giant rhododendrons.

Lochinch. Lochinch Castle, western Scotland. Property of the Earl of Stair; very old rhododendrons; one entire alley 300 m./300 yds. long of *Araucaria araucana*, many evergreen, and conifers. Not far from here is a further garden, *Logan Park*, which also contains many treasures.

Gardens in Germany

Aurich-Haxtum. Research and experimental gardens. Very large range, perhaps the largest in Germany, particularly as regards hybrids; few wild varieties, however. Open on Sundays also.

Baden-Baden. In the last twenty years a great many rhododendrons have been planted here, particularly those cultivated by D. Hobbie. About 11,000 rhododendrons of 120 different varieties.

Bremen. Rhododendron park (founded 1936) measuring 35 hectares/87 acres together with the botanical gardens, easily reached from the Autobahn. Comprehensive range of rhododendrons and evergreen trees, large selection of wild varieties. This park is also the headquarters of the Deutsche Rhododendron Gesellschaft. (Plate 4.)

Dortmund. Two gardens with large quantities of rhododendrons. The Westfalenpark, 65 hectares/162 acres, was completely remodelled and enlarged in 1967, and specialises in displaying the latest Knap Hill varieties. The botanical gardens in Dortmund Brünninghausen (the 'Rombergpark'), 53 hectares/133 acres, has a large rhododendron forest begun in 1952 and several times enlarged. It contains about 15,000 rhododendron bushes up to 5 m./15 ft. high, comprising around 400 varieties, mainly hybrids, with perhaps eighty wild sorts.

Essen. Botanical gardens, together with the Gruga-Park measuring 45 hectares/112 acres in all. Includes a rhododendron valley. Best visited when the plants are in flower. (Plate 4.)

Gristede near Bad Zwischenahn. Rhododendron wood belonging to the Johann Bruns nurseries. 1·5 hectares/4¼ acres, started in 1949, contains show plants of 80 varieties and 100 hybrids. Entry is possible at all times and is free. But announce your arrival first at the nursery in Bad Zwischenahn.

Hamburg. Show park (Planten un Blomen, at Dammtor, founded in 1935 together with the neighbouring botanical gardens, 36 hectares/90 acres. The Elbpark and the Hirschpark are also interesting. Here are reputed to stand the first rhododendrons planted on the European continent. They were introduced by John Booth, whose father had come from Scotland to be head gardener to Baron Voigt, founder of the Holstein horticultural school. Also, the cemetery at Othmarsch, with its sixty-year-old rhododendrons, is worth a visit.

Linswege bei Westerstede. Dietrich Hobbie's rhododendron park, 65 hectares/162 acres, with meadows, deciduous and pine woods. Best visited from the middle of April until the end of May. About 25 hectares/62½ acres of the entire area are planted with rhododendrons and similar plants. Many imports from North America and from Asia. The park usually receives around 50,000 visitors each year. About 200 wild varieties in cultivation, the largest selection in Germany.

Munich. Botanical gardens in München-Nymphenburg, founded 1914, 18 hectares/45 acres. Contains a 'Rhododendron Grove' with about 500 plants consisting of about 60 wild varieties and 100 hybrids up to 2·5 m./5½ ft. high. Probably the most important collection in southern Germany.

Oldenburg i. O. State botanical gardens on the Philosophenweg, founded 1882, 3·7 hectares/approx. 9 acres. Contains a very varied collection of rhododendrons and evergreen plants. Best visited May–September.

Rodenkirchen near Cologne. Research botanical gardens of the city of Cologne. Large variety of wild sorts, also several rare species. Open only at specified times, but usually open on Saturdays and Sundays from 10 a.m. Also many conifers.

Stuttgart-Bad Cannstatt. 'Wilhelma', founded 1837, 25 hectares/62 acres, easily reached via the Autobahn; large collection of hundred-year-old azaleas and camellias which are on display in April in the greenhouses. No longer contains the 'Wilhelma' rhododendrons which originated here.

Würn über Pforzheim. Garden 1 hectare/2½ acres in size with considerable collection of wild and hybrid rhododendrons. Best visited between April and June, open daily.

Gardens in Belgium

Kalmthout. Arboretum de Belder. Grew up from the original Van Geert nurseries; 9 hectares/22½ acres, large quantity of rhododendrons, evergreens and conifers; open Wednesdays and Saturdays.

Gardens in Holland

Boskoop. Although there are rhododendrons and azaleas virtually all over Holland, the largest collection is found in the experimental nurseries in Boskoop. Here are collected all the varieties which are hardy in Holland, planted in rows. The only garden in Europe where rhododendrons from New Guinea can be seen. In this neighbourhood there are 600 nurseries, many of which export rhododendrons to all parts of the world.

The Hague. Park Clingendael; This is a new rhododendron park which was created to house the plants for which there was no longer room in Boskoop. There is also a good Japanese garden in this park.

Wageningen. The largest collection of trees in the country, but not nearly so many rhododendrons as in Boskoop.

Gardens in Italy

Lago Maggiore. Isola Bella, cultivated as a garden since 1600, 2·5 hectares/6¼ acres, very many rhododendrons and evergreens. —*Isola Madre,* 5 hectares/12½ acres, horticulturally and botanically more interesting than the previous garden and happily not so overrun with visitors as Isola Bella. Many rhododendrons, azaleas, evergreens and conifers. Both islands are reached by ship on the Stresa–Baveno–Pallanza line.

Also in Pallanza–Verbani is the *Giardini Taranto,* about 30 km./18½ miles to the south of the Swiss border, on the northern shore of Lago Maggiore, 40 hectares/100 acres, founded 1930, now the property of the Italian state; very large collection of plants, including many wild and hybrid species of rhododendrons.

Tremezzo, Lago di Como. Villa Carlotta, founded 1847. 2 hectares/3 acres, easily accessible by bus from Como or from Lugano, between Tremezzo and Cadenabbia; rich selection of rhododendrons and azaleas; best visited at the end of April and the beginning of May.

Gardens in Austria

Frohnleiten. Alpine gardens of Franz Mayr-Melnhof, many unusual conifers and evergreens.

Linz. City botanical gardens, Roseggerstrasse 20. 4·5 hectares/11¼ acres, around 170 wild species and strains of rhododendrons; largest collection in Austria. Landscaped plantation on a north-facing hill beneath fir trees, together with other evergreens.

Gardens in Sweden

Göteberg SV. Botaniska Trädgården; Frölundagatan 22; founded 1922, 22 hectares/55 acres. Contains a large amount of rhododendrons hardy in Sweden, mainly collected in Japan; many evergreens and conifers. Best visiting times: May–June.

Sofiero. King Gustav Adolf of Sweden's Rhododendron Park. In southern Sweden not far from Malmö, contains nearly 250 wild varieties of rhododendrons and azaleas from America, Asia and Europe.

Gardens in Switzerland

Brissago. Parco Botanico del Cantone Ticino. Founded 1950. 2·5 hectares/6¼ acres. Under the auspices of the botanical gardens of Zürich. Accessible from Porto Ronco by boat, or from Lago Maggiore. Not all that many rhododendrons, but quite a lot of evergreens.

In both Lugano and Locarno are many private gardens with imposing clumps of rhododendrons.

IMPORTANT VARIETIES OF WILD RHODODENDRONS

The division rhododendron belongs to the Ericaceae family. Several systems have been evolved in order to provide clear and intelligible groupings of the members of the rhododendron family. The best known systems are those devised by A. Rehder and, more recently, that by H. Sleumer. However, the terms are for the most part used only in scientific botanical literature. Amateur literature on the subject (particularly that from England and America) split the genus up into series and subseries only. Within the series, varieties are listed alphabetically. This may not be scientific, but it is certainly practical.

To begin with, the amateur will not be able to make much sense out of all the series and subseries, but after a while he will begin to notice how all the varieties in a series have one or more characteristics in common. For example, the series Falconeri and Grande all have large leaves; the Fortunei series have scented, seven-pointed flowers; those belonging to the Triflorum series have aromatically scented foliage. It is therefore useful to get to know the scientific names as well as the common names. In this way you will eventually be able to place and recognize even those varieties which were previously unknown to you.

I have tended to give the wild varieties more space in this book than is normally allotted to them, since they are now coming more and more into fashion.

British rhododendron experts prefer wild varieties because they find them more individual than the majority of hybrids, although the latter are often more robust and flower more profusely.

By far the largest proportion of wild varieties mentioned in this book are hardy in winter; the few that are not are listed because of their importance in modern cultivation.

It is very difficult to explain the main points in the classification of rhododendrons in terms understood by the amateur. Identification by means of a code would also have been too complicated. One important characteristic, however, must always be looked out for: the presence or absence of squama. These are shield- or star-shaped 'hairs' which can occur on all parts of the plant and always form a characteristic shape. Their size varies considerably, as does the distance of the squama from each other—but this is really a subject for the specialist in wild rhododendrons.

Although this book follows the general practice of grouping plants under series and subseries, a better appreciation of how the genus is composed can be obtained from a brief glance at the family as a whole. If the next couple of pages look either too difficult or irrelevant to the reader, come back to them when you have studied the subject a little further and feel more ready to cope with it.

Subfamily I: EURHODODENDRON

Leaves evergreen, scaled or hairy, either not ciliate or ciliate and scaly at the same time; occasionally deciduous and scaly; stamens 5–20; ovaries bare, scaled or hairy, never setaceous, often with more than five cells.

A. Two or more flowers from a single bud, seldom with additional corolla; long-lasting leaves.
  1. Section: Leiorhodion
    Leaves without squama, bare or hairy underneath, usually large or fairly large; ovaries bare; stamens 10–20.
    To these belong the series *Falconeri, Grande, Irroratum, Arboreum, Argyrophyllum, Ponticum, Fortunei, Thomsonii, Fulvum, Glischrum, Griersonianum, Lacteum, Campanulatum, Neriiflorum, Taliense.*

    × Leaves more or less thickly covered with squama (hardly ever completely covered with hairs), small to medium; ovaries scaly.—To these belong Sections 2 and 3.
  2. Section: Lepipherum
    Corolla wheel shaped or bell shaped; stamens 10, protruding from the corolla.
    To these belong the series *Maddenii, Triflorum, Cinnabarinum, Edgeworthii, Heliolepis, Moupinense, Saluenense, Carolinianum, Ferrugineum, Glaucophyllum, Uniflorum, Campylogynum, Micranthum* and *Lapponicum.*
  3. Section: Pogonanthum
    Corolla plate shaped, tubular under the outspread lobes, hairy at the tips; stamens 5–10 together with the short pistil; Only the series *Anthopogon* belong to this section.

B. Single flower or more from individual buds, grouped together at the ends of the short stems; leaves mainly evergreen, scaly; corolla wheel or bell shaped; stamens 10.—Series *Virgatum, Dauricum* and *Trichocladum.*

(*Between subfamilies I and II stands the hybrid subfamily* AZALEODENDRON; *natural wild hybrids unknown.*)

Leaves deciduous, hairy, often setaceous or ciliate, never covered with squama; stamens 5–10; ovary setaceous, seldom bare five-celled.
A. Flowers occur on leafless buds at the ends or sides of shoots, single or manifold and umbelliferous; no higher leaves on flower stems; stamens 5–10; erect shoots.

+ subs. Mamirazalea (R. semibarbatum of Japan)

Wild rhododendrons

Subfamily II: AZALEASTRUM

Flowers single or in pairs from side buds at the ends of secondary shoots

1. Section: Azaleastrum

   Imposing calyx, large and broad at the tip; ovary short, wide, egg-shaped. Not on the market.

2. Section: Chionasturm – *S. to Malay Psm*

   Minute calyx; ovary oblong, fairly long. Series *Stamineum* (not on the market) and *Albiflorum*. ← *Suby. Candidastrum* *close to Rhododendron Hymeno-thess?*

Subfamily III: ANTHODENDRON *(2. Subgenera)*

Flowers at the end of shoots, usually in multiple clusters, seldom single.

a. Flowers and leaf-covered secondary shoots from the same end bud; blooms 1–3, seldom more.

   1. Section: Tsutsutsi – *S. to Luzon + C Vietnam* *algo Tsusiopsis*

      Shoots with closely spaced setaceous hairs; leaves long lasting but sometimes deciduous, disperse; stamens 5–10. Includes the series *Azalea*, subseries *Obtusum*.

   2. Section: Sciorhodion *± Brachycalyx*

      Shoots bare or hairy, but never setaceous; leaves deciduous, grouped in dense whorls at the end of secondary shoots (also widely spaced on robust main shoots); stamens 5–10. Includes series *Azalea*, subseries *Schlippenbachii*.

b. Flowers out of end buds, leaves out of noticeable side buds appearing under the flowers.

   3. Section: Rhodora

      Stamens 8–10, visible; corolla wheel or bell shaped; sometimes with 1–3 divided lobes. Includes series *Azalea*, subseries *Canadense*.

   4. Section: Viscidula

      Stamens 10, enclosed in the tubular-bell shaped corolla. Includes series *Azalea*, subseries *Nipponicum* (not on the market).

   5. Section: Pentanthera

      Stamens 5; corollas funnel shaped. Includes series *Azalea*, subseries *Luteum*.

      6 Section Sciarhodion s.s. subseries Schlippenbachii ss

B. Flowers on leaf-covered stems bearing one, two or three flowers; flower stems bearing higher leaves; corolla wheel-shaped or bell-shaped; stamens 10 or more; shoots narrow or short.

Subfamily IV: THERORHODION

Characteristics as under 'B'. Includes the series *Camtschaticum*. *(2 spp + 1 ssp)*

   List of wild varieties mentioned in this book, arranged under series

Series Albiflorum
   R. albiflorum HOOK.

Pogonanthes Series Anthopogon *+anthopogon*
   R. cephalanthum FRANCH.
   R. trichostomum FRANCH.

Series Arboreum *+ cuspanum-Yannan + SE Tibet*
   Subseries Arboreum
      R. arboreum SMITH *Himalaya (Khasia Mtns, Ceylon, Nilghiri Mtns,*
      ssp. cinnamomeum WALL.
   Subseries Argyrophyllum
      R. argyrophyllum FRANCH. *Szechuan*
      R. floribundum FRANCH. *Szechuan*
      R. insigne HEMSL. & WILS. *Szechuan*

Series Azalea *amagianum*
   Subseries Canadense

52

Auriculatum - Auriculatum

J R. albrechtii MAXIM. *close to Ledum*
Am R. canadense (L.) TORR. – *close to Ledum gray?*
   R. × fraseri W. WATS.
J R. pentaphyllum MAXIM.
Am R. vaseyi A. GRAY

Subseries Luteum
   Am R. arborescens (PURSH) TORR.
   Am R. atlanticum (ASHE) REHD.
   Am R. bakeri LEMM. & McKAY *orange*
   Am R. calendulaceum (MICHX.) TORR. *orange*
   Am R. canescens (MICHX.) TORR.
   J R. japonicum (GRAY) SURING. *pink to orange = R. glabrius Nakai*
   Eu R. luteum SWEET *yellow*
   As R. molle (BLUME) G. DON *yellow* → *? 2 ssp of molle?*
   Am R. nudiflorum (L.) TORR.
   Am R. oblongifolium (SMALL) MILLAIS
   Am R. occidentale A. GRAY
   Am R. prunifolium (SMALL) MILLAIS *orange*
   Am R. roseum (LOISEL.) REHD.
   Am R. viscosum (L.) TORR.

Subseries Obtusum
   J R. indicum (L.) SWEET *scabrum*
   J R. kaempferi PLANCH. *etc*
   J R. kiusianum MAKINO
   J R. linearifolium S. & Z. – *macrosepalum*
   J R. mucronatum G. DON – *ripense*
   J R. obtusum (LINDL.) PLANCH. – *kiusianum*
   J R. pulchrum SWEET
   J R. serpyllifolium MIQ.
   As R. simsii PLANCH.
   As R. yedoense MAXIM. – *poukhanense*

Subseries Schlippenbachii
   J R. quinquefolium BISS. & MOORE
   J R. reticulatum D. DON ex G. DON *Section with calyx (= subsection of Tsutsusi)*
   J R. schlippenbachii MAXIM.

Series Barbatum *anhweiense, ba-batum*
   Subseries Crinigerum
      R. crinigerum FRANCH.
   Subseries Glischrum
      R. habrotrichum BALF. F. & W. W. SM.
      R. hirtipes TAGG
      R. rude TAGG & FORREST

R Series Boothii *auritum*
   Subseries Megeratum
      R. leucaspis TAGG

Series Campanulatum
   R. campanulatum D. DON
   R. sherrifii COWAN
   R. wallichii HOOK. F.

Series Camtschaticum – *Korea, Manchuria & Japan to S. Alaska!*
   J R. camtschaticum PALL.

R Series Carolinianum
   R. carolinianum REHD. *; chapmanii; N. Carolina & Tennessee to*
   R. minus MICHX. *Georgia + Alabama*

R Series Cinnabarinum *× 6 "Madenodendron : Keysii"*
   × 6 R. cinnabarinum HOOK. F.
   × 6 R. concatenans HUTCH.
   × 6 R. xanthocodon HUTCH.

R Series Dauricum *= Rhodorastrum*
   R. dauricum L.

∫R. mucronulatum TURCA.

R Series Edgeworthii *u Rhododendron: Bullatoradion*
  R. bullatum FRANCH.
  R. edgeworthii HOOK. F.

Series Falconeri *+ coriaceum Lactanthys*
  R. arizelum BALF. F. & FORREST
  R. basilicum BALF. F. & W. W. Xm.
  R. falconeri HOOK. F.
  R. fictolacteum BALF. F.
  R. rex LEVL.

R Series Ferrugineum *= Rhododendron*
  R. ferrugineum L.
  R. hirsutum L.
  R. × intermedium TAUSCH
  R. kotschyi SIMONK.
  R. × laetevirens REHD.

Series Fortunei *+ deoprepes ×2,3 - Yunnan*
  Subseries Calophytum
    R. calophytum FRANCH. *Szechuan*
  Subseries Davidii
    R. sutchuenense FRANCH. *Szechuan, Hupeh + praevernum - Hupeh*
  Subseries Fortunei *+ serotinum 'w. china'*
    R. decorum FRANCH. *Yunnan, Szechuan*
    R. discolor FRANCH. *Szechuan, Hupeh*
    R. fortunei LINDL. - *Chekiang*
    R. vernicosum FRANCH. *Yunnan, Szechuan*
  Subseries Griffithianum
    R. griffithianum WIGHT *Sikkim, Bhutan*
  Subseries Orbiculare
    R. orbiculare DCNE. *W. Szechuan*
  Subseries Oeiodoxa *+ scabese in Szechuan*
    R. fargesii FRANCH. *Hupeh, Szechuan, Yunnan*
    R. oreodoxa FRANCH. *W. Szechuan + Kansu*

Series Fulvum
  R. uvarifolium DILES

R Series Glaucophyllum
  R. brachyanthum FRANCH. *, charitophyllum*
  R. glaucophyllum REHD.

Series Grande *+ coryphaeum Lactanthes ?*
  R. giganteum FORREST ex TAGG
  R. grande WIGHT
  R. macabeanum WATT ex BALF. F.
  R. sinogrande BALF. F. & W. W. SM.

Series Griersonianum
  R. griersonianum BALF. F & FORREST

R Series Heliolepis *+ brevistylum*
  ×6 R. heliolepis FRANCH.
  ×4,6 R. rubiginosum FRANCH.

Series Irroratum *, subsessile to Sumatra*
  R. aberconwayi COWAN *, agastum, annae*
  R. venator TAGG

Series Lacteum *Lactanthes*
  R. beesianum DIELS
  R. przewalskii MAXIM.
  R. traillianum FORREST & W. W. SM.
  R. wightii HOOK. F.

R Series Lapponicum *27 spp. + complexum, cuneatum, Yunnan*
  R. chryseum BALF. F. & WARD *Yunnan, Szechuan, SE Tibet*
  ×2,4 R. fastigiatum FRANCH. *Yunnan*
  R. hippophaeoides BALF. F. & W. W. SM. *Yunnan*

Edgarianum - Szechuan, Yunnan, SE Tibet
flavidum - W Szechuan + SE Tibet
glomerulatum Yunnan
() tapetese Yunnan
(?solepis - Szechuan
microleucum - Yunnan
orthocladum - Yunnan, Szechuan
ravum - Yunnan, Szechuan
stictophyllum - W. Szechuan
telmateium - Szechuan + Yunnan

Lepidoton - Bailey

R. impeditum BALF. F. & W. W. SM. *Yunnan, Szechuan*
×2,4 R. intricatum FRANCH. *Szechuan*
×2,4 R. lapponicum WAHL. *Arctic Regions*
R. parvifolium ADAMS. *Mongolia to Kamchatka*
×4,6 R. russatum BALF. F. & FORREST *√ W Yunnan + Szechuan*
R. scintillans BALF. F. & W. W. SM. *Yunnan*
R. tapetiforme BALF. F. & WARD *Szechuan, Yunnan*

R Series Maddenii *about 38 spp. Rhododendron: also burmanicum, ciliato-*
  Subseries Ciliicalyx *Maddenia johnstoneanum, valentinianum*
    R. ciliicalyx FRANCH. *crassum ×4,6*
  Subseries Maddenii *crassum ×4,6*
    ×4,6 R. maddenii HOOK. F. *Tetraploid + Hexaploid polyandrum ×6*
  Subseries Megacalyx *taggianum rhabdotum*
    R. dalhousiae HOOK. F.
    R. lindleyi MOORE
    R. megacalyx BALF. F. & WARD
    R. nuttallii BOOTH

R Series Micranthum
  R. micranthum TURCZ.

R Series Moupinense *Rhododendron: Moupinense lepidotum*
  R. moupinense FRANCH.

Series Neriiflorum *beanianum + catacosmum, chaetomallum, chamaethomsonii*
  Subseries Forrestii *+ trinifolium*
    R. forrestii BALF. F. & DIELS
  Subseries Haematodes
    R. haematodes FRANCH.
  Subseries Neriiflorum
    R. neriiflorum FRANCH.
  Subseries Sanguineum
    R. dichroanthum DIELS
      ssp. apodectum BALF. F. & W. W. SM.
      ssp. scyphocalyx BALF. F. & FORREST
    R. sanguineum FRANCH.
      ssp. didymum BALF. F. & FORREST
      ssp. haemaleum BALF. F. & FORREST

Series Ponticum *-, adenopodum Szechuan, Hupeh ; chrysanthum - Siberia, Manchuria, Japan*
  Subseries Ponticum *hypoglaucum - Taiwan*
    R. catawbiense MICHX. *E. US*
    R. macrophyllum D. DON ex G. DON *W us*
    R. maximum L. *E. N Am*
    R. ponticum L. *Caucasus + Spain*
  Subseries Caucasicum
    ∫R. brachycarpum D. DON *Japan*
    R. caucasicum PALL. *Caucasus*
    ∫R. degronianum CARR. *Japan*
    ∫R. makinoi TAGG *Japan*
    ∫R. 'metternianum' WADA *Japan*
    ∫R. metternichii S. & Z. *Japan*
    R. smirnowii TRAUTV. *Caucasus*
    R. ungernii TRAUTV. *Caucasus + NE Asia*
    ∫R. yakusimanum NAKAI *Just S. of Japan*

R Series Saluenense
  ×2,4 R. calostrotum BALF. F. & WARD *+ chamaeunum ×2,4 nitens nmogariflorum chamaeunum*
  R. keleticum BALF. F. & Forrest
  R. radicans BALF. F. & FORREST
  R. prostratum W. W. SM.
  ×2,4 R. saluenense FRANCH.

R Series Scabrifolium
  R. racemosum FRANCH.
  R. spinuliferum FRANCH.

Wild rhododendrons

Series Taliense, *agapetum*, *alutaceum*, *bathyphyllum* *luctne-thai*
  Subseries Adenogynum
    R. adenogynum DIELS
    R. adenophorum BALF. F. & W. W. SM.
    R. bureavii FRANCH.
  Subseries Roxieanum
    R. roxieanum FORREST
  Subseries Taliense
    R. clementinae FORREST
    R. taliense FRANCH.
    R. vellereum HUTCH. ex TAGG
  Subseries Wasonii
    R. rufum BATAL.
    R. wiltonii HEMSL. & WILS.
Series Thomsonii + *calvroulum*
  Subseries Campylocarpum
    R. callimorphum BALF. F. & W. W. SM.
    R. campylocarpum HOOK. F.
  Subseries Cerasinum
    R. cerasinum TAGG
  Subseries Souliei
    R. puralbum BALF. F. & W. W. SM.
    R. souliei FRANCH.
    R. wardii W. W. SM.
  Subseries Thomsonii
    R. cyanocarpum (FRANCH) W. W. SM.
    R. hookeri NUTT.

    R. thomsonii HOOK. F.
  Subseries Williamsianum
    R. williamsianum REHD. & WILS.
Series Trichocladum
    R. lepidostylum BALF. F. & FORREST + *catsium* + *conorianum*
Series Triflorum 18?? *bauhiniiflorum* *Rhododedron* *melanthudro*
  Subseries Augustinii
    R. augustinii HEMSL.
  Subseries Hanceanum
    R. hanceanum HEMSL.
  Subseries Triflorum
    R. ambiguum HEMSL.
    R. keiskei MIQ.
    R. lutescens FRANCH.
    R. triflorum HOOK. F.
  Subseries Yunnanense   + *davidsonianum* ×6
    R. concinnum HEMSL.
    R. hormophorum BALF. F. & FORREST
    R. oreotrephes W. W. SM.
    R. rigidum FRANCH. + *bodnieri*
    R. yunnanense FRANCH.
Series Uniflorum   *M. trinodolen* = *Rebodoha*
    R. imperator HUTCH. & WARD
    R. ludlowii COWAN
    R. pemakoense WARD
Series Virgatum
    R. oleifolium FRANCH.

INTRODUCTION OF RHODODENDRONS INTO GARDEN CULTIVATION

It is not generally known that many varieties of rhododendrons were known to botanical scientists many years before they became available for the garden. This is chiefly because botanical collectors usually worked in very out-of-the-way places; what's more, they were usually too busy preparing and drying flowers and twigs for their own purposes to spend time looking for fertile seeds. In order to bring living plants back from their natural environment all the way to Europe painstaking and careful preparations had to be undertaken. In those days there was no such thing as plastic, one of the botantist's chief standbys in our own day and age; and it is difficult to imagine how the early collectors managed without the aid of plastic bags when transporting plants over long distances.

Before 1815 the few varieties to be found in Europe were nearly all growing in botanical gardens. Only a very few, if any at all, grew in the gardens of amateurs. Only when certain English collectors started bringing seeds back from the Himalayas did the spread of rhododendrons to the Continent get under way. I should now like to show at what stage the varieties listed in this book were first introduced into Europe. Almost without exception, the dates given are for the first introduction into British gardens; where this refers to another country, the country in question is listed in brackets afterwards. Fr. = France; Russ. = Russia; NL = Netherlands.

The plants place of origin is listed first.

1656 to 1799
Alps: R. hirsutum 1656; R. ferrugineum 1752
Gibraltar: R. ponticum 1763
Caucasus: R. luteum 1792
East Asia: R. dauricum 1780; R. chrysanthum 1796; R. camtschaticum 1799
North America: R. canascens, R. nudiflorum, R. viscosum 1734; R. maximum 1736; R. canadense 1767; R. minus 1786

1800 to 1844
Caucasus: R. caucasicum 1803
Scandinavia: R. lapponicum 1825
Japan: R. obtusum 1803; R. simsii (= 'Azalea indica', not from India!) 1808; R. mucronatum 1819; R. reticulatum 1832; R. kaempferi 1843; R. obtusum 1844; R. indicum (not R. simsii!) 1833
China: R. molle (= 'Azalea Sinensis') 1833
India, Himalayas: R. arboreum 1815; R. campanulatum 1825
North America: R. calendulaceum 1806; R. catawbiense 1809; R. roseum 1812; R. arborescens 1818

1845 to 1855
India, particularly from the Himalayas: R. campanulatum var. aeruginosum, R. cinnabarinum, R. fulgens, R. grande, R. griffithianum, R. lindleyi, R. maddenii, R. thomsonii, R. wallichii 1849, R. ciliatum, R. dalhousiae, R. falconeri, R. glaucophyllum, R. triflorum 1850; R. campylocarpum, R. edgeworthii, R. griffithianum, R. wightii 1851; R. nuttallii 1851; R. hookeri 1855
China: R. fortunei 1855
North America: R. californicum 1849

1856 to 1899
Caucasus: R. smirnowii 1880; R. ungernii 1886
Japan: R. brachycarpum, R. japonicum (= Azalea mollis; to NL) 1861; R. linearifolium 1865; R. yedoense (Russ.) 1884; R. albrechtii 1892; R. schlippenbachii 1893; R. quinquefolium 1896; R. keiskei 1898; R. mucronulatum 1897
China: R. decorum, R. fictolacteum, R. racemosum (Fr.), R. rubiginosum, R. yunnanense 1889; R. ciliicalyx 1892; R. beesianum, R. brachyanthum, R. cyanocarpum, R. dichroanthum, R. oleifolium, R. oreotrephes, R. neriiflorum 1896; R. spinuliferum 1897; R. insigne, R. williamsianum 1898; R. moupinense 1899.

1900 to 1911
China and Tibet: R. discolor 1900; R. adenopodum, R. augustinii, R. fargesii (Fr.), R. micranthum, R. sutchuenense 1901; R. floribundum, R. taliense 1903; R. ambiguum, R. argyrophyllum, R. bullatum, R. calophytum, R. concinnum, R. haemaleum, R. intricatum, R. lutescens, R. orbiculare, R. oreodoxa, R. vernicosum 1904; R. forrestii var. repens, R. souliei 1905; R. haematodes, R. impeditum 1911

1912 to 1919
China: R. apodectum, R. campylogynum, R. chryseum, R. heliolepis, R. sinogrande 1912; R. hippophaeoides, R. litiense, R. puralbum, R. roxieanum, R. russatum, R. scintillans, R. uvarifolium, R. wardii 1913; R. glischrum, R. saluenense, R. trichostomum var. ledoides 1914; R. arizelum, R. griersonianum 1917
Himalayas and Tibet: R. forrestii, R. megacalyx, R. myrtilloides 1914; R. didymum 1917; R. calostrotum, R. caloxanthum, R. keleticum 1919;
Japan: R. pentaphyllum 1914; 50 Kurume varieties to USA 1919
North America: R. oblongifolium 1917; R. prunifolium 1918

1920 to 1939
Tibet: R. radicans 1921; R. cerasinum, R. tsangpoense, R. venator, R. xanthocodon 1924; R. concatenans, R. leucaspis 1925; R. pemakoense 1930; R. ludlowii 1936
Himalayas: R. imperator, R. pruniflorum 1926; R. elliottii 1927; R. macabeanum 1928
China: R. aberconwayi 1937
Japan: R. yakusimanum 1937

Since 1939
Chief among these are the tropical varieties brought back by H. Sleumer from his expeditions to Malaysia (1961–63). These will not, however, be discussed in this book, since they are very difficult to grow and need hothouse treatment.

Since 1945 there have been occasional expeditions by English collectors, but no new varieties were discovered. Which brings us to the question: Are there any new rhododendrons to be found? Luckily, there is the opinion of a considerable expert on the subject to fall back on when answering this question. E. H. M. Cox, who as a young man collected rhododendrons in China with Farrer, has expressed the following views in the *Rhododendron and Camellia Year Book* (1967: 21–24):

'Sixty years ago Sir Harry Veitch told Ernest H. Wilson, who was just off on his first collecting expedition to China, that by now every variety which could possibly be grown in Europe must have been discovered and brought back. But when you consider how much Wilson, Forrest, Kingdon Ward, Farrer and Rock have imported during the past sixty years you realize that it cannot be assumed everything has been discovered and catalogued. The great French missionaries Delavay, David, Farges and Soulié collected only for science; collecting seeds and live plants was incidental to their work. It is unlikely that the English collectors managed to send home all the species to be found in China. In that country there are wide areas which can be attained only with considerable difficulty. Since many varieties have such a small area of distribution, one can state with near certainty that there are still many unknown varieties. Perhaps when political conditions in China are not so fraught, botanical exploration of this country will be permitted by means of helicopters. When this happens, varieties with a large area of distribution will probably be discovered, as well as those contained within a smaller area. It seems very likely that there are a good many more fishes in the rhododendron sea.

F. Kingdon Ward answered the question more succinctly and precisely: 'It is not only in the tropical jungles that new varieties await discovery. In the fantastic rhododendron fairyland stretching from the snow mountains of Burma, Assam, China and Tibet no doubt many as yet unknown varieties grow, hardy as well as sensitive types. The eager discoverer must merely seek for them.'

List of the more important collectors of rhododendrons

Name	Home	Collection Area	Time
GRIFFITH, W.	England	India	1810–45
WALLICH, N.	England	India	1815–45
WIGHT, ROBERT W.	England	India	1830–50
FORTUNE, ROBERT	England	East Asia	1843–61
HANCE, HENRY F.	England	China	1844–88
HOOKER, JOSEPH D.	England	Himalayas	1849–51
THOMSON, TH.	England	Himalayas	1949–51
MAXIMOWICZ, K.	Russia	Amur, Japan	1853–64

DAVID, A.	France	China, Mongolia	1866–72
FAURIÉ, LOUIS	France	China	1870–1900
PRZEWALSKI, N. VON	Russia	Central Asia, Tibet	1873–80
MARIES, CHARLES	England	Central China	Since 1879
HENRY, AUGUSTINE	Ireland	South-west China	From 1881
DELAVAY, J. M.	France	China, Tibet	1882–95
SOULIÉ, J. A.	France	South-west China	Around 1890
FARGES, PAUL	France	North-east Setschuan	1890–1907
FORREST, GEORGE	Scotland	China	1895–1931
WILSON, ERNEST H.	England	China	1899–1900, 1905
WILSON, ERNEST H.	For USA	China	1907–10
WARD, KINGDON F.	England	China	1910–53
FARRER, REGINALD	England	North-west China	1914–15, 1919
ROCK, JOSEPH	For USA	South-west China	1923–32
LUDLOW & SHERRIFF	England	China, Tibet	1933–49
HU, Prof. (with his collector YU)	China	South-west China	1937
SLEUMER, H.	For Holland	Malaysia	1961–63

DESCRIPTIONS OF THE WILD SPECIES

S. = Series; SS. = Subseries. For explanation of code see page 27.

R. aberconwayi COWAN (Plate 13, *2*)

Named after a previous president of the Royal Horticultural Society in London. Evergreen, upright shoot up to 1 m./3 ft. high. Leaves elliptical; 5–8 cm./2–3$\frac{3}{16}$ in. long, leathery, spreading, brittle, noticeably rolled at the edge; flowers in clusters of 6–12, wide, bell or saucer shaped, white, often with pink tone and dark red points, May, June. Western China, Yunnan, 1937. ∧∧∧***#.

R. adenogynum DIELS (Fig. 13)
S. Taliense; SS. Adenogynum

Evergreen, slow-growing bush, 1–2 m./3–6 ft. high, shoots pale green; leaves oval, 5–12 cm./2–4$\frac{3}{4}$ in. long, covered with dense yellowish down underneath, stem 2 cm./1 in. long; flowers in clusters of about 12, funnel or bell shaped, fleshy, white to lilac pink, with carmine flecks, about 4·5 cm./1¾ in. wide, April: calyx to 1·5 cm./½ in long, tomentose. China, North-west Yunnan, grassy slopes at an altitude of 3,000 m./9,000 ft. Sparse flowers, but fine foliage. *#

R. adenophorum BALF. F & W. W. SM.
S. Taliense; SS. Adenogynum

Evergreen bush, 1–2 m./3–6 ft. high, young shoots very downy and tomentose; leaves lanceolate, 6–10 cm./2–4 in. long, rusty brown and downy underneath, tomentose beneath the hairs; flowers in groups of about 10, funnel shaped, 5 cm./2 in. long, pink with a few carmine flecks, April. China, central Yunnan, stony meadows at an altitude of 4,000 m./12,000 ft. Few flowers. *#

R. albiflorum HOOK (Fig. 14)
S. Albiflorum

Deciduous bush, up to 1·8 m./approx. 5 ft. high, young shoots hairy; leaves oval, 3–6 cm./1³⁄₁₆–2³⁄₈ in. long; flowers singly or in pairs on the previous year's shoots, bell shaped, 2 cm./¾ in. wide, white with 10 stamens and a large calyx, June until July, not particularly beautiful. North America, Rocky Mountains, at altitudes of 1,000–3,000 m./3,000–9,000 ft. Hardy, but very difficult to cultivate. Interesting perhaps for crossing purposes.

R. albrechtii MAXIM.
S. Azalea; SS. Canadense   *close to Ledum!*

Named after Dr. M. Albrecht, Russian doctor who discovered this variety. Deciduous bush, 1–3 m./3–9 ft. high, loosely bush shaped; leaves narrow and oval, usually in groups of 5, 4–15 cm./1⅝–6 in. long, short stemmed; flowers in groups of 4–5, appearing with the leaves or before them, wide bell shaped, corona not divided all the way to the base, purplish-red, April–May, with 10 stamens. Central and northern Japan, at the edges of forests. ∧–∧∧***

R. ambiguum HEMSL. (Plate 15, 4)   *tetraploid*
S. and SS. Triflorum

Evergreen compact bush, in cultivation to 1 or 1–5 cm./3 or 4½ ft. high, shoots thin, upright, tomentose; leaves oval, 6–9 cm./2⅜–3⅝ in. long, very aromatic, differently shaped squama on the undersides; flowers in groups of 2–7, funnel shaped up to 5 cm./2 in. wide, yellow with green flecks, occasionally also purple, slightly hairy inside, April–May. China, Western Setschuan, 2,500–4,500 m./7,500–13,500 ft. **#   *Central szichuan*

R. arborescens TORR.
S. Azalea; SS. Luteum

Deciduous bush, up to 4–6 m./12–18 ft. high in its natural habitat, in our gardens barely 3–4 m./9–12 ft., branches unevenly distributed, young shoots bare, sometimes tinged with blue; leaves elliptical or lanceolate, 4–8 cm./2–4 in. long, mainly bluish underneath; flowers 3–6, long, funnel shaped, up to 5 cm./2 in. wide, white often also tinged with pink, filaments purple and very long, smelling strongly of heliotrope. June. Eastern USA, in the high lands and in the forests. ***#   *S. Pennsylvania + Kentucky to Georgia Alabama*

R. arboreum SM. (Colour plate 1, *1*)
S. and SS. Arboreum

Evergreen growing to a high tree 6–12 m./18–36 ft. tall in its homeland; leaves robust, lanceolate, 10–20 cm./4–8 in. long, shiny above, mainly silvery beneath; flowers in groups of up to 20 in

Fig. 13. R. adenogynum

umbelliferous bunches, tube or bell shaped, 4–5 cm./1⁹⁄₁₆–2 in. wide, normally deep red with black flecks, but with many other tints occurring, January to April. Himalayas, Cashmir to Bhutan and Ceylon. Captain Hardwicke found the first plant in 1796, but it was not until 1815 that one was successfully grown in England; ten years later this plant flowered for the first time in England. Some of these beautiful giant plants are to be found in Britain now, but probably nowhere else in Europe. Unfortunately they are not hardy on the Continent. Nevertheless, this variety was long ago crossed with *R. catawbiense*, from which many of the hardy older Catawbiense hybrids have come. ∧∧∧***#   *+ Nilghiri Mts etc.*

R. argyrophyllum FRANCH. (Plate 14, *1*)
S. arboreum; SS. Argyrophyllum

Evergreen, very slow growing, man-size, roundish bush, young shoots downy to begin with; leaves oblong, 6–13 cm./2⅜–5¼ in., dark green above, silvery and downy below, flowers in bunches of 6–10, bell shaped, about 3 cm./1³⁄₁₆ in. wide, white to pink, faintly scented, very richly flowering, May. China, Western Setschuan, 1,800–2,500 m./5,400–7,500 ft. Introduced by Wilson in 1904. Very hardy, but flowers irregularly, ∧***# The variety shown on Plate 15, *1* is var. *cupulare* REHD. & WILS, which can be distinguished by its bare young shoots and smaller, goblet-shaped white flowers.

R. arizelum

R. arizelum Balf. F. & Forrest (Plate 13, *3*)
S. Falconeri

Evergreen bush, in its homeland a tree up to 5 m./15 ft. high, young shoots and undersides of leaves velvety brown; leaves oval, 13–20 cm./5$\frac{3}{16}$–8 in. long, wrinkled above; flowers in groups of up to 20, in dense bunches about 15 cm./6 in. wide, bell shaped, 4–5 cm./1$\frac{3}{16}$–2 in. broad, white to yellow or tinged with pink. Basal fleck carmine, 8–lobed edge, 16 stamens, ovaries thickly haired, April. China, in open spaces in rhododendron forests in western Yunnan, Upper Burma and south-east Tibet, at altitudes of 3,300–4,000 m./9,900–1,200 ft. ∧∧∧**#

R. atlanticum Rehd.
S. Azalea; SS. Luteum

Deciduous bush, only up to 50–60 cm./20–24 in. in its homeland, leaves oval, 4–10 cm./2–4 in. long, pale or bluish green; flowers in groups of 4–10, appearing with the leaves or shortly afterwards, funnel shaped, white but often also pink, strongly smelling of roses, May; buds have a crown of long brushlike tomenta at the tip. Eastern North America, Pennsylvania to South Carolina. Cannot be crossed with other white American varieties because of its early flowering period. *** *Delaware to Georgia u. Alabama*

R. augustinii Hemsl (Colour Plate 1, *4*) *tetraploid*
S. Triflorum; SS. Augustinii

Named in honour of the botanist Augustine Henry from Ireland. Evergreen bush, 1·5–3 m./4$\frac{1}{2}$–9 ft. high, aromatic, shoots slightly haired and tomentose; leaves lanceolate, pointed, limp 4–12 cm./2–4$\frac{1}{2}$ in. long, very tomentose beneath; flowers in groups of 2–6, usually in threes, wide, funnel shaped, with 5 deep lobes, very varied in colour, ranging from lavender to violet (including unfortunately many ugly colours among cultivated varieties), corona completely covered with squama, April–May. China, generally found in sunny mountain slopes from West Hupeh to Setschuan, at altitudes up to 3,300 m./9,900 ft. The best blue variety with the largest flowers (from Caerhays, Cornwall) is unfortunately also the most tender, as is Wilson's Nr 4238. If you live in a cold area therefore choose only strongly coloured hardy types. ∧∧***# *Hupehse.Szechuan*

R. augustinii var. *chasmanthum* (Diels) Davidian *tetraploid*

Distinguishable from *R. augustinii* chiefly by bare shoots and its flowering period, which occurs two weeks later. Here, too, colours range from lavender to violet, with olive green flecks (= *R. chasmanthum* Diels). China, Yunnan, south-east Tibet, 3,300 m./9,900 ft. high. ∧∧*** *NNW+NNC +W Szechuan*

R. bakeri Lemmon & Mckay
S. Azalea; SS. Luteum

Named in honour of the American Dr. W. F. Baker. Deciduous bush, about 0·5–2 m./1$\frac{1}{2}$–6 ft. high; leaves oval, 4–6 cm./1$\frac{9}{16}$–2$\frac{3}{4}$ in. long, deep green above, more bluish green beneath; flowers in groups of 4–7, slim funnel shaped to tube shaped, 4–5 cm./1$\frac{9}{16}$–2 in. wide, usually orange to reddish orange, but also salmon coloured to straw yellow, occasionally up to 30 flowers in spherical bunches together, June; North America, from the Cumberland Plateau in Kentucky to the mountains of North Georgia and Alabama (= *R. cumberlandense* Brauno). 1937. Very similar to 'Coccinea Speciosa', but two weeks later; strong growth.

Fig. 14. R. albiflorum

R. basilicum Balf. F. & W. W. Sm. (Plate 8, *3*)
S. Falconeri

Evergreen, imposing bush, also a tree up to 9 m./27 ft. high in its homeland, reddish brown and downy; leaves oblong to oval, up to 30 cm./12 in. long, and 15 cm./6 in. wide, stem 3 cm./1$\frac{3}{16}$ in. long, more or less winged. Leaves reddish brown and downy on the undersides; flowers, 20–25 in 15 cm./6 in. wide bunches, wide bell shaped, creamy white with carmine basal fleck, also often tinged with red on the outsides; edge has 8 lobes, April. 16 stamens, thickly covered ovaries (= *R. regale* Balf. F. & Ward; *R. megaphyllum* Balf. F. & Forrest). China, Yunnan, north-east Upper Burma, in rhododendron forests at a height of 3,500 m./10,500 ft. Beautiful even after flowering period. ∧∧∧***#

R. beesianum Diels
S. Lacteum

Named after the nurseries of that name in Cheshire. Evergreen, stately shrub, also a tree growing to 3–5 m./9–15 ft. high in its homeland, with thick robust shoots; leaves elliptical, 15–20 cm./6–12 in. long, dark green and smooth above, covered with fine brown hairs beneath; flowers in dense bunches of 15–25, wide bell shaped, to 5 cm./2 in. long, pink with a few red flecks, April–May; ovaries brown and downy. China, north-west and central Yunnan. Interesting variety for amateurs; large leaved, buds sticky. ∧*#

R. brachyanthum Hutchins (Fig. 15)
S. and SS. Glaucophyllum

Broad evergreen shrub, barely 1 m./3 ft. high, with reddish young shoots bearing squama; leaves aromatic, oblong, 3–6 cm./1$\frac{3}{16}$–2$\frac{3}{4}$ in.

long, deep blue-green beneath, with pale and darker squama; flowers in 3s or 4s (–8) in little clusters, bell shaped, pale yellow to greenish yellow, 10 stamens, red; calyx 1 cm./⅜ in. long, with 5 deep lobes, tip erect, June–July. China, Yunnan, south-east Tibet, 3,000–3,600 m./9,000–10,800 ft. high in the mountains. Not very useful in the garden. *# *[NCC Yunnan with sspp. to NNW Yunnan, SE Tibet + Nrtn. N Burma]*

var. *hypolepidotum* FRANCH. Smaller than its type, about 30 cm./ 12 in. high, often cushion shaped; leaves smaller, aromatic, much more tomentose on the undersides; 5–6 flowers together about 2 cm./¾ in. long, yellow; China, Tibet, Yunnan, Burma. *R. charitostreptum* BALF. F. & WARD (= *R. hypolepidotum* BALF. F. & FORREST.) *#

R. brachycarpum D. DON
S. Ponticum; SS. Caucasicum

Evergreen shrub, 2–3 m./6–9 ft. high, tips of shoots and of youngest leaves white and downy, fairly thick, later clear green; bare; leaves oblong, 7–15 cm./2¾–6 in. and half as broad, pale green above, thinly covered with brown down beneath; flowers in long bunches of 10–20, wide funnel shaped, up to 3 cm./1³⁄₁₆ in. long, creamy white or with pink tinge and green flecks; pistils shorter than the 10 stamens, June–July, northern and central Japan in the mountains. Very hardy. **#

R. bullatum FRANCH.
S. Edgeworthii

Evergreen, open shrub, up to 2 m./6 ft. high in its homeland; in cultivation half that height; shoots dense and woolly; leaves elliptical, 5–10 cm./2–4 in. long, upper sides vesicular between the veins, underneath, brown and downy; flowers in groups of 2–5, wide funnel shaped, up to 5 cm./2 in. long and 10 cm./4 in. broad, white flesh, strongly scented, with scales and dense hairs, April–May; large calyx, up to 2 cm./¾ in. long, tip leaf-like and often red. China, Yunnan, south-east Tibet, north-east Burma, 3,000–4,500 m./ 9,000–13,500 ft. high in mountainland. Wonderful strain, but best suited to the greenhouse. ^^^***#

R. bureavii FRANCH. (Plate 6, 2)
S. Taliense; SS. Adenogynum

Named after the French botanist, Edouard Bureau, 1830–1918. Evergreen bush, up to 1·5 m./4½ ft. high; young shoots covered with dense rusty red down; leaves tough and leathery, broad, elliptical, up to 12 cm./4¾ in. long and 5 cm./2 in. wide; with rust-coloured down on the undersides; flowers in groups of 10–15, up to 5 cm./2 in. long, tube or bell shaped, white to pink with carmine markings; calyx has five lobes. China, Yunnan. Chiefly grown for their beautiful leaves. ^^^***

R. calendulacum TORR. (Plate 3, 3)
S. Azalea; SS. Luteum

Deciduous bush, densely wooded, 1–5 m./3–15 ft. high; in its homeland usually over 4 m./12 ft. high; young shoots covered with hairs; leaves broad and elliptical, 4–12 cm./1⁹⁄₁₆–4¾ in. long, with fine hairs on both sides; bright orange and carmine in autumn; flowers in groups of 5–7, appearing with the leaves or shortly after-wards, funnel shaped, up to 5 cm./2 in. wide, in all colours between yellow, orange and scarlet; in higher mountain regions, however, mainly orange or red, and with a later flowering period, May–June, almost completely without scent, eastern States of North America, Smoky Mountains, mainly in warm, sheltered spots in chestnut forest. Very hardy. *** *[SW Pennsylvania + SW Ohio to n Georgia + n Alabama]*

R. callimorphum BALF. F. & W., W., SM. (Plate 12, 6)
S. Thomsonii; SS. Campylocarpum

Evergreen bush, up to about 2 m./6 ft. high; leaves broad and elliptical to almost perfectly circular, 4–8 cm./1⁹⁄₁₆–3³⁄₁₆ in. long, dark green and shiny above, blue-green beneath; flowers in groups of 5–8, 4–5 cm./1¹⁵⁄₁₆–2 in. long, wide bell shaped, fine pink colour, either with or without basal fleck, darker in the bud, May–June. China, Yunnan, north-east Burma. 3,000–3,600 m./9,000–10,800 ft. high. ^^–^^^**

R. calophytum FRANCH. (Plate 8, 2)
S. Fortunei; SS. Calophytum

Evergreen, shrub with thick shoots, growing as a tree up to 12 m./ 36 ft. high in its homeland, young shoots first covered with white down, later bare; leaves hanging downwards, lanceolate, 20–30 cm./ 8–12 in. long, very beautiful; flowers in loose bunches of up to 30, open bell shaped, white, pale lilac or pink with dark red fleck at the base, March–April, stamens 15–20, pistils with crowning yellow stigma. China, western Setschuan, Tibet, 2,000–3,000 m./6,000–9,000 ft. high in forests. In our climate it is absolutely essential that this variety should stand in semi-shadow. Given time, this variety will grow into a small tree even in this country. ^^***#

R. calostrotum BALF. F. & WARD *[Diploid + Tetraploid]*
S. Saluenense

Evergreen bush, hardly over 30 cm./12 in. high in cultivation, but in its homeland reaching a height of around 1 m./3 ft.; young shoots covered with scales; leaves elliptical to oval, around 3 cm./1 in. long and half as wide, covered with thick greenish scales above, underneath covered thickly with dry red scales; edge ciliate; flowers usually in pairs, wide funnel shaped, about 30 cm./12 in. long, plate or top-shaped, purplish red to bright carmine, flecked with dark red, soft hairs on outside, but no scales, May. North-eastern upper Burma, Yunnan, south-east Tibet, in the high mountains 4,000 m./12,000 ft. and above. Very hardy. Blooms twice a year. *[N Burma + W Yunnan 3300–4250m]* *[ssp riparium also in N Assam + SE Tibet 1250–4550m]*

R. campanulatum D. DON
S. Campanulatum

Evergreen, mansize shrub, growing to 5–6 m./15–18 ft. in its homeland, sometimes as a small tree; leaves elliptical, 7–15 cm./ 2¾–6 in. long, tough, on opening densely covered with down, under-neath covered with dense rust brown down, later shiny green above, but with no metallic sheen; flowers in bunches of 6–12, 4 cm./1⁹⁄₁₆ in. long, 5 cm./2 in. wide, very varied in colour, from almost white to purple, and in its best form bluish violet; five-pointed edge, April–May; 10 stamens, bare ovaries and pistils. Cashmir to Bhutan. Unfortunately this one does not flower in its youth, as is the case with many others of this species, but it is interesting for its beautiful foliage. ***#

R. Campanulatum var. aeruginosum HOOK. F. (Plate 11, 4)

Similar to previous variety, but mainly distinguishable through its metallic, silvery green leaves when young; these later turn bluish green on the upper sides; flowers reddish purple (= *R. aeruginosum* HOOK, F.), Sikkim, Himalaya; in mountains at about 4,000 m./ 12,000 ft. Few flowers, but very hardy and glorious foliage. ***#

R. campylocarpum HOOK. F. (Fig. 16)
S. Thomsonii; SS. Campylocarpum

Evergreen, bushy shrub, 1–2 m./3–6 ft. high, young shoots thin;

Fig. 15. R. brachyanthum *var.* hypolepidotum

flowers somewhat smaller than on the type, plum coloured, small, but very attractive. Reasonably hardy. **#

R. camtschaticum PALL.
S. Camtschaticum

Deciduous bush, lying on the ground, very slow growing, seldom higher than 10 cm./4 in.; new shoots tomentose and covered with hairs; leaves wedge shaped, very thin, pale green, red in autumn, edge ciliate, flowers singly or in pairs on new shoots on stems 15 cm./6 in. long; wheel shaped, around 3·5 cm./1⅜ in. wide, purplish red with brownish red marks, generally richly flowering, May; calyx large, with leaf-like tips. Alaskas, either side of the Bering Straits, Kamtschatka, northern Japan. Loves cool, moist cliff areas, sheltered but with plenty of direct sunshine. Very hardy. **

R. canadense TORR. (Fig. 17)
S. Azalea; SS. Canadense

Deciduous shrub, 30–70 cm./12–28 in. high, with thin shoots, over covered, leaves narrow, 2–5 cm./¾–2 in. long, dull bluish green; flowers in groups of 3–6, appearing before the leaves, circular, corona split to the base in five divisions, 3 cm./1³⁄₁₆ in. wide, purple-lilac, April. North-eastern and northern America, near the banks of rivers. Very hardy; excellent for damp or wet sites. *
Labrador to Quebec to n. N.J. + c. N.Y.

R. canescens SWEET
S. Azalea; SS. Luteum

Deciduous shrub, growing up to 4 m./12 ft. in its homeland;

leaves oval, dark green and shiny above, blue green beneath; flowers in clusters of 6–10, bell shaped, 4 cm./1⁹⁄₁₆ in. long, yellow, April–May; 10 stamens with reddish anthers, ovaries and calyx tomentose, Himalayas; 3,500–4,500 m./10,500–13,500 ft. in mountains. Very beautiful with its eau-de-nil foliage, yellow flowers and coral pink flower buds. Most of the yellow hybrids to be developed in England stem from this variety. Not very easy to cultivate, but needs a moist soil with good drainage. Of the many hybrid forms available, among the best known are 'Goldsworth's Yellow' (1925), 'Zuider Zee' (1936) and 'Mrs. W. C. Slocock' (1929). ΛΛ–ΛΛΛ***#

R. campylogynum BALF. F. & WARD
S. Campylogynum

Evergreen very low-growing broad bush, generally not growing to more than 30–50 cm./12–20 in. in height in cultivation, shoots tomentose; leaves 1–2 cm./⅜–¾ in. long, with thick tips, oval, blue green underneath and somewhat scaly; flowers in clusters of 1–4 at the tips of shoots, occurring singly on upright stems 3–5 cm./1³⁄₁₆–2 in. long; flowers bell shaped, only 1·5 cm./⁹⁄₁₆ in. long, violet red outside, dark brown inside, but also occurring in other shades, May–June. North-east Burma in the mountains 4,000–5,000 m./12,000–15,000 ft. high, on moist granite slopes. **# *N Assam + Extreme N Burma / W + N C Yunnan + SE SE Tibet*

R. campylogynum var. *myrtilloides* (BALF. F. & WARD)
COWAN & DAVIDIAN

Even smaller than the type, hardly over 15 cm./6 in. high when grown in our country; leaves dark green above, silvery beneath;

Fig. 16. R. campylocarpum

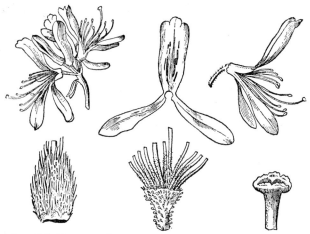

Fig. 17. R. canadense

leaves long to oblong, up to 10 cm./4 in. long, with thick hairs beneath; flowers in groups of 6–15, appearing before the leaves corona funnel or tube shaped, up to 5 cm./2 in. wide, pure white or dirty pink to pink, with red tubes, pleasantly scented; tubes thickly layered with squama outside. (This is the easiest way to distinguish this variety from *R. nudiflorum*, which has no squama.) May; South-eastern U.S.A. Fairly hardy. * *Delaware to Florida, Texas, Arkansas + Tennessee*

R. carolinianum REHD.
S. Carolinianum

Small, evergreen bush, 1–1·5 m./3–4½ ft. high, growth loosely bush-shaped, shoots covered with squama; leaves eliptical, 6–10 cm./2 3/16–4 in. long, with a network of veins on top, hairy underneath; flowers in groups of 4–9, narrow, tube shaped, 3 cm./1 3/16 in. long, pale pink. May–June. Mountains of eastern states of America, Blue Ridge Mountains. Extremely hardy, but needs good drainage in cultivation. *#

R. catawbiense MICHX. (Plate 3, *1* and Fig. 6)
S. and SS. Ponticum

Evergreen, tall bush, 2–4 m./6–12 ft. high or more, often wider than it is high; leaves ovoid, 7–15 cm./2⅞–6 in. long, dark green and shiny above, somewhat arched, pale green beneath; flowers in groups of 15–20, funnel to bell shaped, 5 cm./2 in. wide, mainly purplish lilac with greenish flecks, end of May to beginning June. North America; in exposed, rocky areas of the Smoky Mountains, on sites over 1,300 m./3,900 ft. growing into impenetrable thickets, often intermingling with *R. carolinianum*. Discovered by John Fraser and his son when he was collecting plants in North America for the Russian Czar Paul. This variety bloomed in England in 1813 for the first time, at Lee & Kennedy's nurseries in London. Indestructible, even in the hardest winter. *#

The wild type is hardly cultivated; instead of this we have the 'Grandiflorum' and 'Boursault' selections. Very often used in crossings, above all in England, Holland and Germany.

R. caucasicum PALL. (Fig. 4)
S. Ponticum; SS. Caucasicum

Evergreen bush, which does not usually reach a height of more than 1 m./3 ft in our climate, but in its homeland reaches up to 2·5 m./7½ ft., shoots covered with thick layer of down; leaves long,

5–10 cm./2–4 in., dark green above, covered in brown down beneath; flowers in groups of 7–10, wide bell shaped, yellowish or with pink tint and green markings, May, ovaries thickly covered with white down, fruit capsule upright. Caucasus, north-eastern Turkey. Formerly much used in crossings. The Russian collector Pushkin sent the first plant to Kew Gardens in 1803; at around the same time the German nursery owner living in England, Conrad Loddiges, received seeds of this variety from St. Petersburg. *#

To this belong among others the following garden varieties: 'Cunningham's White', 'Cunningham's Sulphur', 'Boule de Neige', 'Jacksonii' and so on, all excellent for their very early flowers.

R. cephalanthum FRANCH.
S. Anthopogon

Evergreen, small bush, only 30–50 cm./12–20 in. high, with thick scales on young shoots; leaves 3 cm./1 3/16 in. long, 1 cm./⅜ in. wide, coarse and leathery, with dense scales beneath; flowers occurring in groups of 8, in dense, round little heads, narrow and tube shaped, around 1·5–2 cm./9/16–1 in. long and broad, white, with five-pointed edge, May. Interesting variety for the enthusiast. Comes from China, Setschuan, Yunnan, south-eastern Tibet, found in high mountain regions around 4,000–5,000 m./12,000–15,000 ft. ∧∧**#

R. cerasinum YAGG
S. Thomsonii; SS. Cerasinum

Evergreen bush, in its homeland growing to 3 m./9 ft. in height (in Burma it even grows into a tree), leaves long, 5–7 cm./2–2¾ in., underneath eventually bare and bluish; flowers hanging, in groups of 5–6, scarlet red with 5 coal black basal flecks, bell shaped, in other varieties creamy white with broad, cherry red edge, May, long stemmed. When ripe, seed pods bend themselves upwards. Burma, Assam, Tibet, 3,000–4,000 m./9,000–12,000 ft. In its homeland the flowers are mostly white with very wide cherry red edge, often coloured red within, too. The stems are very long and thin, so that the flowers swing in the breeze; as soon as the fruit capsules develop the stems turn upwards and become stiff. ∧∧***#

R. chryseum BALF. F. & WARD *R. rubicola var c.*
S. lapponicum

Evergreen, aromatic small bush, 30–70 cm./12–28 in. high, leaves around 1·5 cm./9/16 in. long, 1 cm./⅜ in. wide, with thick scales on both sides; flowers in groups of 4–5, broad funnel shaped, around 2·5 cm./1 in wide, with short tubes covered with fine hairs, *3300 t* sulphur to yellow, April–May. China, Yunnan, south-eastern *4750* Tibet, Setschuan, in high mountains. Hardy, but somewhat particular. *mil-s* One of the finest yellow dwarf varieties; often blooms in autumn in our climate. **# *Extreme N Burma NW Yunan + SE Tibet other vars + SW Szechuan*

R. ciliicalyx FRANCH.
S. Maddenii; SS. Ciliicalyx

Evergreen bush, not very hardy in our climate, growth loose, up to 2·5 m./7½ ft. leaves narrow, 6–11 cm./2⅜–4¾ in. long, pointed, bluish and covered with scales beneath; flowers mainly in groups of 3, funnel shaped up to 10 cm./4 in. wide, pure white or with yellow marking, edge with 5 lobes, March–May, very finely scented, calyx has 5 lobes, each one 3–8 mm./⅛–5/16 in. long and brushlike. China, Yunnan, Setschuan, south-eastern Tibet, 2,500–3,000 m./7,500–9,000 ft. high in mountain land. Wonderful variety for the hothouse. Profusely flowering. ∧∧***# *NVC+NC Yunnan 81,000ft.*

61

R. cinnabarinum

R. cinnabarinum Hook. F. (Plate 16, 5) *Hexaploid*
S. Cinnabarinum

Evergreen, upright bush, shoots reddish in colour, with some scales at first; leaves oval, bluish underneath, with scales on both sides but many more beneath; flowers mainly in groups of 5, tube shaped, 5–6 cm./2–2$\frac{3}{16}$ in. long, somewhat flattened on top, and with 5 upright tips to the lobes. Colour of the flowers varies considerably, including cinnamon red, orange, but including all the tones to salmon. China, Sikkim, Bhutan, south-eastern Tibet, 3,000–4,000 m./9,000–12,000 ft. high. Wonderful, rich profusion of flowers, but unfortunately rather delicate in our climate. ∧∧∧***# *Nepal to Bhutan & Adjacent Tibet 2,750–3950 m*

Two more varieties are worth a mention:

var. *purpurellum*; flowers shorter, more bell shaped, plum coloured through to lilac pink. Southern Tibet, in the high mountains. Equally beautiful as the type, but more hardy. Less flowers, however.

var. *roylei*, Hook. Shorter, more open flowers, in a glorious carmine colour with violet tint. ∧∧∧***# (Plate 12, 4)

R. clementinae Forrest (Plate 11, 5)
S. and SS. Taliense

Named by the author after his wife. Evergreen bush, growing up to 3 m./9 ft. in its homeland; leaves long to elliptical, up to 18 cm./7$\frac{3}{16}$ in. long and 7 cm./2$\frac{3}{4}$ in. wide, deep green and matt above, underneath covered with think white or brown down; flowers in groups of up to 15, coronas bell shaped, up to 4 cm./1$\frac{5}{16}$ in. long, white to pink with carmine tints, April–May. China, Yunnan, Setschuan, south-east Tibet in the mountains around 3,600–4,600 m./10,800–13,800 ft. Chiefly beautiful for their leaves. ∧–∧∧**

R. concatenans Hutchins *Hexaploid*
A. Cinnabarinum *= cinnabarinum ssp xanthocodon Bhutan, N Assam + Adjacent Tibet*

Evergreen bush, around 1 m./3 ft. high, shoots reddish brown and thickly covered with scales; leaves long, 4–6 cm./1$\frac{3}{16}$–2$\frac{3}{8}$ in. in length, bare above, bluish and scaly beneath, often tinged with red; flowers in groups of 7–8. 'Bell-shaped flowers which look like gleaming copper, and when the wind blows them it is easy to imagine that they sound gently when they knock against the leaves' (Ward); around 4 cm./1$\frac{9}{16}$ in. wide, apricot coloured with purple tinge and veins. South-eastern Tibet. The hardiest of the Cinnabarinum series. The flowers contain large quantities of nectar. ∧∧∧***# *3050–3950 m*

R. concinnum Hemsl. *Tetraploid*
R. Triflorum; SS. Polylepis

Evergreen bush, 1 m./3 ft. high, grows up to 3 m./9 ft in its homeland, thickly wooded, young shoots covered with scales; leaves lanceolate, 4–8 cm./1$\frac{9}{16}$–3$\frac{3}{16}$ in. long, scales on both sides; flowers in groups of 3–6, funnel shaped, 4–5 cm./1$\frac{9}{16}$–2 in. wide, purple, or sometimes nearer to lilac in colour, with or without carmine flecks, usually with scales outside, April–May (= R. yanthinum But. & Franch.). China, Setschuan, Mount Omei. # Good and hardy, but not particularly recommended because of the frequently poor quality of the colour of the flowers; better than this is the var. *pseudoanthinum* (Balf. F.) Davidian, which is chiefly distinguishable through larger darker, ruby red flowers. Western Setschuan, 2,500–4,000 m./7,500–12,000 ft. high. ∧∧ *all Setschuan & W Hupeh 7,600 to 15,000 ft*

R. crinigerum Franch. (Plate 10, 7)
S. Barbatum; SS. Crinigerum

Evergreen bush, growing to 3 m./9 ft. or more in its homeland, young shoots very sticky, and covered with long hairs. Leaves long and lanceolate, 10–15 cm./2–6 in. long, up to 5 cm./2 in. wide, dark green above and generally arched, thickly covered with brown or white down below; flowers in groups of up to 12 together, bell shaped, pure white or with pink tint; sometimes clear pink with carmine fleck inside; May; calyx up to 15 mm./$\frac{5}{8}$ in. long and thickly covered with scales. China, Yunnan, south-eastern Tibet, 3,300–4,600 m./9,900–13,800 ft. ∧–∧∧**

R. cumberlandense Braun = R. bakeri Lemm. & Mckay (See under *bakeri*)

R. cyanocarpum (Franch.) W. W. Sm.
S. and SS. Thomsonii

Evergreen bush, growing up to 5 m./15 ft. high in its homeland, young shoots bluish green; leaves broad and elliptical, dark green above, bluish green beneath, similar to R. thomsonii, 5–11 cm./2–4$\frac{3}{4}$ in. long; flowers in groups of 8–10, in loose bunches, wide funnel or bell shaped, 5–6 cm./2–2$\frac{3}{8}$ in. broad, white or creamy yellow, with pink tinge or, occasionally, completely pink (Different from R. thomsonii) March–April–May; calyx large and goblet shaped, 12 mm./$\frac{1}{2}$ in. long, fruits with plum-coloured tinge. China, Yunnan. ∧–∧∧**#

R. dalhousiae Hook. F. (Plate 10, 3)
S. Maddenii; SS. Megacalyx

Named in honour of Lady Dalhousie, wife of the Governor General of India. Evergreen bush, up to around 3 m./6 ft. high; leaves lanceolate, up to 16 cm./6$\frac{3}{8}$ in. long and 5 cm./2 in. wide; bluish green beneath and covered with thick layer of scales; flowers almost lily-shaped, pale yellow to white, golden yellow at the base, often with pink tint, around 10 cm./4 in. long, strongly scented, May. Sikkim, Bhutan, south-eastern Tibet. Glorious flowers, but only suitable for the greenhouse. ∧– ∧∧*** *Nepal To Bhutan 6,000 to 8,100 ft.*

R. dauricum L. (Plate 9, 2)
S. Dauricum

Named after Dauria or Dahuria, a region of south-eastern Asia, east of Lake Baika. Deciduous or winter green (leaves are shed in spring) bush, up to 2 m./6 ft. high, young shoots covered with hairs and scales; leaves elliptical, 2–4 cm./$\frac{3}{4}$–1$\frac{9}{16}$ in. long, rounded off at both ends; deep green above; some scales above, many more beneath; flowers broad funnel shaped in groups of 1–3; pink, around 2 cm./$\frac{3}{4}$ in. wide, January–March; scales on the flower buds fall off very early; fairly hardy and very beautiful after a mild winter; in this case it will bloom in January in the open ** *& Hokkardo*

var. *sempervirens* Sims is completely evergreen, but is otherwise hardly to be distinguished.

R. decorum Franch.
S. and SS. Fortunei

Evergreen bush, up to 2 m./6 ft. high in our climate, up to 6 m./18 ft. high in its homeland, with thick, pale green shoots; leaves oblong, 5–15 cm./2–6 in. long, covered with waxy substance above, bluish green beneath; flowers in groups of 8–10, open funnel to bell shaped, edge with 6–8 points, mainly pure white, but occasionally with pale pink tinge, slightly scented, March–May, and June; China, Yunnan, Setschuan, on mountain slopes, in heights of 2,500–3,000 m./7,500–9,000 ft. Winter hardiness varies considerably with the place of origin of the plant, but is mainly sensitive. ∧∧∧***#

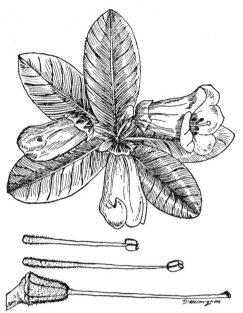

Fig. 18. R. dichroanthum *var.* apodectum

R. degronianum CARR (Plate 10, *1*)
S. Ponticum, SS. Caucasicum

Named after M. Degron, Director of the French Station in Yokohama in 1869. Evergreen, densely growing bush, usually only 1–1·5 m./3–4½ ft. high, thick and usually covered with leaves as far as the base of the shoot, young shoots somewhat downy; leaves long, wider in the centre, 8–15 cm./3 3/16–6 in. long, gleaming dark green above, covered with dense reddish brown or pale brown down beneath; flowers in groups of 10–12, wide funnel shaped or bell shaped, 4–5 cm./1 3/4–2 in. wide, pale pink with dark pink lines on the divisions of the corona, April–May; Japan. Quite frequently confused with the similar *R. metternichii*, which, however, has a corona divided into 7 parts. Very hardy. *#

R. dichroanthum DIELS (Plate 13, *1*)
S. Neriiflorum, SS. Sanguineum

Evergreen bush, only 1–1·5 m./3–4½ ft. high, young shoots covered with white hairs, turning grey the following year; leaves oval, 5–10 cm./2–4 in. long, bare on top, covered with white down beneath; flowers in groups of 4–8, tube or bell shaped, around 4 cm./1 9/16 in. long, 5-lobed edge, very varied in colour, usually orange with pink tinge, but also deep orange to salmon, May–June; calyx very large, coloured the same as the corona. China, Yunnan, in open, rocky ground 3,000–4,000 m./9,000–12,000 ft. high. Fastidious over here. By no means as beautiful as is often made out, the colour is a dirty orange. ∧∧∧***#

Equally beautiful are the following subspecies, which, however, are equally delicate in our climate; *apodectum* BALF. F. & W. W. SM. flowers orange with pink or carmine red tinge, or clear cherry red; flowering period 2 weeks later than the type; May–June; Western Yunnan (Fig. 18). ∧∧∧***. Subspecies *scyphocalyx* BALF. F. & FORREST. Flowers in groups of 3–5, orange to orange-yellow or pink with carmine or copper and yellow (the latter form is easily the

most beautiful with a glorious brownish tone). North-eastern Burma, Western Yunnan. ∧∧∧***# (Colour Plate 1, *3* and Plate 12, *5*.)

R. discolor FRANCH. (Plate 10, *5* and Plate 11, *6*)
S. and SS. Fortunei

Evergreen shrub, barely man-high in Europe, but up to 5–6 m./15–13 ft. or more in its homeland, young shoots and flowers usually appearing together; leaves very large, elliptical, 10–20 cm./4–8 in. long, up to 7 cm./2 3/4 in. wide, dark green above, pale beneath; flowers in groups of about 10, funnel to bell shaped up to 10 cm./4 in. wide and 5–8 cm./2–3¼ in. long, edge with 7 lobes, pale pink to white, scented, often not blooming until about July; China, Setschuan, Hupeh, in woods. Closely related to *R. fortunei*, but blooms later and grows higher. This variety has often been used in an attempt to achieve later-flowering hybrids. Usually hardy over here, but not all plants bloom profusely. ∧–∧∧***#

R. edgeworthii HOOK. F. (Plate 13, *5* and Fig. 9)
S. Edgeworthii

Named after M. P. Edgeworth of the Bengal Civil Service. Loose, often in its homeland epiphytic bush, up to 2·5 m./7½ ft. high, young shoots covered with thick brown down; leaves oval, 5–10 cm./2–4 in. long, wrinkled above, covered with thick brown down beneath; flowers in groups of 2–4, funnel shaped, white, often tinged with pale pink, very strongly scented, April–May. Himalayas. Very beautiful variety, but only possible for us in the greenhouse, although there are hardier types. ∧∧∧***#

from sikkim & Da-Jeeling to N+C Yunnan 2400–3800m (7,800 to 11,800 ft)

R. falconeri HOOK. F.
S. Falconeri

Named after Hugh Falconer, who was director of the Saharampur Gardens in India in 1832. Evergreen tree, a forest tree in its homeland, which occurs everywhere in the fir forests of Sikkim. Grows to around 12 m./36 ft. in height. Even in England these heights have been reached in very many instances. Stems with brown, peeling bark, young shoots thick, covered with brown-grey down; leaves elliptical, 15–30 cm./6–12 in. long, round at both ends, deep green above, matt and somewhat wrinkled; covered with thick rust red down beneath, with 4–6 cm./1 9/16–2 3/16 in. long stem; flowers occurring in groups of up to 20 in round bunches, bell shaped and swollen underneath, creamy white with purple basal fleck ('Like glass frozen with the remains of red wine'; WARD). Edge with 8–10 lobes, April–May. Himalaya, at heights of around 3,000 m./9,000 ft. ∧∧∧***#

R. fargesii FRANCH
S. Fortunei; SS. Oreodoxa

Named after Father Farges of the French Mission in Setschuan. Evergreen bush, 1·5 m./4½ ft., with bare, often reddish shoots; leaves elliptical, 5–8 cm./2–3 3/16 in. long, leathery, dark green above, bluish green beneath; flowers in groups of 6–10, open bell shaped, around 4 cm./1 9/16 in. long, white to dark pink, 6–7 lobes at the edges, March–April; China, Setschuan and Hupeh, in woods in the regions of 2,000–3,000 m./6,000–9,000 ft. high. ∧∧∧***. Much more beautiful than *R. ordeodoxa*, blooms so profusely that the plant can literally flower to death if the dead heads are not removed the moment they have flowered. ∧∧∧***#

R. fastigiatum

R. fastigiatum FRANCH. *Diploid + Tetraploid* (handwritten)
S. Lapponicum

Evergreen bush, growth very upright (can grow up to 90 cm./3 ft. in height), often more cushion shaped, in which case no higher than 30 cm./1 ft. leaves around 1 cm./⅜ in. in length, covered with thick scales on both sides, the scales just touching; flowers in groups of 4–5, wide funnel shaped, purple lilac to purple blue, 12 mm./½ in. long (unfortunately blue tones occur only very seldom), very short stemmed, April–May. China, Yunnan, in the high mountains around 4,000 m./12,000 ft. high. Very hardy. Best to give it rather meagre soil in the garden, so that the plant remains a dwarf. **#

(handwritten notes: 3400–4400; NW + NC Yunnan)

R. ferrugineum L; True Alpine rose (Plate 14, *2* and Fig. 19)
S. Ferrugineum

Evergreen, upright or (particularly often in its natural state) low-lying bush, up to around 1 m./3 ft. high; leaves elliptical to lanceolate, 3–5 cm./1¾₁₆–2 in. long, dark green above, covered with dense red-brown scales beneath, the scales overlapping, edge rolled back; flowers in groups of 6–12, tube shaped, 2 cm./¾ in. long, with spread-out edge, dark reddish purple, June–July, Alps, Pyrenees, Apennines, on volcanic rock. Should be included in all rockeries and all collections of rhododendrons. However, it is not recommended that specimens should be collected from their natural habitats, for they are normally protected plants in the care of various natural trusts, and in any case they do not respond well to transplanting at this stage. Loves humus, chalk-free soil, although it will stand a certain amount of lime. # There is yet another form of this variety, with white flowers and pale green leaves, f. *album* SWEET, which is occasionally found wild in the Alps.

R. fictolacteum BALF. F.
S. Falconeri

Evergreen bush, growing in its homeland as a tree up to 12 m./36 ft. high. In particularly favourable areas the same heights have been achieved in England; leaves elliptical to ovoid, extremely variable in size, 5–10 cm./6–12 in. long, dark green and shiny above, reddish brown, paler and downy below; flowers in groups of up to 25, unevenly bell shaped, up to 6 cm./2⅜ in. long and broad, creamy white to pale pink, always with deep red basal fleck, edge with 7–8 lobes, April–May. China, Yunnan, often in otherwise clear areas 3,000–4,000 m./9,000–12,000 ft. high in the mountains. The easiest large-leaved variety to find in England. ∧∧∧***#

R. flavum, see **R. luteum**

R. floribundum FRANCH.
S. Arboreum; SS. Argyrophyllum

Evergreen bush, growing to man-size over here, but 3–5 m./9–15 ft. in its homeland, young shoots downy; leaves elliptical-lanceolate, 7–15 cm./2⅜–6 in. long, coarse and leathery, dark green above, covered with white down beneath; flowers in bunches of 8–12, wide bell shaped, 4 cm./1⁹₁₆ in. long, purple to lilac or pink, with carmine basal fleck and marks. April. Ovaries brushlike, 10 stamens. China, western Setschuan, Mupin, in forests, 1,300–2,500 m./3,900–7,500 ft. ∧∧∧*#

R. forrestii BALF. F. ex DIELS
S. Neriiflorum, SS. Forrestii

Named in honour of the Scottish plant collector George Forrest, 1873, 1932. Evergreen creeping shrub, only 10–15 cm./4–6 in. high, making a carpet; leaves small, round to broad oval shaped; 1·5–3 cm./⁹₁₆–1³₁₆ in. long, dark green and shiny above, purple beneath; flowers singly or in pairs, narrow bell shaped, 3 cm./1³₁₆ in. long and wide, carmine, April–May. China, north-eastern Yunnan, south-western Tibet, growing in moist mountain soil and on moors. At least as well known in cultivation is the var. *repens* (BALF. F. & FORREST), COWAN & DAVIDIAN (= *R. repens* BALF. F. & FORREST), which can be distinguished by its more or less blue-green undersides to the leaves (not purple); it also has more scarlet-red flowers, ovaries and stems, which are less scaly than on the type. Tibet. ∧–∧∧*–***# (Plate 7, *4*.)

One or two more should be mentioned here: *R. forrestii* and the var. *repens* are renowned as belonging to the most beautiful varieties, and of being completely hardy, yet this is only partly true. There are many bad examples in both varieties, which either do not bloom at all or do so very erratically. This is what WARD has to say on the subject:

'*R. repens* is one of the brightest varieties, and easily obtained, yet I hesitate to recommend it, for it is by far the slowest growing variety; it is very expensive (in the nursery) and rather stubborn, requires a continually damp climate. In England, this variety could

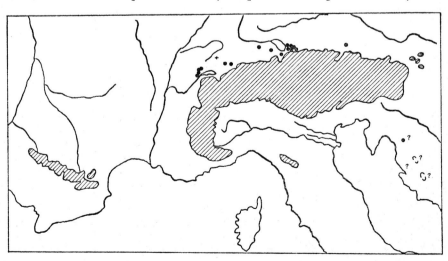

Fig. 19. Distribution area of Rhododendron ferrugineum. *Locali-ties in the Croatian–Dalmatian mountains are considered by Degen to be incorrect and are yet to be verified; they are marked with a question mark.* (After E. Jäger.)

PLATE 17

Wild varieties of
rhododendrons.

1 *R. luteum,* the
'Ponticum azalea'.
2 *R. schlippenbachii.*
3 *R. nudiflorum.*
4 *R. quinquefolium*
(flowers white,
appearing at the
same time as the red-
edged leaves; not
to be confused with
R. pentaphyllum).
5 *R. viscosum.*
6 *R. serpyllifolium*
(having the smallest
leaves of the entire
azalea group).

4

PLATE 18 Garden hybrids. 1 *R.* 'Lady Alice Fitzwilliam' (strongly scented), 2 *R.* 'Galloper Light' (an azaleodendron), 3 *R.* 'Argosy' (blooms first at the end of June), 4 *R.* 'Loderi King George', 5 *R.* 'Narcissiflora' (a double Ghent azalea), 6 *R. indicum* 'Macranthum' (flowers end of June).

not hope to attain the glory it reaches in its native mountains in a million years. It is now slowly going out of cultivation, for out of 10 plants not one will bloom profusely and regularly. I know people who have not seen one single flower on a plant they have owned for 25 years. In fact this plant, in our country, is no more than a green cover for the ground.'

But don't become too gloomy about this situation as, luckily, there is a whole row of hybrids which possess all the good characteristics which we expect. Foremost among these are those grown by D. Hobbie of Linswege, for example 'Scarlet Wonder', 'Elisabeth Hobbie', 'Jewel', 'Gertrud Schäle' and others, which provide us with all that we hoped for in vain from the wild variety.

S. fortunei LINKL. (Plate 7, 3)
S. and SS. Fortunei

Named after Robert Fortune, plant collector in China, 1812–80. Evergreen, wide-growing bush, 2–5 m./6–15 ft. high, up to 7 m./21 ft. in its homeland. Young shoots covered with scales at first, later bare, pale green; leaves long, 10–20 cm./4–8 in., dark green above, blue-green beneath, bare, stem, 2–3 cm./$\frac{3}{4}$–1$\frac{3}{16}$ in. long; flowers in groups of 6–12 in loose bunches, funnel or bell shaped, white to pale pink, often with creamy yellow tinge, up to 9 cm./3$\frac{9}{16}$ in. wide, scented, edge with 7 lobes, May. China, Chekiang, at a height of around 900 m./2,700 ft. Because of its broad growth it needs a lot of space, but it is none the less a wonderful variety, very often used in crossings. Good types must be picked out. Very hardy, and therefore indispensable, in particular because of its late flowering period and glorious scent. ∧–∧∧***#

R. fraseri W. WATS (= R. canadense × R. japonicum)
S. Azalea; SS. Canadense

Known after its grower, G. Fraser of Ucluelet, B.C., Canada. Deciduous shrub, around 1 m./3 ft. high, young shoots and winter buds covered with fine hairs; leaves elliptical, 4–6 cm./1$\frac{9}{16}$–2$\frac{3}{8}$ in. long, with hairs on both sides; flowers two-edged, with very short tubes, pinkish lilac, flecked, under-edge deeply incised, not scented, April. Similar to R. canadense, but larger in every respect. *

R. giganteum, FORREST EX TAGG
S. Grande

Evergreen tree, up to 12 m./36 ft. high, young shoots covered with grey down, leaves lanceolate or oblong, up to 50 cm./20 in. long and 20 cm./8 in. wide, pale green and matt above, pale green beneath; flowers in groups up to 20–25, funnel or bell shaped, dark pink with darker basal fleck, March–April. Yunnan, 3,000–3,600 m./9,000–10,800 ft. ∧∧– Very impressive on account of its particularly gigantic leaves, but is hardly found in Europe apart from a few particularly sheltered and favourable localities in England.

R. glaucophyllum REHD. (= R. glaucum HOOK. F.) (Fig. 20)
S. and SS. Glaucophyllum

Evergreen, aromatic shrub, growing only to about 1 m./3 ft. high, shoots thickly covered with scales; leaves elliptical, 3–7 cm./1$\frac{3}{16}$–2$\frac{3}{4}$ in. long, matt green above, blue-green beneath with small yellow and large dark brown scales; flowers in groups of 5–6, wide bell shaped, around 3 cm./1$\frac{3}{16}$ in. long and 4 cm./1$\frac{9}{16}$ in. wide, paler or darker pink to purple, May; with large calyx, about 1 cm./$\frac{3}{8}$ in. in size, thickly covered with scales outside; pistils becoming thicker towards the large stigma. Himalayas, 3,000–4,000 m./9,000–12,000 ft. Very sensitive to frost. ∧∧∧**#

Fig. 20. R. glaucophyllum.

R. grande WIGHT
S. Grande

Evergreen shrub, growing in its homeland and also in England up to 9 m./27 ft. high; leaves long to oblong, 15–45 cm./6–14 in. long and up to 12 cm./4$\frac{3}{4}$ in. wide, gleaming dark green above and with 20–24 pairs of veins, silvery white beneath or covered with pale brown hairs; flowers up to 25 in number, in semicircular bunches, bell shaped, 5–7 cm./2–2$\frac{3}{4}$ in. long and wide, white, with purple basal fleck and thick yellow stigma, March–April. Himalayas, forming forest at heights of 2,500–3,300 m./7,500–10,200 ft. ∧∧∧***#

R. sinogrande is in every respect larger and more beautiful than this variety, but neither is completely hardy in our very exposed areas.

R. griersonianum BALF. F. & FORREST (Fig. 8)
S. Griersonianum

Named after R. C. Grierson, a friend of G. Forrest in China. Evergreen, somewhat wider, stook-shaped bush, 1·5–3 m./4$\frac{1}{2}$–9 ft. high, young shoots thickly covered with down, and brushlike scales. Terminal buds long and pointed; leaves lanceolate, 10–20 cm./4–8 in. long, dull green above, whitish or pale brown, covered with down, beneath; flowers in groups of 5–12, in loose bunches, trumpet shaped, up to 6 cm./2$\frac{3}{8}$ in. wide and 7 cm./2$\frac{3}{4}$ in. long. Tubes very narrow, geranium red, with darker markings inside, quite different in colour from all other varieties, richly flowering, even when the plants are still young, June. China, northern Yunnan, northern Burma, 2,500–3,000 m./7,500–9,000 ft. high. One of the most beautiful of the Chinese varieties, therefore often used for crossings; only possible in the greenhouse in Europe. ∧∧∧***#

R. griffithianum

R. griffithianum Wight
S. Fortunei; SS. Griffithianum

Named after William Griffith, 1810–45, Director of the Botanical Gardens in Calcutta. Griffith found this variety as early as 1830, but he collected no seeds. This was done by Hooker in 1849. Evergreen shrub, 1–3 m./3–9 ft. high, reddish-brown bark, peeling, young shoots bare, pale green; leaves 10–30 cm./4–12 in. long, bare above and smooth, yellowish green with blue tinge beneath; flowers in groups of 4–6, in loose bunches, wide bell shaped, 12–15 cm./$4\frac{7}{8}$–6 in. wide, around 6–7 cm./$2\frac{5}{8}$–$2\frac{7}{8}$ in. long, white with pink tint and delicate veining, faintly scented, May; calyx plate shaped, 2 cm./$\frac{7}{8}$ in. wide, edge has five lobes. Himalayas; Sikkim, Bhutan, 2,500–3,000 m./7,500–9,000 ft. This very sensitive variety has the largest flowers of all the wild varieties and is incomparably more beautiful than all the hybrids, but it is sensitive and can generally be raised only in the greenhouse. The Rev. H. Ewbank described it in glowing terms as the 'Glory of the Himalayas, the Queen of all flowering shrubs'. It is very important for collectors and cultivators, who often use it for crossings. ΛΛΛ***#

R. habrotrichum Balf. F. & W. W. Sm. (Plate 13, *6*)
S. Barbatum; SS. Glischrum

Evergreen shrub up to 2·5 m./$7\frac{1}{2}$ ft.; young shoots brushlike, covered with thick squama; leaves elliptical, up to 20 cm./8 in. long and 7 cm./$2\frac{7}{8}$ in. wide, dark green and somewhat rough above, pale green above, and the main leaf is a little brushlike at the base; flowers in quantities of up to 20 together, funnel or bell shaped, white to pale pink, with or without marking, April–May. Yunnan; 3,300 in./9,900 ft. ΛΛ*–**

R. haemaleum see *R. sanguineum*, ssp. *haemaleum*
S. Neriiflorum; SS. Haematodes

Evergreen, low-growing, broad shrub, around 1 m./3 ft. high or a little more, young shoots woolly or downy; leaves ovoid, 4–8 cm./$1\frac{3}{5}$–$3\frac{1}{5}$ in. long, deep green above and slightly wrinkled, underneath, covered with thick reddish brown down; flowers in groups of 6–12, tube or bell shaped, 5 cm./2 in. long, fleshy and shining, dark scarlet red, edge with five lobes, calyx 8 mm./$\frac{5}{16}$ in. long, red, May–June. China, Yunnan, 3,500–4,000 m./10,500–12,000 ft. high. One of the most beautiful Chinese varieties, which has, however, only recently begun to be cultivated. Unfortunately the wild variety does not flower until the plant is mature, yet it is worth waiting for. ΛΛ–ΛΛΛ***

R. hanceanum Hemsl (Plate 14, *3*)
S. Triflorum; SS. Hanceanum

Named after H. F. Hance, British consul in Canton, 1827–86. Small, evergreen shrub, hardly 1 m./3 ft. high, young shoots bronze coloured; leaves oval lanceolate, 4–10 cm./$1\frac{3}{4}$–4 in. long and half as wide, covered with fine scales beneath; flowers in groups of 5–10 in small bunches, corona up to 2·5 cm./1 in. long, funnel shaped, creamy white to clear yellow, faintly scented, April; calyx 6 mm./$\frac{1}{4}$ in. long, five lobes extending to the base. Λ*–**

R. heliolepis Franch Hexaploid
S. Heliolepis

Evergreen, man-size shrub, young shoots thickly covered in scales, leaves oval lanceolate, 9–12 cm./4–$4\frac{7}{8}$ in. long, very aromatic, long and pointed, with a dense network of veins on the surface, and scales

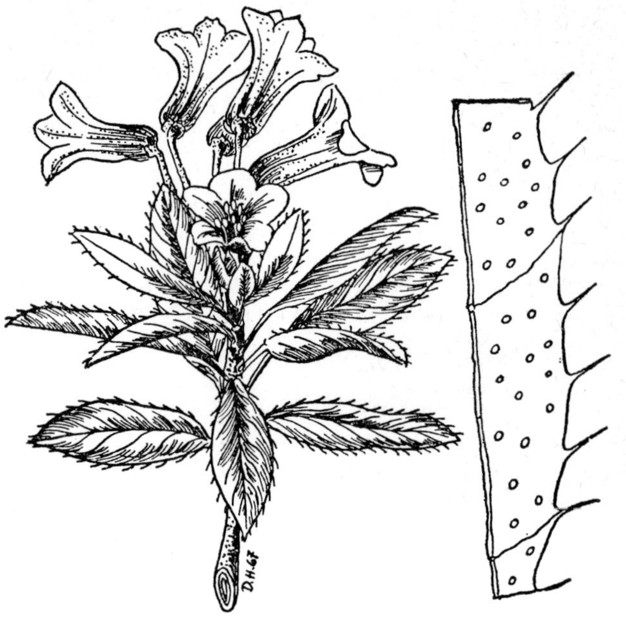

Fig. 21. R. hirsutum

beneath; flowers in groups of 4–6 in loose bunches, broad funnel shaped, 3 cm./$1\frac{1}{4}$ in. long, pink to purplish pink, May–June. China, Yunnan, at heights of 3,500 m./10,500 ft. in mountain regions. One of the best varieties of this series. ΛΛ–ΛΛΛ**#

R. hippophaeoides Balf. F. & W. W. Sm.
S. Lapponicum

Small, evergreen upright shrub, 60–100 cm./24–40 in. high, thickly wooded, shoots thin, scaly, aromatic; leaves narrow, 2–4 cm./$\frac{7}{8}$–$1\frac{3}{4}$ in. long, growing at intervals along the entire shoot; scales on either side, but particularly so on the undersides; therefore has a silver-grey appearance, aromatically scented; flowers in groups of 4–8 cm./$1\frac{3}{4}$–$3\frac{1}{4}$ in., fairly small, funnel shaped, around 2·5 cm./1 in. wide, lavender blue to lilac, not flecked, April. China, Yunnan, particularly in marshy areas. Hardy, but better for open ground and not for dry spots in a rock garden, where it is so often planted. ***#

R. hirsutum L., (Figs. 21 and 22)
S. Ferrugineum

Low growing, only winter green shrub (gradually renews all its leaves in the spring), 0·5–1 m./$1\frac{1}{2}$–3 ft. high, relatively short shoots; leaves elliptical, clear green, slightly curved and ciliate, green underneath; flowers in groups of 3–10, tube to funnel shaped, only around 13 mm./$\frac{1}{2}$ in. in length, carmine pink, June–July. Alps, Tatra, on dry, stony cliffs, also on weathered chalk beds. # Has been in garden cultivation since 1656. Can even be grown in soil containing lime with success. There is also a variety with white flowers and quite pale green leaves, *f. albiflorum* Goiran, which can be found here and there in the Alps.

R. hirtipes TAGG
S. Barbatum; SS. Glischrum

Evergreen shrub, growing here to man-size, but in its homeland is a small tree, young shoots with brushlike hairs; leaves elliptical, 5–12 cm./$2\frac{3}{8}$–$4\frac{1}{2}$ in. long, shiny above, beneath having scaly middle rib and stem; flowers in loose bunches of 3–5, bell shaped, up to 5 cm./2 in. long, pale pink or white, calyx almost 8 mm./$\frac{5}{16}$ in. long, with five irregular lobes, April. South-eastern Tibet, 4,500 m./13,500 ft. high. –∧∧*# Attractive because of its very early flowers; according to Hobbie, it will also withstand a certain amount of lime. Found by F. Kingdon Ward in Tibet, and very highly regarded there, although until now it has been disappointing both in England and in Germany.

R. hookeri NUTT. (Fig. 23)
S. and SS. Thomsonii

Named after the famous English botanist and Director of Kew Gardens, Sir J. D. Hooker, 1817–1911. Evergreen shrub, very similar to *R. thomsonii*, having the same thin, reddish brown bark, long leaves up to 15 cm./6 in., bluish green beneath, but easily recognizable through the brown, pin-shaped groups of hairs on the undersides of the leaves; blooms blood red, April. Bhutan, Assam, 3,600–4,000 m./10,800–12,000 ft. ∧∧∧**

R. hormophorum BALF. F. & FORREST (Plate 15, 3)
S. Triflorum; SS. Yunnanense

Deciduous bush, growing to about 2 m./6 ft. in its homeland, young shoots scaly; leaves lanceolate, 3–7 cm./$1\frac{1}{4}$–$2\frac{7}{8}$ in. long, with yellowish scales beneath; flowers in groups of 3–6, at the end of the stems, but sometimes also growing in the axis of the two top leaves, wide funnel shaped, up to 4 cm./$1\frac{9}{16}$ in. long, pink to lilac, with or without brown marks, May; calyx has a narrow edge of scales, from which it derives its botanical name (= *R. chartophyllum* var. *praecox* DAVIS). China, Yunnan, Setschuan, 2,600–4,000 m./7,800–12,000 ft. Profusely flowering. According to Cox, the only wild variety which the Chinese of Yunnan plant in their gardens. ∧***

R. impeditum BALF. F. & W. W. SM.
S. Lapponicum

Evergreen, very thick and broad, only 15–40 cm./6–16 in. high shrub, growth almost bolster shaped, shoots very short, thickly

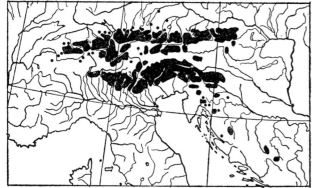

Fig. 22. Distribution of Rhododendron hirsutum. *(After E. Jäger.)*

Fig. 23. R. hookeri

covered with scales; leaves small, elliptical, 1–2 cm./$\frac{3}{8}$–$\frac{3}{4}$ in. long, with thick scales on both sides; flowers singly or in pairs, small, funnel shaped, violet to purple, May–June, often blooming a second time in August–September. China, north-western Yunnan, Lichiang mountains, in fresh and open areas, at a height of around 5,000 m./ *[handwritten: 3300 to 4600 m]* 15,000 ft. Very hardy. One of the best known dwarf varieties for rockeries, but tends to vary in quality in cultivation; the green-leaved types grow higher and are not nearly as beautiful as the grey-leaved ones. ***#– 'Blue Tit' and 'Moerheim'. *[handwritten: NNC Yunnan + SW Szechuan]*

R. imperator HUTCHINS & WARD
S. Uniflorum *[handwritten: R uniflorum var -i]*

Evergreen shrub, growing in mats, at most 30 cm./12 in. high, but usually only 10 cm./4 in.; young shoots with some scales; leaves narrow, oblong, around 2·5–3 cm./1–$1\frac{3}{16}$ in. long, bluish green beneath, and with very fine scales; flowers usually single (but so many together that the observer begins to wonder if as much as one leaf can be seen); funnel shaped, 2·5–3 cm./1–$1\frac{3}{16}$ in. long and 12 mm./$\frac{1}{2}$ in. broad, pink to purplish pink, with no marking, May. *[handwritten: Extreme N]* Burma, 3,300–3,600 in./9,900–10,800 ft. Hardy. ***# *[handwritten: the sp in se tibet]*

R. indicum SWEET
S. Azalea; SS. Obtusum

Must not be confused with 'Azalea indica' found in gardens (For this cf. under *R. simsii*). Evergreen, wide spreading bush, sometimes low lying, 0·7 m./2 ft. high or more, shoots covered with brushlike hairs; leaves lanceolate, 2·5–3 cm./1–$1\frac{3}{16}$ in. long. Edge finely incised and ciliate, with red hairs on both sides, autumn colour usually red to carmine; flowers singly or in pairs, funnel shaped, 3 cm./$1\frac{3}{16}$ in. long, 5 cm./2 in. wide, bright red or scarlet or pink, *[handwritten: 32, 25, 30]* June. South Japan. ∧∧∧** More common and more interesting

Fig. 24. R. kaempferi.

for our gardens is the low-growing form 'Balsaminiflorum' (= *Azalea rosaeflora* R. DEAN) only 10 cm./4 in. high, leaves up to 2·5 cm./1 in. long, but only 3–4 mm./$\frac{1}{8}$–$\frac{3}{16}$ in. wide; flowers well filled (?) salmon red. ∧∧∧***#

R. insigne HEMSL. & WILS (Plate 6, *1*)
S. Arboreum; SS. Artyrophyllum

Evergreen shrub, 1–4 m./3–12 ft. high, young shoots thick, upright, covered with ash-grey down, later bare; leaves lanceolate, coarse and leathery, 7–13 cm./2$\frac{3}{4}$–5$\frac{3}{16}$ in. long, dark green above, with a silvery or sometimes copper-coloured sheath underneath; edge lightly rolled; flowers in groups of 8 or more, wide bell shaped, up to 5 cm./2 in. long, pale pinkish white, with darker tones, and flecked with carmine inside, May–June. China, Setschuan, in forests at heights of 2,500–3,500 m./7,500–10,500 ft. Unfortunately does not flower very well when young, but is always a fine plant on account of its leaves. ∧∧***#

R. × *intermedium* TAUSCH (= *R. halense* GREMBLICH) cross between *R. ferrugineum* and *R. hirsutum*
S. Ferrugineum

Evergreen natural hybrid of our nearest two varieties; the variety looks like a mixture of the two parents; growth small and compact, leaves similar to *R. hirsutum*, but covered with dense scales beneath, not so dense as in *R. ferrugineum*, however. Flowers pink with darker markings, June–July, Tyrol. On limestone cliffs. #

R. intricatum FRANCH. Diploid & Tetraploid
S. Lapponicum

Evergreen, low-growing shrub, 30–90 cm./1–3 ft. high, fairly loose, shoots covered with reddish scales, leaves elliptical, only 6–12 cm./$\frac{1}{4}$–$\frac{1}{2}$ in. long, scaly on both sides, bluish green above, more

grey-green beneath; flowers in 2s or 4s, 1 cm./$\frac{3}{8}$ in. long, tube shaped, lobes standing out, lilac pink to violet or purple, April, tubes with fine hairs on the outsides. China, Setschuan, on grass and moorland in mountains 2800–4900 4,000–5,000 m./12,000–15,000 ft. high. Very hardy. One of the most useful varieties for the rockery. The flower buds which first appear in autumn are particularly pretty, looking very much like pearls. ***# NNC Yunnan & SWtSC Szechwan

R. japonicum (GRAY) SURING. (= *Azalea japonica* GRAY)
S. Azalea; SS. Luteum

Deciduous bush, 1–2 m./3–6 ft. high, thickly wooded, young shoots covered with brushlike hairs or bare, scales of the winter buds finely ciliated; leaves thin, lanceolate, 6–10 cm./2$\frac{3}{8}$–4 in. long, dull green above, bluish beneath, turning red or yellow in autumn; flowers in 6s to 10s, appearing before the leaves, broad funnel shaped, 6–8 cm./2$\frac{3}{8}$–3$\frac{3}{16}$ in. wide, salmon pink to orange, with large orange fleck, not scented, April–May. Northern and central Japan, in the lower mountain regions. From here originate the many cultivated varieties which are even more important than the wild varieties. Completely hardy. ***#

R. kaempferi PLANCH. (= *R. obtusum* var. *kaempferi* WILS.)
S. Azalea; SS. Obtusum

Named after E. Kaepfer, a German botanist, who travelled to Japan in 1690–92 and collected plants. Deciduous bush, partly evergreen in milder areas, 1–2 m./3–6 ft. high, loosely wooded, young shoots densely covered with hairs; leaves elliptical, 5–7 cm./2–2$\frac{3}{4}$ in. long, shiny and green above, paler beneath, with small upstanding hairs on both surfaces; flowers in groups of 1–4, wide bell or funnel shaped, up to 5 cm./2 in. long and broad, pink, orange to scarlet, middle of May; calyx has 5 narrow, hairy points. Northern and central Japan. Completely hardy. Extremely variable with regard to flowering period and colour. *** & mtns of South 18, 25, 30

R. keiskei MIQ. (Plate 15, *2*)
S. and SS. Triflorum

Named after Ito Keisuke, a Japanese botanist. Evergreen, compact

Fig. 25. R. keleticum.

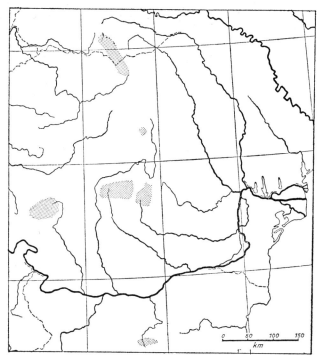

Fig. 26. Distribution of Rhododendron kotschyi.
(After E. Jäger.)

shrub, 1 m./3 ft. high, young shoots somewhat scaly, often lying on the ground; leaves lanceolate to elliptical, 3–8 cm./$1\frac{3}{16}$–$3\frac{3}{16}$ in. long, dark green scaly beneath, young leaves a fine bronze-brown colour; flowers in groups of 3–5, wide bell shaped, 4 cm./$1\frac{3}{4}$ in. across, lemon yellow or dull yellow, without flecks, March–May, Japan. ∧***# *2,000 to 6,100ft.*

R. keleticum BALF. F. & FORREST (Fig. 25)
S. Saluenense *= Rr. calostrotum ssp K· Extreme N Burma + Nw Yunnan + se Tibet + the ss ppto N Assam + w NW Yunnan*

Evergreen bush, growth matlike, 15–30 cm./6–12 in. high, shoots lying on the ground; leaves very small, around 15 mm./$\frac{5}{8}$ in. long and 10 mm./$3\frac{3}{4}$ in. wide, almost olive green, very aromatic, edge ciliated; flowers in groups of 1–3, broad funnel to wheel shaped, around 2·5 cm./1 in. across, quite large for this variety, deep purple or carmine with even darker markings, end of May to beginning of June, calyx with 5 egg-shaped tips. South-eastern Tibet, Yunnan, Burma, in the high mountains around 4,000–5,000 m./12,000–15,000 ft. Completely hardy, flowers appear when the night frosts are over. ***# *1,250–4,550m*

R. kiusianum MAK.
S. Azalea; SS. Obtusum

Evergreen or partly evergreen shrub, hardly more than 70 cm./28 in. high, usually low lying, but spreading and dense; leaves dimorphus, spring leaves elliptical, 1–2 cm./$\frac{3}{8}$–$\frac{3}{4}$ in. long, summer leaves more oblong, and longer; flowers in groups of 2–5, funnel shaped, around 4 cm./$1\frac{3}{4}$ in. wide, salmon pink to carmine or even purple, May–June. Anthers brown (yellow in *R. obtusum*). Southern and central Japan, above all around Mt. Kiushiuma, a volcano still

active today. Hardy (= *R. obtusum* var. *japonicum* WILS). **#
This is now regarded as the wild variety from which the many so-called 'Kurume' azaleas derived (named after the town of Kuruma on the island of Kiushiu). Particularly interesting to note is the fact that the Kurume azaleas are not hybrids, but different forms of *R. kiusianum*. This is a very great difference. *High refined kphershled*

R. kotschyi SIMONK (Fig. 26)

Named in honour of the Austrian botanist Theodore Kotschy, 1813–66. Evergreen, very compact bush, hardly higher than 50 cm./20 in. leaves oblong, 15 cm./$\frac{5}{8}$ in. long and 7 mm./$\frac{5}{16}$ in. wide, round in front with a small tip, edge slightly bowed, bare above, very scaly beneath; flowers in groups of 2–4, tube shaped, with fine short hairs on both surfaces, tip of edge, standing out, pink. Balkans, in high mountains, 2,500–3,500 m./7,500–10,500 ft. #** Will support limestone.

R. × laetevirens REHD (= *R. wilsonii* HORT) (Fig. 27)
S. Ferrugineum

Evergreen, low bush, a cross between *R. carolinianum* and *R. ferrugineum*, up to 1 m./3 ft. high, wide and loose; leaves narrow, lanceolate to elliptical, 3–7 cm./$1\frac{3}{16}$–$2\frac{3}{4}$ in. long, pointed, clear green, with thick scales beneath, aromatic; flowers in small bunches, tube shaped, 3 cm./$1\frac{3}{16}$ in. wide, lilac red, profusely flowering, May–June. Quite hardy. **#

R. lapponicum WAHLBG. (Figs. 28 and 29) *Diploid + Tetraploid*
S. Lapponicum

Evergreen dwarf bush, 15–25 cm./6–10 in. high, shoots with only a few small leaves at the tips of twigs, thickly covered with scales; leaves oblong, 8–12 cm./$3\frac{3}{16}$–$4\frac{3}{4}$ in. long, with deep scales above, fine dense scales beneath; flowers generally in threes, funnel shaped, purple or violet, June–July; calyx small and lobed. Lapland, on bare spots in Fjell. # Hardly ever found in cultivation and difficult to

Fig. 27. R. laetevirens.

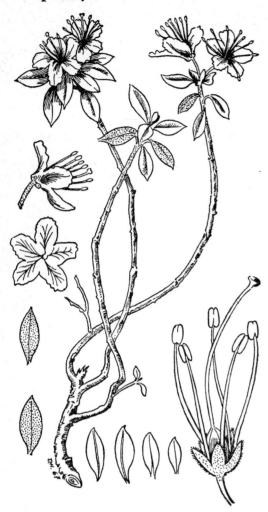

Fig. 28. R. lapponicum.

maintain; more interesting botanically, for it is the only variety to be found right round the pole. Northern Europe, Greenland, Alaska, Siberia.

R. lepidostylum BALF. F. & FORREST (Plate 11, *1*)
S. Trichocladum

Evergreen (in Europe often only winter green) compact shrub, about 50 cm./20 in. high; leaves oval, 3–4·5 cm./1$\frac{3}{16}$–1$\frac{3}{4}$ in. long, beautiful bluish green, edge brushlike and ciliate, bluish and scaly beneath; flowers in pairs, broad funnel shaped, 2·5 cm./1 in. across, pale yellow but unfortunately frequently hidden beneath the new leaves, May–June, ovaries very scaly and hairy. Western Yunnan. Hardy. Beautiful variety, but recommended particularly to the enthusiast and the collector.

R. leucaspis TAGG
S. Boothii; SS. Megeratum

Small evergreen bush, hardly over 40 × 40 cm./16 × 16 in. in size, shoots somewhat angular and hairy; leaves elliptical, clear green, 3–6 cm./1$\frac{3}{16}$–2$\frac{3}{8}$ in. long, dark green and hairy above, bluish green and scaly beneath; young leaves copper red, then pale green, finally dark green; flowers usually in pairs, wheel shaped with short tubes, 5 cm./2 in. wide, milky white with brown anthers, the tips of the edge bending over, February to April. Buds have silvery fringe. Tibet, Burma, 2,500–3,300 m./7,600–6,900 ft. Wonderful variety for rockery; the very early flowers must be protected from night frosts. Blooms at the age of three years! ∧∧–∧∧∧***#
Tsangpo Gorge

R. lindleyi MOORE (Colour Plate 1, *2*)
S. Maddenii; SS. Megacalyx

Named in honour of Dr. John Lindley, English botanist, 1799–1865. Evergreen, somewhat 'long-legged' bush, growing to around 3 m./9 ft. in its homeland and often living epiphytically, growth very loose; leaves elliptical, 6–15 cm./2$\frac{3}{8}$–6 in. long, dark green above with a network of veins, blue green and scaly beneath; flowers usually in groups of 4–6 or more, tube or funnel shaped, around 7 cm./2$\frac{3}{4}$ in. long and wide, milky white with yellow or orange fleck, scented; calyx almost 2 cm./$\frac{3}{4}$ in. long, with 5 points, free to the base, April–May, Himalayas. Wonderful variety, which, although there are hardier varieties, can only be considered for the greenhouse. ∧∧∧***# *Nepal to N Assam + in Manipur 6,600 to*

R. linearifolium S. & Z.
S. Azalea; SS. Obtusum

Evergreen (or only winter green) small bush; entire plant covered with hairs; leaves very narrow, lineal, 5–9 cm./2–3$\frac{3}{4}$ in. long and 3–8 cm./$\frac{1}{8}$–$\frac{5}{16}$ in. across; flowers in groups of 3, corona made of 5 narrow linear, around 3 cm./1$\frac{3}{16}$ in. long and 5 mm./$\frac{3}{16}$ in. broad divisions; pink, scented, April–May; 5 stamens; Japan. This bush is occasionally seen here in botanical gardens and in special collections, but does not grow wild. Even in Japan it occurs only in cultivation. # var. *macrosepalum* MAKINO is the wild variety belonging here which has normally shaped, broad funnel like flowers up to 5 cm./2 in.

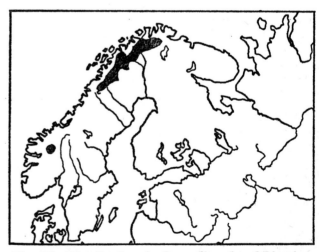

Fig. 29. Distribution in Scandinavia of Rhododendron lapponicum. *In North America this species represents the northern border of the family's distribution.* (After R. Fries.)

broad, pink with purple fleck, April–May, leaves elliptical to lanceolate 4–6 cm./1–$2\frac{3}{8}$ in. long, only deciduous, carmine red in autumn. Central and southern Japan; healthy, hardy and beautiful, growing to about 2 m./6 ft. over here.

R. lochae F. Muell.
Sect. Virea; Subsect. Euvireya; S. Javanica

Evergreen, highly epiphytical shrub, up to 1·75 m./$4\frac{1}{4}$ ft. high, leaves broad and oval, up to 9 cm./$3\frac{9}{16}$ in. long, dark green and shiny above, paler beneath with loose scales; flowers in groups of 2–7 together, tube or funnel shaped, hanging; tubes up to 5 cm./2 in. long, tips standing out. Australia, north-east Queensland. The only Australian variety. Only for the greenhouse; seldom cultivated in Europe. ΛΛΛ

R. ludlowii Cowan
S. Uniflorum

Named after F. Ludlow, plant collector in the Himalayas. Evergreen dwarf bush, hardly over 30 cm./12 in. high, usually smaller; leaves oval, around 2 cm./$\frac{3}{4}$ in. long, usually waved at the edge and slightly curved; flowers singly or in pairs, at the end of shoots, tube shaped with a wide edge, about 2·5 cm./1 in. long and wide, primula yellow with brown marks, April–May; calyx large, with leaf-like tip. South-eastern Tibet, 4,500 m./13,500 ft. in the mountains. Not yet seen much in cultivation, but fine and hardy. ***#

R. lutescens Franch.
S. and SS. Triflorum

Evergreen shrub, usually only growing to 1 m./3 ft. high over here (2–3 m./6–9 ft. or even higher in its homeland), young shoots green, somewhat scaly leaves fine bronze-red colour on emerging, lanceolate, with long points, 4–8 cm./$1\frac{9}{16}$–$3\frac{3}{16}$ in. long, pale green and shiny, not very numerous, turning yellow or brown in the autumn; flowers usually in groups of 3–6, broad funnel shaped, 4–5 cm./$1\frac{9}{16}$–2 in. wide, clear primrose yellow with 5 noticeable greenish flecks outside, over the base, March–April; China, Setschuan, Yunnan, 700–3,300 m./2,100–9,900 ft. high. Tends to freeze back here occasionally, but usually pushes through again soon. The brown colour of the autumn leaves is not so beautiful as the reddish brown spring colour. ΛΛ–ΛΛΛ***#

R. luteum Sweet (= *R. flabum* [Hoffm.] G. Don; *Azalea Pontica* L.) (Plates 2, *2* and 17, *1*; Figs. 4 and 30)

Well-known deciduous shrub, 1–4 m./3–12 ft high, and wide (with us usually no more than 2 m./6 ft. high), thickly wooded, young shoots first scaly and sticky; leaves lanceolate, 6–12 cm./$2\frac{3}{8}$–$4\frac{3}{4}$ in. long, ciliate, hairy when young, yellow in autumn, turning to orange or red; flowers in groups of 7–12, appearing shortly before the leaves, funnel shaped, up to 5 cm./2 in. across, golden yellow, strongly scented, scaly and sticky outside. Caucasus, eastern Europe. Very useful variety, very often used for crossings, but also excellent when allowed to grow wild in woods, where it is completely hardy. ***

R. macabeanum Watt (Plate 8, *1*)
S. Grande

Named after Mr. McCabe, an official in India. Evergreen shrub or tree, growing to 14 m./42 ft. in its homeland, young shoots covered thickly with chestnut down; or bud scales red; leaves broad and elliptical, tough, up to 30 cm./12 in. long and 20 cm./8 in. wide, dark green and smooth above, grey and downy beneath; flowers in clusters, bell shaped, 5–6 cm./2–$2\frac{3}{8}$ in. long, dark or creamy yellow, with purple basal fleck, edge with 8 lobes, March–April. India; Manipur, Assam, 3,000 m./9,000 ft. ΛΛΛ***# One of the best tree varieties, similar to *R. falconeri.*

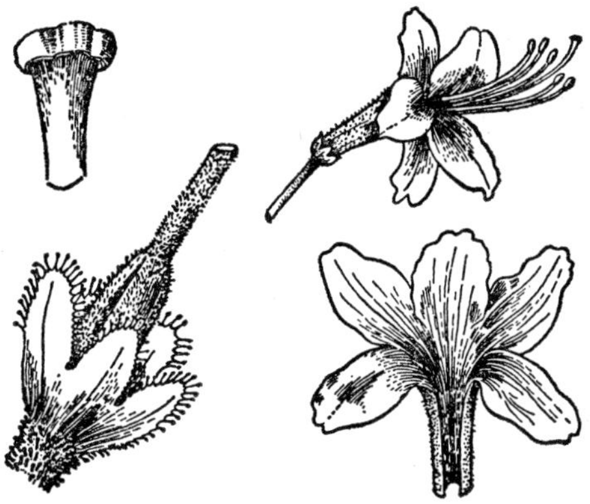

Fig. 30. R. luteum.

R. macrophyllum D. Don (= *R. californicum* Hooi. F.) (Plate 2, *1*)
S. and SS. Ponticum

Evergreen shrub, growth very upright, usually not more than 1·5 m./$4\frac{1}{2}$ ft. here, in its homeland up to 6 m./18 ft., young shoots green; leaves long and oval, 7–15 cm./$2\frac{3}{4}$–6 in. long, dark green above, pale beneath; flowers in arched clumps of about 20, wide bell shaped, 3–4 cm./$1\frac{3}{16}$–$1\frac{9}{16}$ in. long, purplish pink with yellow marks, becoming paler inside, edge waved, ovaries thickly covered with white hairs (as opposed to *R. catawbiense* which has brown hairs), May–June. North America, Pacific coast, from British Columbia to California; replaces *R. catawbiense* in these areas. #

R. makinoi Tagg (= *R. metternichii* var. *angustifolium* Bean)
S. Ponticum; SS. Caucasicum

Named after T. Makino, Japanese botanist. Evergreen, round and compact shrub, 1–2 m./3–6 ft. high, young shoots first loosely covered with white down, later brownish, lasting several years, appearing first in autumn; leaves narrow and lanceolate, 10–17 cm./4–$6\frac{3}{4}$ in. long, but only about 2 cm./$\frac{3}{4}$ in. wide, edge rolled in, dark green above, covered with thick pale green down beneath; flowers in groups of around 6–8, funnel or bell shaped, up to 4 cm./$1\frac{9}{16}$ in. wide, with or without carmine flecks, edge has 5 lobes (important characteristic!), June. Japan. Λ–ΛΛ***#

R. maximum L. (Plate 7, *5*)
S. and SS. Ponticum

Evergreen bush, 1–4 m./3–12 ft. high (up to 7–10 m./21–30 ft. in its homeland) growth loose, young shoots first covered with pink tomenti, leaves lanceolate, 10–30 cm./4–12 in. long, bare above, with a fine film of hairs, stem 2–4 cm./$\frac{3}{4}$–$1\frac{9}{16}$ in. long, flowers in groups of 16–24, bell shaped, 3 cm./$1\frac{3}{16}$ in. long, pale or darker pink, with yellow or green flecks, June–July; North America; in moist marshes of the Rocky Mountains, can tolerate a great deal of shadow, but late flowers are usually hidden by new growth. Hardy. #

Fig. 31. R. micranthum.

R. metternianum WADA (provisional name)
S. Ponticum; SS. Caucasicum

Evergreen bush, very similar to *R. metternichii*, bushy, growth somewhat stronger; flowers larger, waxy, pale pink, edge had 7–8 lobes, blooms 3–4 weeks earlier and is much more beautiful than the older type. Japan, collected by K. Wada. Very hardy and early flowering. ***#

R. metternichii S. & Z. (Plate 7, *1*)
S. Ponticum; SS. Caucasicum

Named after the Austrian Prince Metternich. Evergreen bush, 1–2 cm./3–6 ft. high, young shoots thinly covered with down; leaves arranged almost in whorls, long, 10–15 cm./4–6 in., 1·5–3 cm./$\frac{9}{16}$–1$\frac{3}{16}$ in. across, shiny above, with thin pale brown or reddish down beneath; flowers in groups of 10–15, irregularly bell shaped, pink, darker flecks inside, edge has 7 lobes, stamens 14, April–May. Japan, not usually pure specimens over here, more often crossed with *R. makinoi* or *R. degronianum*. **# 5 C+5 Japan

R. micranthum TURCZ (Fig. 31)
S. Micranthum

Evergreen shrub, very woody, 1–1·5 m./3–4$\frac{1}{2}$ ft. high, at first glance looking more like a spiraea than a rhododendron, shoots very thin and woody, scaly; leaves lanceolate, 2–5 cm./$\frac{3}{4}$–2 in. long and 1–1·5 cm./$\frac{3}{8}$–$\frac{9}{16}$ in. wide, pale brown scales beneath; flowers in dense clumps, wide bell shaped, milky white, edge star shaped, May–June. China, Hupeh, Setschuan, Kansu, 2,000–2,600 m./6,000–7,800 ft. Very hardy. #

R. minus MICHX (= *R. punctatum* ANDR.) (Plate 14, *4*)
S. Carolinianum

Evergreen shrub, 1 m./3 ft. high (up to 3 m./9 ft. in its homeland) dense foliage, shoots with loose scales; leaves elliptical, with points at each end, 3–7 cm./1$\frac{3}{16}$–2$\frac{3}{4}$ in. long, scales beneath; thickness of the scales half the size of their diameter; flowers in bunches of 6–12, narrow funnel shaped, purplish pink, thick scales outside, 25 mm./1 in. across, greenish or brownish flecks, May–June, calyx 3 mm./$\frac{1}{8}$ in. long, ciliate. South-eastern States of America. Completely hardy. **# Similar to *R. macrophyllum*, but growing taller and flowering earlier. 59 Mtns + Piedmont

R. molle (BL.) G. DON (= *R. sinense* SWEET: *Azalea sinensis* LODD)
S. Azalea; SS. Luteum

Deciduous shrub, 1–3 m./3–9 ft. high (generally over 1 m./3 ft.), branches fairly stiffly erect, young shoots hairy and setaceous, leaves oblong 5–15 cm./2–6 in. long, hairy above (at least in youth), thick, velvety grey-white down beneath; flowers appearing before the leaves, many together, without scent, broad funnel shaped, golden yellow with large greenish fleck (composed of several smaller flecks), May; calyx small, ciliate. Eastern and central China, Chekiang, Hupeh, Hunan, above all in mountains and pine forests. ∧–∧∧*** This variety used to be used in crossings quite frequently, but nowadays, because of its sensitivity to winter, it is hardly ever found in cultivation. (Do not confuse this variety with 'Azalea mollis': the latter plant is now called *R. japonicum*.)

R. moupinense FRANCH.
S. Moupinense

Evergreen spreading shrub, hardly more than 50–70 cm./20–28 in. high, young shoots setaceous; leaves oval or elliptical, round at both ends, 2–4 cm./$\frac{3}{4}$–1$\frac{9}{16}$ in. long, half as wide, shiny above, covered with fine scales beneath, edge ciliate, flowers in groups of 1–3, funnel shaped, up to 5 cm./2 in. wide, usually white or pale pink, but also with occasional purple flecks, scented as early as February–March; calyx 4 mm./$\frac{3}{16}$ in. long, ciliate. Western China, 2,000–2,600 m./6,000–7,800 ft. Needs winter protection on account of its particularly early flowering period. Very beautiful variety, similar to *R. leucaspis*, but slightly inferior. ∧∧*** Central Szechuan 6,700ft to 13,400ft.

R. mucronatum G. DON (= *Azalea ledifolia* HOOK.)
S. Azalea; SS. Obtusum

Evergreen, or only winter green, very widespread and woody shrub, semicircular, up to 1·5 m./4$\frac{1}{2}$ ft. high, but broader than it is high, young shoots very hairy; leaves dimorphous; spring leaves elliptical, 4–9 cm./$\frac{9}{16}$–3$\frac{9}{16}$ in. long, pointed at both ends, deciduous; summer leaves lanceolate, 1–4 cm./$\frac{3}{8}$–1$\frac{9}{16}$ in. long, dark green, staying on through the winter, both leaf types hairy on both sides; flowers in groups of 1–3, funnel shaped, up to 6 cm./2$\frac{3}{8}$ in. wide and 5 cm./2 in. long, pure white, scented, May; calyx green, with lobes 12 mm./$\frac{1}{2}$ in. long. Japan and China, in garden cultivation; not known in a wild state. ***# The wild form belonging to it, which was not discovered until much later is var. *ripense* WILS. with pale lilac flowers; Japan, at the edge of rivers in the south of the country. The garden variety 'Van Noordt' is still important, having even large, pure white flowers, in groups of 3–7, calyx larger. ***

R. mucronulatum TURCZ. (= *R. dauricum* var. *mucronulatum* SIMS) (Plate 9, *3*)
S. Dauricum

Deciduous, dense, short-growing bush, shoots brown, thin, somewhat scaly; leaves lanceolate, 4–12 cm./$1\frac{9}{16}$–$4\frac{3}{4}$ in. long, with marked point (thus not so rounded as *R. dauricum*), very thin, somewhat scaly; flowers singly, appearing from the buds grouped at the tips of the shoots, appearing before the leaves, broad funnel shaped, 3 cm./$1\frac{1}{4}$ in. wide, edge has five lobes, purple pink, January–March. Japan. Wonderful winter-flowering variety, whose glorious blooms appear as early as January during a mild winter, although they are susceptible to frost. *** Worth mentioning is also the American selection 'Cornell Pink', with reddish pink flowers, which bloom somewhat later. *S+SC Japan + Korea, China (+Hup shahtang) + mongolia + Siberia*

R. neriiflorum FRANCH.
('With Oleander flowers'; the flowers do not in any way resemble Oleander flowers, for this scientific name is the result of an error. The author had written 'neriifolium'—i.e. with *leaves* like that of an Oleander, did not notice the error, and the mistake cannot now be rectified.)
S. and SS. Neriiflorum

Evergreen shrub, growing to 1–1·5 m./3–$4\frac{1}{2}$ ft. in cultivation, a little more in its homeland, young shoots first covered with white down, later bare and red; leaves 5–10 cm./2–4 in. long, round at both ends, dark green and smooth above, waxy and white or bluish white beneath; flowers in groups of 5–12, tube or bell shaped, fleshy, 3–4 cm./$1\frac{3}{16}$–$1\frac{9}{16}$ in. long and broad, clear carmine red, calyx very large and similarly coloured, edge has five lobes, May. China, Yunnan, Tibet, 3,000–4,000 m./9,000–12,000 ft., in shady valleys. ∧∧∧***# There are also hardier races of this variety.

R. nudiflorum TORR. (= *Azalea nudiflora* L.) (Plate 17, 3) *R prioncphilleum*
('naked flowers'; that means, flowers before leaves) *(also incl "restum"?)*
S. Azalea; SS. Luteum

Deciduous, approximately man-size bush, shoots setaceous, leaves elliptical, 3–10 cm./$1\frac{3}{16}$–4 in. long, middle rib setaceous, clear green above; flowers in groups of 6–12, appearing shortly before the leaves, tube or funnel shaped, up to 4 cm./$1\frac{9}{16}$ in. wide, scented, lobes longer than the tubes, white to pale pink, with or without yellow fleck, filaments three times as long as the tubes, May. North America; hardy. Once much used in crossings. Fast growing and highly recommended. * *Mass to Ga – E to Ill.*

R. nuttallii BOOTH.
S. Maddenii; SS. Megacalyx

Named after Thomas Nuttall, English botanist. Evergreen bushy or treelike variety, growing up to 8 m./24 ft. in its homeland, with rigid thick young shoots; leaves elliptical, stiff and leathery, up to 30 cm./12 in. long, reddish on emergence; flowers in groups of 3–6 almost lily-shaped, 10–12 cm./4–$4\frac{3}{4}$ in. long and broad, very fleshy, ivory white to yellow, red at the edges, April–May, strongly scented, calyx 2–5 cm./$\frac{3}{4}$–2 in. long. Himalayas, Bhutan, in the mountains 1,300–1,600 m./3,900–4,800 ft. high. This variety has the largest individual flowers of all the wild varieties to be found in cultivation, but it is so very sensitive that it will survive only in the greenhouse. W. Hooker named this variety 'Prince of Rhododendrons', because of its huge flowers; F. Kingdon Ward termed it 'Madonna of Rhododendrons'. ***∧∧∧#

R. oblongifolium MILLAIS
('with oblong leaves')
S. Azalea; SS. Luteum

Deciduous shrub, about man-size; leaves elliptical to oblong, 5–10 cm./2–4 in. long, dark green above, paler beneath, flowers in groups of 7–12, appearing after the leaves, tube to funnel shaped, white, June–July, with faint scent of clover. South-eastern states of America. Very closely related to *R. viscosum*, although flowering somewhat earlier. Hardy. *

R. obtusum PLANCH (Colour Plate 3, *1*)
('stubborn')
S. Azalea; SS. Obtusum

Evergreen or only winter-green shrub, up to about 0·7 m./2 ft. high, growth very dense and widespreading, remaining low, young shoots covered with thick brown hairs; leaves dimorphous spring leaves elliptical-oval, 1·5–4 cm./$\frac{9}{16}$–$1\frac{9}{16}$ in. long, clear green, with setaceous brown hairs on both sides; summer leaves smaller, narrower, tougher and darker; flowers in groups of 1–3, funnel shaped, about 2·5 cm./1 in. wide, with large variations in colour, between bright red, carmine and orange, May. North-western Japan. The type is very seldom found in cultivation in its pure state, but there are innumerable garden varieties, among which the many 'Kurume' Azaleas, of which Ernest Wilson in 1919 brought no less than fifty varieties back to America; all of these had Japanese names. ***#

R. occidentale GRAY (Plate 3, *4*)
('occidental, western')
S. Azalea; SS. Luteum

Deciduous shrub, 1–2 m./3–6 ft. high, young shoots with fine hairs, later bare; and brown; winter buds with long points; leaves elliptical–lanceolate, 4–10 cm./$1\frac{9}{16}$–4 in. long, ciliate, few hairs on either side, in autumn yellow or carmine; flowers in groups of 6–12, appearing at the same time as the first leaves, funnel shaped, up to 6 cm./$2\frac{3}{8}$ in. wide, white to pale pink, with yellow fleck, hairy outside, sweetly scented, June. Western States of America. Hardy. From this come the Occidental hybrids, valuable because of their late flowering period. ***

T. oleifolium FRANCH.
('with leaves like an olive')
S. Virgatum

Evergreen shrub with long, thin, scaly shoots, 0·5–1·2 m./$1\frac{1}{2}$–$3\frac{1}{2}$ ft. high; leaves narrow and lanceolate, 6 cm./$2\frac{3}{8}$ in. long, thick scales beneath flowers singly or in pairs, standing in the axle, with bud-scales which do not fall off; tube or bell shaped, around 2·5 cm./1 in. long, pink or white, very hairy outside and scaly; April–May. China, Yunnan, south-eastern Tibet, 2,500–3,000 m./7,500–9,000 ft. Flowers profusely, but the long shoots unfortunately tend to freeze easily. Very similar in appearance to *R. virgatum*, but the flowers are hairy outside. ∧∧*#

R. orbiculare DC. (Colour Plate, 1, *5*; Plate 12, *2* and Fig. 33)
('circular', referring to the shape of the leaves)
S. Fortunei; SS. Orbiculare

Low-growing evergreen, very compact shrub, roundish, hardly over 1 m./3 ft. high and wide over here (but up to 3 m./9 ft. in its homeland), young shoots pale green with bluish tinge; leaves round, 4–10 cm./$1\frac{9}{16}$–4 in. long, and broad, base heart-shaped, dull green above, blue green beneath; flowers in groups of 7–10, in loose bunches, very regularly bell shaped up to 5 cm./2 in. long, edge has 7 lobes, carmine pink, often with a bluish tinge, somewhat paler inside, profusely flowering, April. China, Western Setschuan,

R. oreodoxa

Mupin and Tatsien-lu, at heights of around 3,000 m./9,000 ft. Only sensitive because of its early development; so beautiful that it needs an area of grass all to itself for its true beauty to be fully appreciated. ∧∧–***#

R. oreodoxa FRANCH. (Plate 12, *3*)
('Glory of the Mountains')
S. Fortunei; SS. Oreodoxa

Evergreen, very rigidly erect, somewhat 'long-legged' shrub, 2–3 m./6–9 ft. high, young shoots downy at first, thereafter bare; leaves appearing only at the tips of new shoots, otherwise no leaves, narrow and elliptical, 5–10 cm./2–4 in. long dark green above, bluish beneath, rolling up in frosty weather; flowers in groups of 10–12, broad bell shaped, about 5 cm./2 in. wide, pale or dark pink, with occasional purple flecks, edge has 7 lobes, March–April, above the leaves. Western to north-western China; Setschuan, Mupin Kansu, in forests at heights of 3,000 m./9,000 ft. Often damaged by frost because of its early flowering period. ∧∧***# George Arends of Wuppertal (Germany) crossed this variety with the dark red garden hybrid 'Doncaster' and achieved the so-called 'Ronsdorfer Frühblühnde', with better foliage and richer flowers; can be obtained in various shades of pink.

R. oreotrephes W. W. SM. (= *R. artosquameum* BALF. F. & FORREST)
('Lives in mountains')
S. Triflorum; SS. Yunnanense   *Hexaploid*

Evergreen shrub, 1·5–2 m./4½–6 ft. high, growth pretty and rounded, shoots with thin scales, reddish; leaves longish-elliptical, both ends rounded, 4–7 cm./$1\frac{9}{16}$–$2\frac{3}{4}$ in. long, with scales on both sides, but thicker and bluish beneath; flowers in groups of 5–10, in loose bunches, funnel shaped, 4–7 cm./2–$2\frac{3}{8}$ in. long, lilac-pink, with or without carmine flecks, April–May. China, Setschuan, Tibet, Burma, 3,000–5,500 m./9,000–16,500 ft. Originates from a relatively dry region. Flower buds freeze very easily; often only winter green in colder areas. ∧∧∧***#   *NNW1NNC Yunan StSeTibt, +SwSzechuan 9,100 to 14,000 ft.*

R. parvifolium ADAMS
('small leaved')
S. Lapponicum

Evergreen dwarf shrub, only 30–40 cm./12–16 in. high, growth very dense and compact; leaves oblong–lanceolate, up to 2 cm./$\frac{3}{4}$ in. long, 7 mm./$\frac{5}{16}$ in. wide, thick scales and greyish green on both sides; flowers usually in groups of 5, broad funnel shaped, beginning of April, purplish pink. North-eastern Asia, Altai to Kamtschatka. Hardy. In very mild areas will flower as early as January. #

R. pemakoense WARD
('from the province of Pemako in eastern Tibet')   *Diploid &Tetraploid*
S. Uniflorum

Evergreen dwarf bush, only about 30 cm./12 in. high, occasionally putting out offshoots, fairly dense, often twice as broad as it is tall; leaves oval or oblong, around 4 cm./$1\frac{9}{16}$ in. long, dark green above, bluish green and scaly beneath; flowers singly or in pairs, funnel shaped about 3 cm./$1\frac{3}{16}$ in. long and wide, lilac pink to purple, blooming at the end of March and therefore susceptible to frosts. Tibet, 3,300 m./9,900 ft. Hardy, ***# but difficult to cultivate, and recommended only to the enthusiast or the specialist.

N. Assam+SETibet   2900 to 3,050m

R. pentaphyllum MAXIM (= *R. nikoense* NAKAI)
('five leaved')
S. Azalea; SS. Canadense

Deciduous bush, man-size in our gardens, shoots relatively bare; leaves usually in groups 5 together at the tips of the shoots; elliptical-lanceolate, 4–7 cm./$1\frac{9}{16}$–$2\frac{3}{4}$ in. long, ciliate and finely incised, dark green above, carmine and orange in autumn; flowers singly or in pairs appearing before the leaves, 5 cm./2 in. wide, wheel or bell shaped, purplish pink, without flecks, March–April. Central and southern Japan, Nikko, in forests. Very sensitive and fragile as young plants, but become hardy later on; flowering period occurs immediately after *R. mucronulatum* (not to be confused with *R. quinquefolium* with white flowers which appear after the leaves!). ∧***

R. ponticum L. (Fig. 3)
('from the Pontus mountains, near Eawt')
S. and SS. Ponticum

Evergreen very woody shrub, 3–5 m./9–15 ft. high, sometimes growing into a small tree, usually wooded from the base, bare; leaves oblong–lanceolate, 10–15 cm./4–6 in. long, dark green above, paler beneath; flowers in loose bunches of 10–15, wide funnel shaped, almost star shaped in appearance, 4–5 cm./$1\frac{9}{16}$–2 in. wide, bright purple with yellowish green marking, end of May to beginning of June. Near East, Caucasus, Armenia; also in Spain and Portugal (the latter also being described occasionally as *R. baeticum* BOISS. & REUT.). Somewhat sensitive in colder areas, therefore should be protected in winter. Not so important as *R. catawbiense*. First discovered in the Caucasus in 1700 by Tournefort, but he did not bring it into cultivation. Around 1740 it was discovered in Spain by C. Alstroemer between Cadiz and Gibraltar, and in 1763 was brought from Gibraltar back to England.

To this species belongs the remarkable garden variety 'Imbricatum', a short-stemmed, very slow-growing small bush with elliptical leaves lying over one another like roof tiles, and small violet flowers (= *R. imbricatum* HORT.). 'Roseum', on the other hand, grows almost as strongly as the type, is very dense, and its young shoots have noticeably red bark, the leaves are a little smaller and narrower, flowers lilac pink with paler centre, appearing in the middle of June. Very useful as a late flowerer. The variegated garden form 'Variegatum' has very irregular leaves, blooms very seldom and is therefore of interest only to collectors and specialists.

R. praecox CARR. (= *R. ciliatum* × *R. dauricum*) (Plate 9, *1*)

Only winter-green shrub, 1–2 m./3–6 ft. high over here, growth loose; leaves elliptical, 4–7 cm./2–$2\frac{3}{8}$ in. long, very shiny, dark green, extremely aromatic, brown scales beneath, becoming partly yellow in autumn, and some leaves falling off; flowers occurring in groups of three on the shoots, 4 cm./$1\frac{9}{16}$ in. wide, lilac pink, February–April, very profusely flowering. Achieved by I. Davies in England in 1855; the best known and most popular early flowering variety, with flowers appearing at the same time as the forsythia; however, the blooms are quite frequently attacked by frost. ∧∧***

R. prostratum W. W. SM.
('laid out')
S. Saluenense

Evergreen, low-lying shrub, only about 10 cm./4 in. wide, although growing as high as 30 cm./12 in. in cultivation, young shoots and leaf-stems setaceous; leaves oblong-elliptical, 12–20 cm./$\frac{1}{2}$–$1\frac{3}{16}$ in. long, smooth above, scaly beneath; flowers in groups of 1–3, wheel to

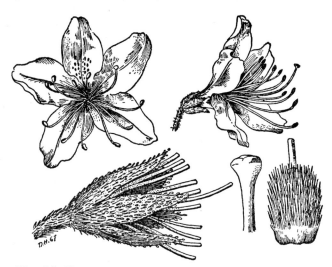

Fig. 32. R. mucronatum.

funnel shaped, up to 3 cm./1⅜ in. wide, purple pink to carmine, with darker flecks, May (often blooming again in autumn). China, Yunnan, in the high mountains, right up to the treeline. *#

R. prunifolium (SMALL) MILLAIS
('with leaves like a plum')
S. Azalea; SS. Luteum

Deciduous shrub, up to 2 m./6 ft. high, growth roundish, young shoots bare, purplish red; leaves elliptical–oval, 3–12 cm./1³⁄₁₆–4¾ in. long, dark green above, paler beneath, central rib hairy, flowers do not appear until July–August, in groups of 4–5, tube or funnel shaped, up to 5 cm./2 in. wide, 2·5 cm./1 in. long, orange to carmine. South-eastern ~~and northern~~ States of America. Completely hardy and very useful on account of its extraordinarily late flowering period. *** S. G. at Ala

R. przewalskii MAXIM
S. Lacteum

Named after the Russian explorer N. M. Przewalski. Evergreen roundish shrub, growth very dense, usually not more than 1 m./3 ft. high in Europe, although generally much smaller, young shoots yellow and bare; leaves oval, brown and downy beneath, but eventually usually more or less bare, dark green above with a noticeable blue-green tinge; flowers in groups of 12–15 (but unfortunately it flowers so seldom that it is possible to go for years without seeing a single flower!), bell shaped, 3–4 cm./1³⁄₁₆–1⁹⁄₁₆ in. wide, white to pink, April–May. North-western China, Kansu, Setschuan, Tibet, completely hardy—and has fine foliage. #

R. pulchrum SWEET (Colour Plate 3, 5)
('beautiful')
S. Azalea; SS. Obtusum

Perhaps only a hybrid, possibly a cross between *R. mucronatum* and *R. scabrum*; not known in a wild state. Low shrub, rarely over 1 m./3 ft. high, young shoots covered with grey-brown hairs; leaves evergreen, elliptical–lanceolate, up to 5 cm./2 in. long; flowers in groups of 1–4 together, funnel shaped, purple with darker marking,

about 5 cm./2 in. wide, May; 10 stamens (= *R. indicum* var. *smithii* SWEET). Known in Japan and in China in garden cultivation in many forms. ∧∧** Here belong the variety illustrated on Colour Plate 3, 5, 'Maxwellii'; flowers bright red with darker marking; large-flowered.

R. puralbum BALF. F. & W. W. SM.
('pure white')
S. Thomsonii; SS. Souliei

Evergreen shrub, about man-size over here (in its homeland up to about 4 m./12 ft.); leaves oblong–elliptical, 5–12 cm./2–4¾ in. long, 3–5 cm./1³⁄₁₆–2 in. wide, round at both ends, dark green above, very bluish green beneath and eventually bare; flowers in groups of about 8, loosely together, broad saucer shaped, pure white, wide, has five rounded lobes, May; buds dark red; calyx large, 12 mm./½ in. deep, lobe tomentose and green. Yunnan, 4,000 m./12,000 ft. Similar to *R. wardii* (yellow flowers) and *R. souliei* (pink flowers), but deceptive in cultivation. ∧–∧∧***#

R. quinquefolium BISS. & MOORE (Plate 17, 4)
('five leaved')
S. Azalea; SS. Schlippenbachii

Deciduous, stiffly upright shrub, 1–3 m./3–9 ft. high, shoots thin, partly spiral, partly in whorls; leaves in groups of 4–5 at the end of new shoots; oval shaped, 4–6 cm./1⁹⁄₁₆–2⅜ in. long and 2–4 cm./¾–1⁹⁄₁₆ in. wide, ciliate, often with a narrow red rim; flowers singly or in pairs, appearing shortly before the leaves or with them, hanging, broad funnel shaped, 4 cm./1⁹⁄₁₆ in. wide, white with greenish flecks, April–May. Central Japan. –∧∧*** Does not bloom very profusely as a young plant, but later becomes very beautiful during its flowering season and in the autumn.

R. racemosum FRANCH.
('with flowers like grapes')
S. Scabrifolium

Evergreen shrub, up to about 1 m./3 ft. high, growth upright, bushy, branches partly lying on the ground, young shoots red; leaves oblong–elliptical, 2–5 cm./¾–2 in. long, bluish green beneath with thick scales; flowers positioned in the axles along the branches, one or two in the angle of the leaves, funnel shaped, up to 2·5 cm./1 in. wide, pink or verging on white, March–April. China, Yunnan, Setschuan, 2,500–3,000 *+,700* m./7,500–9,000 ft. high. Pretty, but very sensitive on account of its early flowering season; however, it normally recovers satisfactorily. ∧–∧∧***# Here belong also two cultivated varieties from Ronsdorf: 'Delicatum', dark pink, and 'Roseum' clear pink. *Nw Yunnan tSw Szechuan*

R. radicans BALF. F. & FORREST
('having roots')
S. Saluenense

Evergreen, mat-forming shrub, or sometimes growing into a round 'Hill', 5–15 cm./2–6 in. high, shoots putting out roots, bare, scales on buds not falling off; leaves small, narrow–lanceolate, up to 15 mm./⅝ in. long, with loose scales above, denser scales beneath, flowers singly on stems 15 mm./⅝ in. long, wheel shaped, 2 cm./¾ in. long, 5 deep lobes, purple hairy and scaly outside, May–June, often blooming a second time in the autumn. South-eastern Tibet, Tsarong, 4,500–5,000 m./13,500–15,000 ft. Very fine for rockeries, even in sunny areas; does not bloom as profusely as *R. keleticum*. ***#

Fig. 33. R. orbiculare.

R. reticulatum D. DON (= *R. rhombicum* MIQ.; *R. wadanum* MAK.)
(Plate 1, *2*)
('with network of veins')
S. Azalea; SS. Schlippenbachii SL.

Deciduous shrub, 1–2 m./3–6 ft. (up to 5 m./15 ft.) high, very thickly wooded, young shoots pale brown, soon becoming bare; leaves usually in 2s and 3s at the end of new shoots, broad oval shaped, 3–7 cm./$8\frac{3}{16}$–$2\frac{3}{4}$ in. long with network of veins beneath. Veins hairy, colour in autumn wine red to purple; flowers singly or in pairs (up to 4) appearing before the leaves; corona wheel to funnel shaped, 4–5 cm./$1\frac{9}{16}$–2 in. wide, purple to purplish pink, not usually flecked, April–May, Japan; widely distributed on volcanic ash. Fairly hardy. Grows well in a sunny position and flowers best there. ***

R. rex LEV. (Plate 8, *5*)
('king')
S. Falconeri

Evergreen shrub, hardly growing to more than 1·5 m./$4\frac{1}{2}$ ft. here, but in a favourable climate can reach 5 m./15 ft., shoots very thick (up to 15 mm./$\frac{5}{8}$ in.) covered with grey-white down, leaves oblong, up to 25 cm./10 in. long, dark green above, grey to pale grey down beneath, stem about 4 cm./$1\frac{9}{16}$ in. long; flowers in groups of 20–30, tube or bell shaped, 5 cm./2 in. long, pink or white, with dark red basal fleck and similar points, April–May, edge of corona has 7–8 lobes, calyx small with 8 downy, wide triangular teeth (?). China, north-eastern Yunnan, south-western Setschuan, 3,000–4,000 m./9,000–12,000 ft. Easily the hardiest of the large-leaved varieties; similar to *R. fictolacteum*, but larger and better in all respects. ∧∧***#

R. rigidum FRANCH.
('stiff')
S. Triflorum; SS. Yunnanense

Evergreen, upright shrub, 1–2 m./3–6 ft. high, shoots rather rigid, hardly scaly; leaves elliptical, 4–6 cm./$1\frac{9}{16}$–$2\frac{3}{8}$ in. long, covered with scales on both sides; flowers appearing in the upper axils of leaves, in groups of 2–6, small, funnel shaped, clear pink with carmine marking edge has 5 lobes, March–May. China, Yunnan, on cliffs, 2,500–3,000 m./7,500–9,000 ft. Very pretty, profusely flowering, but sensitive. ∧∧–∧∧∧#

R. roseum REHD. (Plate 3, *2*) = *R. Prionophyllum (see also nudiflorum)*
('pink')
S. Azalea; SS. Luteum

Deciduous shrub, 1–3 m./3–9 ft. high, young shoots covered with fine hairs, winter buds grey; leaves elliptical to oval, 3–7 cm./$1\frac{3}{16}$–$2\frac{3}{4}$ in. long, dull blue green above, grey hairs beneath; flowers in groups of 5–9, appearing with the leaves, wide tube shaped, up to 4 cm./$1\frac{9}{16}$ in. wide, pink, strongly scented, May, profusely flowering. East and northern America. *** Fairly hardy and highly recommended. *Maine to Quebec to W. Va, Tenn, + Mo.*

R. roxieanum FORREST
S. Taliense; SS. Roxieanum

Named after Mrs. Roxie Hanna. Evergreen, very compact and slow-growing shrub, hardly over 50 cm./20 in. in our country, in its homeland up to 2 m./6 ft. Young shoots thickly covered with down, bud scales remaining for several years; leaves narrow and lanceolate, 5–10 cm./2–4 in. long, edge rolled, thick rust red down beneath, flowers in bunches of 10–15, bell shaped, white to pale pink, with or without carmine marking, edge has 5 lobes, April–May. China, Yunnan, on open, moist, mountain meadows, 4,000 m./12,000 ft. Does not bloom until it is an old plant. ∧∧***#
var. *oreonastes* (Plate 6, *3*) is an alpine dwarf variety with narrower leaves.

R. rubiginosum FRANCH. (Plate 12, *1* and Fig. 34)
('reddish brown')
S. Heliolepis *Tetraploid + Hexaploid*

Evergreen shrub growing to 2–3 m./6–9 ft. over here, but becoming a small tree in its homeland, young shoots reddish, scaly; leaves elliptical–lanceolate, pointed, 3–7 cm./$1\frac{3}{16}$–$2\frac{3}{8}$ in. long covered with thick rust brown scales beneath; flowers usually in groups of 4–8, funnel shaped, around 4 cm./$1\frac{9}{16}$ in. long, lilac-pink, scaly outside, particularly on the tips of the edge, April–May. China, Yunnan, 2,000–3,000 m./6,000–9,000 ft., in open forest areas. Generally completely hardy over here, but is better for the larger garden on account of its size. Good experiments with this variety have been made in areas not completely free of lime. ∧***#

R. rude TAGG & FORREST (Plate 10, *4*)
('rough')
S. Barbatum; SS. Glischrum

Evergreen man-size shrub, young shoots rough and setaceous, with scales remaining for one or two years; leaves broad, oblong-lanceolate, up to 20 cm./8 in. long and 7 cm./$2\frac{3}{4}$ in. wide, dark green, hairy, with depressed middle rib, paler beneath with long, curled hairs; flowers wide bell shaped, carmine pink with darker lines; calyx at least 12 mm./$\frac{1}{2}$ in. long; April–May; China, Yunnan. ∧∧∧**

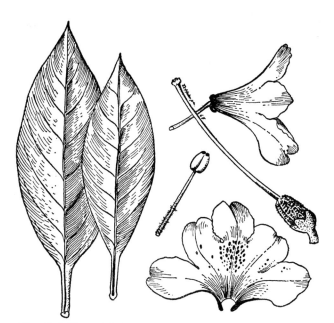

Fig. 34. R. rubiginosum.

young shoots thickly scaled and setaceous; leaves oblong–elliptical, 3 cm./$1\frac{3}{16}$ in. long, 1 cm./$\frac{3}{8}$ in. wide, with loose scales and shiny above, with thick scales beneath, aromatic, stem setaceous, flowers in groups of 1–7, wide bell shaped, 3 cm./$1\frac{1}{4}$ in. long and 4 cm./$1\frac{9}{16}$ in. wide, purple-red with darker markings, April–May, often blooming again in June. China, Yunnan, Setschuan, 4,000 m./12,000 ft. on cliffs. Hardy. Very useful for rockeries because of the large flowers. ***#

R. sanguineum FRANCH.
('blood red')
S. Neriiflorum; SS. Sanguineum

Evergreen shrub, hardly higher than 70 cm./28 in., upright, shoots thin, short, covered with white down; leaves oval-oblong, leathery, 4 cm./$1\frac{9}{16}$ in. long, tube or bell shaped, fleshy, 3 cm./$1\frac{3}{16}$ in. long, bright carmine red, May, unfortunately does not flower very frequently, Yunnan, Tibet. Fairly hardy. ∧–∧∧***#

Here belong also the ssp. *didymum* TAGG & FORREST (= *R. didymum* BALF. F. & FORREST) (Fig. 36), with whorl-like leaves and dark red, fleshy blooms; June. South-eastern Tibet, on the limestone cliffs of moist alpine meadows. ∧∧**#

ssp. *haemaleum* BALF. FL. & FORREST (= *R. haemaleum* BALF. FL. & FORREST). Equally small, shoots covered with hairs, as are the calyx and flower stems, leaves larger—up to 8 cm./$3\frac{3}{16}$ in. long; flowers blackish carmine, May. South-eastern Tibet, Salween–Mekong area, 4,000 m./12,000 ft. ∧–∧∧***# Very resistant to frost.

R. schlippenbachii MAXIM (Plate 17, *2*)
S. Azalea; SS. Schlippenbachii

Named after Baron von Schlippenbach, Russian marine officer and traveller. Deciduous shrub, growing to about 2 m./6 ft. high here, but up to 5 m./15 ft. in its homeland, branches short and erect; leaves in groups of 5, at the end of new shoots, oval, 6–10 cm./

R. rufum BATAL. (Plate 1, *1*)
('fox red')
S. Taliense; SS. Wasonii

Evergreen shrub, growth compact and roundish over here, in its homeland it reaches up to 5 m./15 ft., leaves elliptical–oblong, 7–11 cm./$2\frac{3}{4}$–$8\frac{3}{4}$ in. long, covered with rust brown down beneath; flowers in groups of 6–10, funnel to bell shaped, 3 cm./$1\frac{3}{16}$ in. long, white to purplish pink with carmine marks, April; China, Setschuan, Kansu, 3,500–4,000 m./10,500–12,000 ft., in woods. Hardy. Unfortunately does not flower very well as a young plant, but has beautiful foliage. #

R. russatum BALF. F. & FORREST (= *R. cantabile* BALF. F.)
('reddened')

Tetraploid + Hexaploid

S. Lapponicum

Small, upright, evergreen shrub 50–80 cm./20–32 in. high, shoots thickly covered with scales, leaves lanceolate, up to 3 cm./$1\frac{3}{16}$ in. long and 1 cm./$\frac{3}{8}$ in. wide, dark green above, rust brown and scaly beneath; flowers occurring at the end of shoots in groups of 4–5, open funnel shaped, dark violet and purple with white inside, about 2·5 cm./1 in. wide, pretty large for such a small bush, end of April to beginning of May. China, north-western Yunnan, 4,000 m./12,000 ft. One of the most beautiful dwarf varieties and quite hardy. ***#

Here belong also two selections from the J. Bruns Nurseries in Zwischenahn: 'Bad Zwischenahn', growth somewhat stronger, leaves pale green, flowers pale blue; 'Gristede', flowers dark purple blue.

NNC + NNW Yunnan + SW Szechuan

R. saluenense FRANCH (Fig. 35) *Tetraploid + Hexaploid*
S. Saluenense

Named after the River Salween. Evergreen dwarf variety, 40–50 cm./16–20 in. high, growing to twice this size in its homeland,

Fig. 35. R. saluenense.

$2\frac{3}{8}$–4 in. long, turning an attractive yellow or carmine in autumn; flowers in groups of 3–6, with or just before the leaves, broad funnel shaped, pale to dark pink, 7–8 cm./$2\frac{3}{4}$–$3\frac{3}{16}$ in. broad, April–May, Korea, north-eastern Manchuria, central Japan, in light woodland. *** Wonderful, fairly hardy variety, very elegant.

R. scintillans, BALF. F. & W. W. SM. (Plate 15, *5*)
('sparkling')
S. Lapponicum

Evergreen, small shrub, 50–70 cm./20–28 in. high, young shoots upright, thin, very scaly; leaves oblong–lanceolate, very small, 1–2 cm./$\frac{3}{8}$–$\frac{3}{4}$ in. long, covered with thick grey-green scales on both sides, but scales on the underside overlap or touch; flowers in groups of 3–6, open funnel shaped, up to 2·5 cm./1 in. wide, blue or nearly blue, bare outside, April–May; Yunnan, Lichiang, open grass or cliffs, 4,000–4,500 m./12,000–13,500 ft. Hardy and beautiful; not cultivated nearly often enough. ***#

R. serpyllifolium MIQ. (Plate 17, *6*)
('with leaves like thyme')
S. Azalea; SS. Obtusum

Deciduous, broad spreading and very finely wooded shrub, up to 1 m./3 ft high, leaves heaped on to the shoots, elliptical to oval, up to 1 cm./$\frac{3}{8}$ in. long, although usually smaller; flowers singly or in pairs, pink, May; Central and southern Japan. Only for enthusiasts; has the smallest leaves of the azalea group.

R. sherriffii COWAN (Plate 11, *3*)
S. Campanulatum (?). Grouping not yet ascertained

Named after G. Sherriff. Evergreen shrub, hardly ever cultivated; grows to 4 m./12 ft. or more in its homeland; leaves elliptical–oblong, up to 7 cm./$2\frac{3}{4}$ in. long, dark brown, thick down underneath; flowers in groups of 4–6, funnel or bell shaped, about 4 cm./$1\frac{9}{16}$ in. long, deep carmine red, calyx similarly coloured, with blue tinge, April. South-eastern Tibet. ∧*

R. simsii PLANCH. (= *Azalea indica* AIT.)
S. Azalea; SS. Obtusum

Named after John Sims, editor of the *Botanical Magazine* from 1800 to 1826. This is the plant which amateurs (and gardeners too) normally know as '*Azalea indica*' and grow indoors. Wide, evergreen shrub; leaves elliptical to oblong, dull green above, paler beneath, setaceous, 3–7 cm./$1\frac{3}{16}$–$2\frac{3}{4}$ in. long, pink to dark red in the type (in cultivated forms appears in all colours from white to deep red and violet, even two-toned, single and double), 10 stamens, often only 8 (this point is important, for the true *R. indicum* only has 5), May. East China, Formosa. *** Not hardy. ∧∧∧# 30-32+

R. sinogrande BALF. F. & W. W. SM. (Plate 8, *4*)
('Chinese River Grande')
S. Grande

Evergreen, very impressive shrub, either a large bush or a small tree, young shoots very thick and covered with grey down; leaves up to 75 cm./30 in. long and half as wide, although much smaller on plants which have already flowered, dark green and very shiny above, with 17 impressed pairs of veins; covered with a silvery grey sheath beneath; flowers in groups of about 20 in round bunches, bell shaped, bulging, 5–6 cm./2–$2\frac{3}{8}$ in. long; edge has 8–10 lobes, narcissus yellow with carmine basal fleck, April. China, Burma, Tibet, 3,000–4,500 m./9,000–13,500 ft., in rhododendron forests.

This imposing wild variety has the largest and most beautiful leaves normally 50 cm./20 in. long and 20 cm./8 in. wide. But these sizes are found only on plants which have not yet flowered; after this the leaves are markedly smaller and never reach again their former size. Until now there has been no type which has been completely hardy, even in England. ∧∧∧***#

R. smirnowii TRAUTV. (Fig. 3)
S. Ponticum; SS. Caucasicum

Named after the Russian doctor and botanist M. Smirnow. Evergreen shrub, 1–2 m./3–6 ft. high and broad, bushy but also somewhat stiff-branched covered with white down; young shoots white and downy, only bare after 2 years; leaves oblong–lanceolate, tough, 6–15 cm./$2\frac{3}{8}$–$5\frac{7}{8}$ in. long, dark green above, white underneath to begin with, later covered with pale brown down; flowers in loose bunches of 10–12, funnel or bell shaped, up to 5 cm./2 in. wide, pale or dark pink, May–June. Caucasus, 1,500–2,000 m./4,500–6,000 ft. Extra hardy, but the flowers are not particularly beautiful; interesting for its leaves. *#

R. souliei FRANCH.
S. Thomsonii; SS. Souliei

Named after Father J. A. Soulié, French missionary in Tibet. Interesting shrub, 1–2·5 m./3–$7\frac{1}{2}$ ft. high, young shoots reddish or bluish and tomentose; leaves broad heart- to oval-shaped, to near circular, 3–7 cm./$1\frac{3}{16}$–$2\frac{3}{4}$ in. long, dark green above, pale bluish green beneath; flowers in groups of 5–8, broad goblet shaped, from pale to dark pink, also sometimes with carmine basal fleck, 5 cm./2 in. wide, edge having 5 or 6 lobes, May. Tibet, Western Setschuan, in woods and thickets. Attractive shrub, growth slow, and not flowering until the plant is some years old. Many fine types. ∧–∧∧∧ ***#

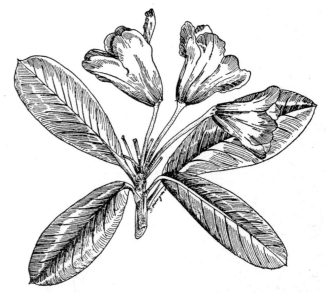

Fig. 36. R. sanguineum *var.* didymum.

R. spinuliferum FRANCH.
('bearing small thorns')
S. Scabrifolium

Evergreen, very 'long-legged' shrub, 1–2 m./3–6 ft. high, young shoots with soft hairs, setaceous, red; leaves 5–7 cm./2–2¾ in. long, oblong–elliptical, somewhat blistered on top, with network of veins; scaly and hairy beneath; flowers standing in the axils of new shoots, in groups of 3–5 in upright groups, almost tubular, 2·5 cm./1 in. long, tip bent in towards the centre and never opening out, bright red to carmine, stamens and pistils protruding, April–May. China, Yunnan. Very interesting and remarkable variety, but meant chiefly for enthusiasts and collectors. ∧∧∧#

R. sutchuenense FRANCH. (Plate 7, 2)
('From Setschuan')
S. Fortunei; SS. Davidii

Evergreen, strong growing, upright shrub, 2–5 m./6–15 ft. high, young shoots thick, first covered with grey-white down, later bare, buds walnut sized, round; leaves oblong–lanceolate, heaped on the growing branches and facing the side, 10–25 cm./4–10 in. long, dull dark green, paler beneath; flowers in bunches of 8–10, wide bell shaped, 5–7 cm./2–2¾ in. long, fine pink or rosy lilac, with purple marks, but no basal fleck, February–March, anthers nearly black. China, Setschuan, Hupeh, 2,000–3,000 m./6,000–9,000 ft. in forests. One of the most beautiful varieties from China, but because of its early flowering period this otherwise hardy plant sometimes succumbs to frost. ∧∧***#
The var. *geraldii* HUTCHINS. is a deeper pink in colour and has a noticeable chocolate brown basal fleck.

R. taggianum HUTCHINS.
S. Maddenii; SS. Megacalyx

Named after the Scottish botanist H. F. Tagg. Evergreen shrub with long, loose shoots, 1–1·5 m./3–4½ ft. high, young shoots scaly; leaves oblong–elliptical, 7–16 cm./2¾–6 in. long, bluish underneath and fairly thickly covered with scales; flowers in groups of 3–4, very large, broad funnel or tube shaped, 7–10 cm./2¾–4 in. long and broad, pure white with pale yellow basal fleck, very pleasantly and strongly scented, April–May. China, Yunnan, Burma, 2,000–3,600 m./6,000–10,800 ft. Wonderful variety, but only possible for the greenhouse. ∧∧∧***#

R. taliense FRANCH.
('from the Tali mountains')
S. and SS. Talienss

Evergreen shrub, 1–3 m./3–9 ft. high, usually growing as a compact shrub here, to about 1 m./3 ft., very thickly wooded, young shoots thick and downy, later bare; leaves broad lanceolate, 4–10 cm./1⁹⁄₁₆–4 in. long, edge rolled, dark green above, covered with thick brownish down beneath, flowers in groups of 10–15, funnel or bell shaped, 3·5 cm./1⅜ in. long, creamy white or with pink tinge, edge has 5 lobes, May; flower stems covered with dense hairs. China, Yunnan, Tali mountains, in open places. # A word of warning about the whole *Taliense* Series: all the varieties belonging to this Series (see page 53) grow very slowly and do not bloom until they are quite old. Despite their strongly smelling leaves, many people will be disappointed in them.

R. tapetiforme BALF. F. & WARD
('like a carpet') S. Lapponicum

Evergreen shrub, growing to a height of 50 cm./20 in. but usually mat-like in shape and much smaller, young shoots scaly; leaves broad and elliptical, 1·5 cm./⅜ in. long, scaly both sides, but denser and reddish brown on the underside, flowers in groups of 2–4, open funnel shaped, about 1·5 cm./½ in. long, lilac pink to deep purplish blue, April. China, Yunnan, Tibet, in the high mountains, 5,000 m./15,000 ft. Hardy. *#

R. thomsonii HOOK. F. (Plate 6, 5 and Fig. 37)
S. and SS. Thomsonii

Named after Th. Thomson, former Director of the Botanical Gardens in Calcutta. Evergreen, wide shrub, growing into a small tree in milder areas, bark of older plants fleshy pink and peeling, quite smooth, young shoots covered with waxlike substance, leaves oval, 5–10 cm./2–4 in. long, base heart shaped, dark green above, bluish white beneath; flowers in groups of 5–8, wide bell shaped, fleshy and waxy, blood red, April–May; calyx goblet shaped, up to 15 mm./⅝ in. long, green or red. Sikkim, Nepal to Tibet, in mountain forests. Unfortunately does not bloom until it is an old plant; the blood red flowers are breathtakingly beautiful when seen through filtering sunshine, and even after the flowering period the calyxes which remain are worth seeing. ∧∧***#
var. *candelabrum* (HOOK. F.) CLARKE with paler flowers and smaller calyx is quite hardy and grows to 2 m./6 ft. high and wide.

R. traillianum FORREST & W. W. SM. (Plate 11, 2)
S. Lacteum

Named after the botanist G. W. Trail. Large, evergreen shrub, treelike in its homeland (over here hardly reaches over 1·5 m./4½ ft.); young shoots pale brown or grey and downy; leaves elliptical to lanceolate, 6–11 cm./2⅜–4⅜ in. long, but only 2–4 cm./¾–1⁹⁄₁₆ in. wide, pleasantly aromatic and with a scent of resin, upper veins impressed, brown and downy beneath; flowers in groups of 10–15, funnel to bell shaped 3·5 m./1⅜ in. long, white to pink, with or without dark red points, April–May. China, Yunnan, Setschuan, 3,600–4,700 m./10,800–14,100 ft. Completely hardy, but we have had one for twenty years which is now 70 cm./28 in. high and still not flowering! Even the scent of the leaves on warm summer days does not compensate for the lack of flowers. *#

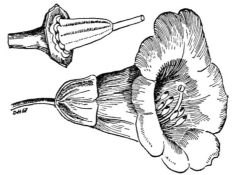

Fig. 37. R. thomsonii.

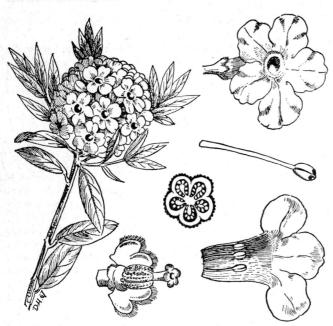

Fig. 38. R. trichostomum *var.* ledoides.

R. trichostomum var. *ledoides* (BALF. F. & W. W. SM.) COWAN & DAVIDIAN (Fig. 38)
S. Anthopogon

(The type of this plant is very sensitive to frost, and because of its similarity to the completely hardy variety mentioned here remains undiscussed.)

Small, evergreen shrub, about 1 m./3 ft. high, shoots short, wooded, scaly; leaves linear–lanceolate, dull green above, yellowish and thickly scaled beneath, 2–3 cm./$\frac{3}{4}$–1$\frac{3}{16}$ in. long; flowers in groups of 12–20 in dense, round heads, the individual flowers being narrow and tubular with protruding tip, 1 cm./$\frac{3}{8}$ in. long, pale pink, no scales outside (as opposed to the type which does have scales), May–June, scented. Yunnan, Setschuan. Quite pretty for the rockery; probably the easiest maintained of this series. ∧***#

R. triflorum HOOK. F.
('three-flowered')
S. and SS. Triflorum

High, loose evergreen shrub, shoots thin, with black tomenti; bark of older stems red-brown, peeling off; leaves oblong–lanceolate 3–7 cm./1$\frac{3}{16}$–2$\frac{3}{4}$ in. long, tomentose and scaly underneath; flowers in 3s, not appearing until after the development of new young shoots, broad funnel shaped, 4–5 cm./1$\frac{9}{16}$–2 in. across, lemon yellow with amber tint and green points, strongly scented, May–June. Himalayas, Sikkim, Bhutan, 2,500–4,600 m./7,500–13,800 ft. high, in woods. Very valuable and beautiful shrub, but should be grown in woods. Also hardier types. ∧∧***# One wild form with noticeable brownish red flecks and points is known as var. *mahogani*.
Nepal to Extreme N. Burma

80

R. ungernii TRAUTV. (Fig. 3)
S. Ponticum; SS. Caucasicum

Named after Professor Ungern-Sternberg from Dorpat. Evergreen shrub, growth upright, dense, hardly over 2 m./6 ft. over here (up to 6 m./18 ft. in its homeland), young shoots at first covered with white down, later bare; leaves oblong–lanceolate, 10–15 cm./ 4–6 in. long, thick and leathery, dark green and with marked small cusps, covered with dense pale brown down beneath; flowers in large bunches of 20–30, funnel shaped, 3·5 cm./1$\frac{3}{8}$ in. long and 5 cm./2 in. wide, clear pink, edge has 5 lobes, appearing in July. Caucasus. # Very hardy variety with beautiful foliage; unfortunately the late-appearing flowers are often completely hidden by the leaves.

R. uvarifolium DIELS (= *R. niphargum* BALF. F. & WARD)
('with uvaria shaped leaves')
S. Fulvum

High evergreen shrub (hardly over 1 m./3 ft. here) young shoots and underneath of leaves covered with glorious snow white down and very delicate; leaves oblong, 10–20 cm./4–8 in. long, dark green, undersides eventually turning greyish; flowers small, but in dense clusters of 15–20, bell shaped, 3–5 cm./1$\frac{3}{16}$–2 in. long, white to purplish pink with carmine basal fleck, pleasantly scented, March–April. Yunnan, Lichiang mountains. ∧∧–∧∧∧*#

R. vaseyi GRAY (Plate 2, *3* and Fig. 39)
S. Azalea; SS. Canadense

Named after the discoverer of this plant, G. S. Vasey. Deciduous shrub, up to 2 m./6 ft. high, growth very outspread and irregular. Shoots reddish brown; leaves elliptical, oblong, 5–10 cm./4–8 in. long, dark green above, edge slightly waved; flowers in groups of 5–8, appearing before the leaves, having five deep lobes, 3 cm./ 1$\frac{3}{16}$ in. wide, pale to dark pink, with red or orange marks, April–May. North America, Blue Ridge Mountains. Completely hardy, fast growing, one of the best wild varieties, which should be planted more often, particularly in woodlands and parks. *North Carolina*

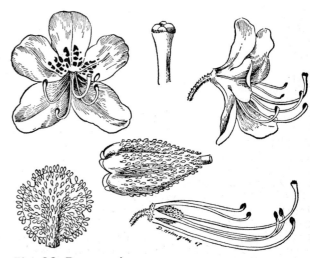

Fig. 39. R. vaseyi.

PLATE 19 Garden hybrids. 1 *R.* 'Attraction', 2 *R.* 'Sappho', 3 *R.* 'Gomer Waterer', 4 *R.* 'Helen Koster', 5 *R.* 'Prince Camille', 6 *R.* 'Louis Pasteur', 7 *R.* 'Fragrans', 8 *R.* 'Prof. F. Bettex'.

PLATE 20

1 Transplanting an old rhododendron bush to give it a new lease of life.
2 Before planting out soak the ball of earth round the roots.
3 An effective way of supporting a newly planted bush from the wind.
4 Once the plant has flowered, the dead flower heads should be removed.
5 The rhododendron bug; *left*, larvae and *right*, two adult, winged insects.
6 Spraying is an effective way of dealing with the rhododendron bug.
7 Leaf damage caused by the bug.
8 A close-up of the bug itself enlarged. Its actual size is $\frac{1}{3}$ inch.
9 Damage caused by frost.

R. vellereum HUTCHINS.
('fleecelike')
S. and SS. Taliense

Evergreen shrub, man-size over here, wide growing, dense, young shoots only slightly downy and soon quite bare; leaves oblong–lanceolate, 6–11 cm./$2\frac{3}{8}$–$4\frac{3}{8}$ in. long, with thick silvery white or pale grey down; flowers in dense bunches of 15–20, funnel or bell shaped, 3·5 cm./$1\frac{3}{8}$ in. long white or pink with red marks, edge having five crenated lobes, calyx consisting of only one waved edge, April. South-eastern Tibet. This variety, like most of those in this Series, does not flower until it is comparatively old, and is therefore designed only for the patient or the specialist collector. ∧∧#

R. venator TAGGO
('huntsman')
S. Irroratum; SS. Parishii

Evergreen shrub, 2 m./6 ft. high or more, but far smaller over here, very bushy; young shoots with long-stemmed tomenta (?) and white hairs; leaves oblong, 5–12 cm./2–$4\frac{3}{4}$ in. long, clear green and slightly rough on upper surface, blue green beneath; flowers in groups of 4–11, tube or bell shaped, 4 cm./$1\frac{9}{16}$ in. long, scarlet with five carmine-black basal flecks, edge has five lobes. South eastern Tibet. Very hardy, but not very well tested here. #

R. vernicosum FRANCH. (= *R. adoxum* BALF. F. & FORREST)
('lacquered')
S. and SS. Fortunei

Evergreen shrub, 1·5–5 m./$4\frac{1}{2}$–15 ft. high, similar to *R. decorum*, but flower stems and calyx have petiolate tomenta; leaves elliptical, 6–12 cm./$2\frac{3}{8}$–$4\frac{3}{4}$ in. long, bare, bluish green beneath; flowers in groups of 10, funnel or bell shaped, white to pink or lilac, with or without carmine flecks, edge has 7 lobes, April–May. Tibet. A somewhat variable variety, but unassuming. ∧–∧∧***#

R. viscosum TORR. (Plate 17, 5)
('sticky')
S. Azalea; SS. Luteum

Deciduous shrub, 1·5–2 m./$4\frac{1}{2}$–6 ft. high, growth loose, branches often lying on the ground, irregular whorls; young shoots covered with rough hairs; leaves oval, 3–5 cm./$1\frac{3}{16}$–2 in. long, very short stemmed, dark green above, generally blue green beneath; flowers appearing after the leaves in groups of 5–10, narrow, tube shaped with protruding tip, 5 cm./2 in. long and 4 cm./$1\frac{9}{16}$ in. wide, white, but also sometimes pinkish in tone, smelling very much like clover, July, although sometimes also in August; filaments white. Eastern states of North America in swampy areas near the coast. Completely hardy, likes moist conditions. *   *Maine to Florida(?)*

R. wallichii HOOK. F. (Plate 10, 2)
S. Campanulatum

Named after V. Wallichi, one-time director of the Botanical Gardens in Calcutta. Evergreen shrub, 2–4 m./6–12 ft. high, also a small tree in its homeland, bark dark brown, shoots rather twisted, young shoots bare; leaves elliptical, leathery, 7–10 cm./$2\frac{3}{4}$–4 in. long, base heart shaped, dark green above, with rust-coloured clumps of hairs beneath, which, however, do not form a continuous cover (as they do in *R. campanulatum*); flowers in groups of 6–10, wide bell shaped, lilac to lilac pink, with pink points, April. Himalayas, Sikkim, Nepal, 3,300–4,600 m./9,900–13,800 ft. Best for enthusiasts and collectors. ∧∧–∧∧∧*#

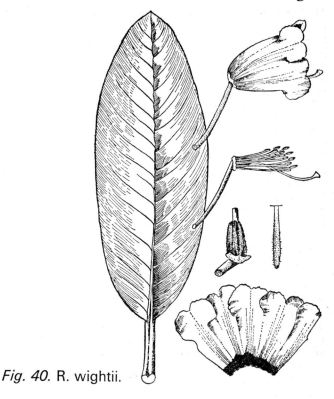

Fig. 40. R. wightii.

R. wardii W. W. SM. (= *R. croceum* BALF. F. & W. W. SM; *R. astrocalyx* BALF. F. & FORREST)
S. Thomsonii; SS. Souliei

Named after the famous plant collector F. Kingdon Ward. Evergreen shrub hardly over 2 m./6 ft. high over here, but up to 5 m./15 ft. in its homeland; young shoots tomentose to begin with; leaves leathery, broad elliptical, 5–10 cm./2–4 in. long and round at both ends, bare above, bluish green beneath; flowers in groups of 7–14, broad goblet shaped, fleshy, 3–4 cm./$1\frac{3}{16}$–$1\frac{9}{16}$ in. long, pure yellow or sometimes lemon yellow, occasionally with green tinge and a carmine basal fleck, May; ovaries and pistils tomentose (important distinguishing characteristic); calyx has 5 marked lobes and is tomentose. Yunnan, Setschuan, south-eastern Tibet. The two synonyms listed above are occasionally used. Very important wild variety, which, however, likes a sheltered spot and plenty of moisture during dry weather. Many plants have coral-coloured buds, which, however, develop into pure yellow flowers. ∧–∧∧***#

R. wightii HOOK. F. (Plate 10, 6 and Fig. 40)
S. Lacteum

Named after R. Wight, former Director of the Botanical Gardens in Madras. Evergreen shrub, growth loose, man-size here, but growing into a small tree in its homeland; young shoots thick and at first covered with grey-white down; leaves elliptical, tough, 12–18 cm./$4\frac{3}{4}$–$7\frac{1}{16}$ in. long, clear green above, white and downy beneath at first, then orange to brown and finally bare; flowers in wide bunches of 12–20 with very sticky scales, bell shaped, 4 cm./$1\frac{9}{16}$ in. long clear yellow to lemon yellow with red basal fleck and points,

R. williamsianum

April–May. Eastern Himalaya; Sikkim, Bhutan. This plant looks like a small version of *R. falconeri*, but it is much hardier; since the flowers are to a certain extent susceptible to frost, this plant should be given a sheltered spot. ∧–∧∧*#

R. williamsianum REHD. & WILS. (Fig. 7)
S. Thomsonii; SS. Williamsianum

Named after J. C. Williams in Caerhays, Cornwall. Evergreen, semi-circular bush, generally not over 1 m./3 ft. high, growth spreading, shoots short; young shoots and leaves copper coloured and very delicate; leaves broad and oval with heart-shaped base, 2–4 cm./$\frac{3}{4}$–1$\frac{9}{16}$ in. long, clear green above, blue green beneath; flowers in 2s and 3s, hanging, bell shaped, 3–4 cm./1$\frac{3}{16}$–1$\frac{9}{16}$ in. long, pure pink, April; edge has 5 lobes (NB. The similar *R. orbiculare* has 7 lobes.). Setschuan, 2,500–3,000 m./7,500–9,000 ft. Unfortunately the wild variety does not flower very often, but there are many hybrids (Plate 9), which bloom profusely and are also hardier. The brown young leaves, which in the hybrids are also salmon and even orange in colour, appear so early that they quite often perish in the frost if they are not given some sort of protection. ∧–∧∧***#

R. wiltonii HEMSL. & WILS (Plate 13, *4*)
S. Taliense; SS. Wasonii

Named after E. C. Wilton. Evergreen shrub, growing to 3 m./9 ft. in its homeland, young shoots greenish-white, downy; leaves oblong–oval, up to 12 cm./4$\frac{3}{4}$ in. long and arched; first covered with white, then with reddish brown down beneath; flowers in groups of up to 10 together, funnel to bell shaped, 4 cm./1$\frac{9}{16}$ in. long, white to pale pink with red marks and basal fleck, May. China, western Setschuan. ∧**

R. xanthocodon HUTCHINS *Hexaploid*
('yellow bell')
S. Cinnabarinum *see concatenans*

Evergreen, upright shrub, narrow, hardly over 1 m./3 ft. high here, but 3·5–6 m./10$\frac{1}{2}$–18 ft. high in its homeland, young shoots covered with golden scales; shoots fine blue green colour; leaves elliptical, 3–7 cm./1$\frac{3}{16}$–2$\frac{3}{4}$ in. long, dull green above, blue green beneath, thick scales on either side, aromatic; flowers in groups of 5–10, fleshy, bell to funnel shaped, 3 cm./1$\frac{3}{16}$ in. long, creamy or pure yellow, without any flecks, very pretty, edge has 5 lobes, May. South-eastern Tibet, 3,500–4,000 m./10,500–12,000 ft. Very pretty variety, similar to *R. cinnabarinum*, but with yellow flowers. The hardy types are very useful. ∧∧***#

R. Yakusimanum NAKAI (= *R. metternichii* var. *yakusimanum* [NAKAI] OHWI)
('from Yakushima', the southernmost island of Japan)
S. Ponticum; SS. Caucasicum

Evergreen shrub, growth rounded, dense, gentle growth, hardly over 1 m./3 ft. in height, young shoots covered with silvery down, finally bare; leaves oblong, edges rolled under (almost like upside-down spoons), 5–10 cm./2–4 in. long, stiff and coarse and leathery, deep green beneath, with thick brown down beneath; flowers in groups of 6–10, or more, in loose bunches, about the leaves; buds deep pinkish red, corona wide bell shaped, 3 cm./3$\frac{3}{16}$ in. long, 5–6 cm./2–2$\frac{3}{4}$ in. across, pale pink to begin with, later pure white; profusely flowering and very beautiful, May. Southern Japan, island of Yakushima. Because of its gentle growth, beautiful flowers, rich profusion of blooms and hardiness, this is one of the most important varieties in cultivation. Unfortunately it is very expensive. ***#

R. yedoense REHD. (= *Azalea yodogawa* GRIG.) (Colour Plate 3, *6*)
S. Azalea; SS. Obtusum

'Yedo' or 'Jeddo' is the earlier name of the Japanese capital Tokyo. Deciduous shrub, although sometimes also winter green, growth spreading, thickly wooded, hardly more than 1 m./3 ft. high and wide, branches thin; leaves narrow, elliptical–lanceolate, 3–7 cm./1$\frac{3}{16}$–2$\frac{3}{4}$ in. long, dark green above, paler beneath, with tough hairs on both surfaces; flowers in groups of 1–3, appearing before the leaves, filled (?), about 4 cm./1$\frac{9}{16}$ in. wide, purple with darker marks, April. Japan; occurring as a garden variety only—wild variety not known. The wild type of this plant was discovered later, and bears the name of a variation, var. *poukhanense* NAKAI (= *R. poukhanense* LEVL.). Growth a little higher, 1–1·5 m./3–4$\frac{1}{2}$ ft., flowers not filled, funnel shaped, lilac with darker markings, scented, the 5 lobes almost circular and waved. Korea. *4·4*

R. yunnanense FRANCH. (incl. *R. aechmophyllum* BALF. F. & FORREST) (Fig. 41).
('from Yunnan')
S. Triflorum; SS. Yunnanense *Hexaploid*

Evergreen, although sometimes also winter-green shrub, growth dense and fairly upright, 2–3 m./6–9 ft. high, young shoots have blackish tomenta; leaves elliptical–lanceolate 5–7 cm./2–2$\frac{3}{4}$ in. long, with dense scales, aromatic; flowers in groups of 3–5, occurring at the end and in the axils of shoots, profusely flowering, broad funnel shaped, up to 5 cm./2 in. wide, very variable in colour, white to pale pink with red or green markings; faintly scented, stamens protruding considerably, May. China, Yunnan, south-western Setschuan, 4,000 m./12,000 ft. Forest shrub. ∧∧***# Because of the great variation among this form, many types have been raised to the rank of Species (e.g. *R. aechmophyllum* BALF. F. & FORREST, *R. chartophyllum* *Hex* FRANCH), but these are now all listed under *R. yunnanense*. It is worth noting that here many plants shed their leaves completely during particularly cold winters. Deer tend to eat large amounts of these leaves.

NN-Burma, NW+NNC Yunnan, W-Szechuan
7,000 to

Fig. 41. R. yunnanense.

IMPORTANT GARDEN VARIETIES OF RHODODENDRONS AND AZALEAS

Although this chapter is very far reaching, it nevertheless includes only those cultivated rhododendrons which are actually available today in European rhododendron gardens.

A large number of less important, now superseded, varieties have not been mentioned. On the other hand, very nearly all the available varieties are listed here.

Because of the large number of entries, details have been kept as brief as possible; the important details seem to be: the name of the grower, the year of introduction on to the market, the group to which the plant belongs, the parents and the colour of the flowers. The plant's usefulness in the garden has already been indicated by means of stars elsewhere (page 27).

(a) Evergreen varieties

All those under this heading are 'evergreen' in the botanical sense, but this is in fact not quite correct, for, like the wild varieties, these plants' leaves fall after two or three years.

It would be possible but probably too confusing to list all the following under their place of origin. Instead, they appear in alphabetical order.

To name just a few important groups: *R. catawbiense*, *R. williamsianum* and *R. repens* hybrids are among the most common.

'Abendglut' (HOBBIE, 1967); 'Essex Scarlet' × *forrestii repens*; dark blood red.

'Adriaan Koster' (KOSTER & ZONEN, 1920); *campylocarpum* hybrids × 'Mrs. Lindsay Smith'; creamy white, red marks inside.

'Aksel Olsen' (HOBBIT, 1965); 'Essex Scarlet' × *forrestii repens*; dark scarlet, profusely blooming, late.

'Albert Schweitzer' (ADR. VAN NES, 1960); origin unknown; flowers in groups of 13–14, pale pink with red fleck.

'Album Elegans' (H. WATERER, before 1876); *catawbiense* × ; pale lilac, becoming white.

'Album Novum' (L. VAN HOUTTE); *catawbiense* × ; white with rosy lilac tinge and green-yellow flecks.

'Alfred' (SEIDEL, 1899); 'Everestianum' × 'Everestianum'; lilac, middle early.

'Alice' (J. WATERER, 1910); *griffithianum* hybrids; dark pink, paler later, early.

'Alice Street' (M. KOSTER & ZONEN, 1953); ('Diane' × *wardii*; clear yellow (= 'Miss Street').

'Allah' (SEIDEL, 1926); *catawbiense* × ; lilac pink, centre paler, late.

'Ambassadeur' (P. VAN NES, 1960); 'Jan Dekens' × 'Mme de Bruin'; flowers 7 cm./2¾ in. wide, deep pink, up to 20 together, central lobes paler.

'America' (M. KOSTER & ZONEN, 1904, but first introduced in 1920) 'Parsons Grandiflorum' × dark red hybrids; dark red.

'Annie E. Endtz' (ENDTZ, 1939); 'Pink Pearl' × ; pale pink.

'Antoon van Welie' (ENDTZ); 'Pink Pearl' × ; pure dark pink.

'Ardy' (Proefstation Boskoop, 1954); 'Britannia' × *williamsianum*; gentle growth, flat, semi-circular shape; leaves dull green, yellow central vein; flowers bell shaped, large, pink, in groups of 7–8 together, second half of April; profusely flowering.

'Argosy' (ROTHSCHILD, 1933); *auriculatum* × *discolor*; white, strongly scented (Plate 18).

'Aristocrat' (M. KOSTER, before 1963); origins unknown; pink, darker flecks above, flowers in clusters of 10–14, measuring about 8 cm./3³⁄₁₆ in.

'Armistice Day' (C. B. VAN NES, 1930); *griffithianum*–hybrids × 'Maxwell T. Masters'; scarlet.

'Attraction' (M. KOSTER & ZONEN); *ponticum* × ; lilac, late; wide growth (Plate 19, 1).

'Baccarat' (ADR. VAN NES, 1960); Garden hybrids × 'Max Sye'; carmine with large black fleck, 14–15 flowers in round cluster.

'Bad Eilsen' (HOBBIE, 1964); 'Essex Scarlet' × *forrestii repens*; strong growth, broad; buds red-brown, flowers scarlet, beginning of May.

'Baden-Baden' (HOBBIE, 1956); 'Essex Scarlet' × *forrestii repens*; delicate growth, leaves dark green, noticeably twisted; flowers bell shaped, dark scarlet, May.

'Bagshot Ruby' (J. WATERER, 1900); *thomsonii* hybrids, blood red.

'B. de Bruin' (A. WATERER); *catawbiense* × ; scarlet, fringed.

'Bengal' (HOBBIE, 1960); 'Essex Scarlet' × *forrestii repens*; flat growth, leaves dark green; branches arched; flowers scarlet.

'Berlin' (J. BRUNS, 1964); *williamsianum* × ; roundish growth, flowers large, bell shaped, pink, overhanging; very hardy.

'Betty Wormald' (M. KOSTER & ZONEN, before 1922); 'George Hardy' × red garden hybrids; like 'Pink Pearl', but a slightly paler pink.

'Bismarck' (SEIDEL, 1900); *catawbiense* × 'Viola'; white with pink veins.

'Bluebird' (ABERCONWAY, 1930); *augustinii* × *intricatum*; violet, small flowered, 8–10 flowers together.

Garden varieties

'Blue Diamond' (CROSFIELD, 1935); *augustinii* × 'Intrifast'; small, violet, good for the rockery. ℞

'Blue Ensign' (SLOCOCK, 1934); pale lavender with black marks.

'Blue Peter' (WATERER, SONS & CRISP, 1933); pale lavender with purple marks, fringed.

'Blue Tit' (J. C. WILLIAMS, 1933); *augustinii* × *impeditum*; one of the best blue dwarf rhododendrons. ℞

'Bodnant Yellow' (ABERCONWAY, 1944); yellow *cinnabarinum* form × 'Royal Flush'; butter yellow with reddish tinge; very beautiful. ∧∧∧ (Plate 16, 6). ℞

'Boskoop' (ADR. VAN NES, 1960); garden hybrids × 'Max Sys', pinkish red with dark brown fleck, 12–13 flowers in round clump.

'Boule de Neige' (OUDIEU, around 1878); *caucasicum* × hardy hybrids, white.

'Bow Bells' (ROTHSCHILD, 1934); 'Corona' × *williamsianum*; shoots red, flowers cherry red, buds red.

'Bremen' (J. BRUNS, 1962); *williamsianum* × ; growth roundish, leaves bright green, flowers glowing carmine, needs a sheltered area.

'Britannia' (C. B. VAN NES, 1921); 'Queen Wilhelmina' × 'Stanley Davies'; scarlet, fringed, 12–14 together; foliages yellowish green, grown compact. ∧

'Burgemeester Aarts' (KOSTER & ZONEN, 1915P); 'L. L. Liebig' × *maximum*; dark red, tall growing.

'Butterfly' (SLOCOCK); *campylocarpum* × 'Mrs. Milner'; quite pale yellow, with light red dots.

'Canary' (M. KOSTER & ZONEN, 1920); *campylocarpum* × *caucasicum luteum*; lemon yellow, leaves yellowish green.

'Caractacus' (A. WATERER, before 1865); *catawbiense* × ; lilac-red.

'Catalgla' (GABLE); only a selection from *catawbiense* 'Album', white catawbiense 'Album' (A. WATERER); *catawbiense* × or selection; white, buds pale lilac.

catawbiense 'Boursault' (BOURSAULT); *catawbiense* × or selection; lilac with pink tint

catawbiense 'Grandiflorum' (A. WATERER); *catawbiense* × or selection; lilac.

'Catharine van Tol' (J. C. VAN TOL); *catawbiense* × ; carmine pink.

'C. B. Van Nes' (C. B. VAN NES); 'Queen Wilhelmina' × 'Stanley Davies' scarlet, early.

'Charles Dickens' (A. WATERER, 1865); *catawbiense* × ; carmine, flecked.

'Charlie Waterer' (A. WATERER, before 1922); red, centre paler.

'China' (SLOCOCK, 1936); *fortunei* × *wightii* 1936; creamy yellow, red inside.

'Chevalier Félix de Sauvage' (SAUVAGE, around 1870); *caucasicum* × ; hardy hybrids; pink with darker markings.

'Clementine Lemaire' (MORE & FILS); pale pink with yellow markings late.

'Concinn' (WILLIAMS); *concatenans* × *cinnabarinum*; yellow, tube or bell shaped, profusely flowering. ∧∧. ℞

'Cornish Cross' (SM. SMITH); *griffithianum* × *thomsonii*; pink, very large flowered. ∧∧∧

'Corry Koster' (M. KOSTER & ZONEN, 1919); origins unclear, pale pink with carmine, fringed.

'Countess of Athlone' (C. B. VAN NES, 1923); *catawbiense* 'Grandiflorum' × 'Geoffrey Millais'; pale lilac, very large clusters of flowers.

'Countess of Derby' (WHITE, SUNNINGDALE, 1913); 'Cynthia' × 'Pink Pearl'; somewhat darker pink than 'Pink Pearl', carmine points at the base.

'Crown Prince' (J. WATERER); pink, yellow marks, large clusters of flowers.

'C. S. Sargent' (A. WATERER, 1888); *catawbiense* × ; red.

'Cunningham's White' (CUNNINGHAM, 1850); *caucasicum* × *ponticum album*; white with greenish yellow marks.

'Cynthia' (STANDISH & NOBLE, before 1870); *catawbiense* × *griffithianum* (?); carmine, very hardy (= 'Lord Palmerston').

'Dairymaid' (SLOCOCK, 1930); *campylocarpum* × ; lemon yellow with pink tinge and rose fleck.

'Daphne' (SEIDEL, 1902); *metternichii* × ?; pure white, greenish spots.

'Darius' (SEIDEL, 1902); 'Mrs. Milner' × *smirnowii*; purplish red.

'Day Dream' (ROTHSCHILD); *griersonianum* × 'Lady Bessborough'; carmine; paler shadows, becoming much paler as it opens out and goes over.

'Diane' (KOSTER & ZONEN, 1920); *campylocarpum* hybrids × 'Mrs. Lindsay Smith'; creamy white with primula yellow clusters of flowers.

'Dietrich' (SEIDEL, 1902); 'Mrs. Milner' × *smirnowii*; carmine.

'Direktor E. Hjelm' (D. A. KOSTER); *fortunei* × 2nd generation; dark carmine pink with bronze markings.

'Doncaster' (A. WATERER); *arboreum* × ; glowing carmine.

'Dortmund' (HOBBIE, 1953); *souliei* × *wardii* Hu 14675; pale yellow with pale pink, flowers in groups of 8–12.

'Douglas McEwan' (C. B. VAN NES); *griffithianum* hybrids × 'Monsieur Thiers'; rosy red.

'Dr. A. Blok' (ENDTZ, 1937); *catawbiense* hybrids × 'Pink Pearl'; pale pink, centre paler (= 'Dr. O. Blok').

'Dr. Arnold W. Endtz' (ENDTZ, 1927); *catawbiense* hybrids × 'Pink Pearl'; carmine, edge fringed.

'Dr. Ernest Schäle' (HOBBIE, 1967), 'Prometheus' × *forrestii repens*; glowing red, beginning May, broad, richly flowering, very hardy.

'Dr. H. C. Dresselhuys' (DEN OUDEN, 1920); 'Atrosanguineum' × 'Doncaster'; aniline red.

'Dr. H. C. Karl Foerster' (HOBBIE, 1952); 'Inswegeanum' × *williamsianum*; growth rounded, low, leaves small, dark green, base round; flowers dark pink to rosy red; in groups of 3–5 together.

'Dr. H. J. Lovink' (DEN OUDEN, 1925); 'Charles Dickens' × 'Lord Roberts'; aniline red, edge fringed.

'Dr. W. F. Wery' (C. B. VAN NES); 'Queen Wilhelmina' × 'Stanley Davies'; scarlet.

'Duchess of Edinburgh' (J. WATERER); *brookeanum gracile* × *lobbii*; clear carmine, centre paler.

'Duke of York' (PAUL, 1894); *fortunei* × 'Scipio'; pink, creamy yellow markings.

'Earl of Athlone' (C. B. VAN NES, 1933); 'Queen Wilhelmina' × 'Stanley Davies'; blood red.

'Earl of Donoughmore' (M. KOSTER & ZONEN, 1953); *griersonianum* × (hardy garden hybrid × 'Mrs. L. A. Dunnett'); red with orange.

'Edward S. Rand' (A. WATERER, 1870); *catawbiense* × ; carmine with yellow eye.

'El Alamein' (KLUIS, 1946); *griffithianum* × ; dark blood red with dark brown fleck.

'Elisabeth Hobbie' (HOBBIE, 1958); 'Essex Scarlet' × *forestii repens*; low growing, scarlet, transparent, in groups of 6–10 flowers together.

'Elizabeth' (ABERCONWAY, 1933); *forrestii repens* × *griersonianum*; deep red, very profusely flowering, low. ∧∧–∧∧∧ (Colour Plate 2, 3).

'Ella' (SEIDEL, 1903); 'Mrs. Milner' × *smirnowii*; carmine.

'Elsi Straver' (STRAVER); *campylocarpum* hybrids; large leaved, flowers bell shaped, large, creamy yellow in large, closed clusters.

'Emasculum' (WATERER); *ciliatum* × *dauricum*; pinkish lilac, similar to *R. praecox*, but higher, later and quite without stamens.

'Empire Day' (KNAP HILL); *griersonianum* × 'Moser's Maroon'; blood red (= Romany Chai var. Empire Day).

'English Roseum' (A. WATERER); *catawbiense* ×; pink—presumably a mutation of 'Roseum Elegans', and generally sold under this name.

'Essex Scarlet' (G. PAUL, 1899); dark carmine red with blackish fleck.

'Everestianum' (A. WATERER, before 1850); *catawbiense* ×; rosy lilac dots, edge fringed.

'Fabia Tangerine' (ABERCONWAY, 1940); *dichroanthum* × *griersonianum*; scarlet with large calyx. ∧∧ (Colour Plate 2, 6).

'Faggetter's Favourite' (SLOCOCK, 1933); accidental seedling from *fortunei*; creamy white, with pink tinge and bronze marks, scented, buds pink.

'Fancy' (M. KOSTER & ZONEN, 1955); 'Mrs. Helen Koster' × 'Mrs. Lindsay Smith'; quite pale lilac with large, dark red fleck.

'Fastuosum Plenum' (FRANCOISI, before 1946); *catawbiense* × *ponticum*; lilac with yellow markings; filled.

'F. D. Godman' (A. WATERER, 1888); *catawbiense* ×; dark carmine.

'Fire' (M. KOSTER, 1962); origins unknown, rosy red, somewhat paler within, darker flecks above, up to 15–17 in closed bunches.

'Floriade' (ADR. VAN NES, before 1960); origins unknown; red with dark brown markings, 16–20 flowers in round bunches.

'Fragrans' (PAXTON, 1843); Azaleodendron; *catawbiense* × *viscosum*; pale lilac, white in the centre (Plate 19, 7).

'Friesland' (ENDTZ); *catawbiense* hybrids × 'Pink Pearl'; pale pinkish lilac.

'Frühauf' (ALBERTZARD); probably *caucasicum* hybrids; ruby red, normally blooming in April, but suitable for Christmas flowering.

'Frühlingstag' (J. BRUNS, 1962); 'Essex Scarlet' × *forrestii repens*; very similar to the two following sorts, glowing red and level growing.

'Frühlingstrau' (J. BRUNS, 1962); 'Essex Scarlet' × *forrestii repens*; growth level, flowers glowing red, richly flowering even as a young plant.

'Frühlingszauber' (JOH. BRUNS, 1962); selection from a crossing of 'Essex Scarlet' × *forrestii repens*; growth broad and bushy, not very level, leaves deep green, flowers scarlet red, profusely flowering, good and hardy.

'General Eisenhower' (ANTH. KLUIS, 1946); *griffithianum* ×; deep carmine; large flowered.

'Genoveva' (SEIDEL); *catawbiense* hybrids; pale lilac white with yellowish green fleck.

'George Cunningham' (CUNNINGHAM, before 1875); *arboreum* × *campanulatum* (?); white, but inside and on the edges marked with black dots.

'Gertrud Schäle' (HOBBIE, 1951); *forrestii repens* × 'Prometheus' scarlet, large flowered, flowers in groups of 6–12 together.

'Gina Lollobrigida' (FELIX DIJKHUIS, 1962); 'Marion' × 'Mrs. C. S. Sargent'; broad funnel shaped, orchid purple, brown flecks above; 10 cm./4 in. wide, up to 15 flowers in dense clusters;

'Goldsworth Orange' (SLOCOCK, 1938); *dichroanthum* × *discolor*; pale orange with pink tinge, growth low.

'Goldsworth Yellow' (SLOCOCK, 1925); *campylocarpum* × *caucasicum*; yellow with greenish and brown marks; buds apricot coloured.

'Gomer Waterer' (J. WATERER, before 1900); *catawbiense* ×; pale

pink with lilac tinge, almost white when finished flowering profusely blooming, very late (Plate 19, 3).

'Graf Zeppelin' (C. B. VAN NES); 'Mrs. C. S. Sargent' × 'Pink Pearl'; flesh pink.

'Gräfin Kirchbach' (V. VON MARTIN); hybrid from *Forrestii repens*; particularly small leaved; flowers large, blood red, hardy.

'Granat' (SEIDEL, 1916); *catawbiense* hybrid, carmine.

'Gudrun' (SEIDEL, 1905); 'Eggebrechtii' × 'Mme Linden'; white with dark red marks; middle late.

'Halopeanum' (HALOPE, 1896); *griffithianum* × *maximum*; completely pink, after flowering pure white; better known as 'White Pearl'.

'Harvest Moon' (M. KOSTER & ZONEN, 1948); *campylocarpum* hybrid × 'Mrs. Lindsay Smith'; pale lemon yellow with carmine markings.

'Hassan' (SEIDEL, 1906); *catawbiense* × 'Carl Mette'; carmine.

'Hero' (SEIDEL, 1906); *catawbiense* hybrid; white with pale lilac tint and yellowish green markings.

'Holbein' (SEIDEL, 1906); 'Alexander Adie' × 'Carl Mette', lilac to pink.

'Holger' (SEIDEL, 1906); 'Eggebrechtii' × 'Mme Linden'; bright purple with greenish yellow or reddish brown markings, late.

'Hollandia' (ENDTZ); 'Charles Dickens' × 'Pink Pearl'; pure carmine (= 'G. Stresemann').

'Homer' (SEIDEL, 1906); 'Agnes' × 'Kaiser Wilhelm'; clear pink.

'Hugh Koster' (M. KOSTER & ZONEN, 1933); 'Doncaster' × hybrids × 'George Hardy'; clear carmine.

'Humboldt' (SEIDEL, 1926); *catawbiense*-hybrids; pink with darker flecks.

'Humming Bird' (J. C. WILLIAMS, 1933); *haematodes* × *williamsianum* growth and foliate similar to *R. williamsianum*, but flowers darker.

'Hymen' (SEIDEL, 1926); *catawbiense*-hybrids; pale lilac with yellowish brown or greenish brown markings.

'Ignatius Sargent' (A. WATERER); *catawbiense* ×; clear carmine.

'Imbricatum' see *ponticum* 'Imbricatum'.

'Inamorata' (ROTHSCHILD, 1950); *discolor* × *wardii*; sulphur yellow with small, carmine marks.

'Independence Day' (A. WATERER, 1915); red, centre paler, darker fleck.

'Isaac Newton' (HOBBIE, 1952); (*catawbiense* × *thomsonii*) × *forestii repens*; carmine red, 6–10 flowers together; leaves very dark green.

'Jacksonii' (HERBERT, 1835); *caucasicum* × 'Nobleanum'; low, pale pink, darker stripes outside, very early (Fig. 42).

'Jackwill' (HOBBIT, 1967); 'Jacksonii' × *williamsianum*; cherry red, buds pink, young leaves bronze.

'James Marshall Brooks' (A. WATERER, 1870); scarlet red with brown marks.

'Jan Dekens' (BLAAUW, 1940); strong pink, fringed.

'Jewel' (HOBBIE, 1960); 'Essex Scarlet' × *forrestii repens*; scarlet, wide spreading.

'Jewess' (LIEBIG, before 1860); *caucasicum* ×; pale lilac, very nearly white, early.

'John Walter' (J. WATERER, before 1860); *arboreum* × *catawbiense*, carmine.

'John Willis Fleming' (W. H. ROGERS); *griffithianum* hybrid, pink.

'Joseph Whitworth' (J. WATERER, before 1867); *ponticum* hybrid; deep purple with darker flecks.

'Karin' (Proefstation Boskoop, before 1966); 'Britannia' × *williamsianum*; growth rounded and very slow; leaves dull green; flowers plate shaped with depressed middle, pink, fringed, long stemmed,

Garden varieties

in groups of 8–9 together, end of April–beginning May.

'Kate Waterer' (J. WATERER, before 1890); pink with yellow centre, late.

'Kluis Sensation' (KLUIS, 1946); 'Britannia' × unknown; scarlet with black flecks.

'Koster's Cream' (M. KOSTER & ZONEN); *campylocarpum* ×; creamy yellow with green markings.

'Lady Alice Fitzwilliam' (Grower and year unknown, but before 1881); pure white, large flowered, scent very strong and pleasant; needs all-year-round glasshouse treatment. ∧∧∧ (Plate 18, *1*).

'Lady Annette de Trafford' (A. WATERER, 1874); *maximum* ×; pale pink with dark brown fleck, late.

R 'Lady Chamberlain' (ROTHSCHILD, 1930); *cinnabarinum roylei* × 'Royal Flush', orange variety; salmon or orange-red with bluish tinge; flowers almost tube shaped, hanging, fleshy. ∧∧∧ (Plate 16, *5*).

'Lady Eleanor Cathcart' (J. WATERER, before 1850); *arboreum* × *maximum*; pure pale pink with purple-red markings.

'Lady Stuart of Wortley' (M. KOSTER & ZONEN, 1909); *griffithianum* ×?; rosy red.

'Laetevirens' see page 69.

'Lavender Girl' (SLOCOCK, 1950); *fortunei* × 'Lady Grey Egerton'; pale lilac, pink edge, more white in the centre.

R 'Lavendula' (HOBBIE, 1967); [*russatum* × *saluenense*] × *rubiginosum*; lavender, compact, very hardy; scented foliage.

'Lamplighter' (K. KOSTER & ZONEN, 1955); 'Britannia' × 'Mme Fr. J. Chauvin'; sparkling clear red with salmon tint; flowers in groups of 10–12.

'Lee's Dark Purple' (LEE, before 1851); *catawbiense* ×; deep purple.

'Leopardi' (METHUEN, 1868); *arboreum album* ×; white with light red tinge and large brown markings.

'Leopold' (SEIDEL, 1909); *catawbiense* hybrid; dark lilac with greenish yellow or brown markings.

'Linda' (Proefstation Boskoop, 1953); 'Britannia' × *williamsianum*; growth round, young shoots bronzy brown, flowers open bell shaped, rosy red, in groups of 7–8 together; profusely flowering, mid-May.

'Linswegeanum' (HOBBIE, 1946); 'Britannia' × *forrestii repens*; Grex;* dark scarlet.

'Lissabon' (V. VON MARTIN, 1964); *williamsianum* ×; growth round, leaves deep green; flowers carmine, completely hardy.

'Locarno' (M. KOSTER, 1965); origins unknown; pink, darker markings above, in clusters of 12–16 flowers.

'Loderi' (LODER, 1901); *fortunei* × *griffithianum*; white to pale pink (grex). About 30 clones are listed here, all from Loder (Plate 18, *4*).

'Lord Palmerston' = 'Cynthia'.

'Lord Roberts' (MASON); dark red, black markings.

'Louis Pasteur' (ENDTZ, 1923); 'Mrs. Tritton' × 'Viscount Powerscourt'; bright red, centre rosy white (Plate 19, *6*).

'Macrantha' is the general horticultural name for *R. indicum*. Cf. page 67 (Plate 18, *6*).

'Madame Carvalho' (J. WATERER, 1866); *catawbiense* ×; white, with yellowish green marks.

'Madame de Bruin' (M. KOSTER & ZONEN, 1904); 'Doncaster' × 'Prometheus'; bright red.

'Madame Masson' (BERTIN, 1849); *catawbiense* × *ponticum*; white with yellow marks.

* Grex = collective term for the bastards of a particular crossing; those selected among these and further propagated are called 'clones'.

Fig. 42. R. *'Jacksonii', one of the most early-flowering varieties.*

'Madame Néjedly' (M. KOSTER, 1965); origins unknown; leaves fairly broad, edge waved; flowers pink, slightly paler inside, darker marks above, 9 flowers together in clusters about 7 cm./ 2¾ in. high.

'Marcel Moser' (MOSER & FILS, before 1914); bright red.

'Marchioness of Lansdowne' (A. WATERER, before 1915); *maximum* ×; pale pinky violet with black marks.

'Marcia' (SWAYTHLING, 1944); *campylocarpum* × [*campylocarpum* × *fortunei*]; yellow (the generally yellow *campylocarpum* hybrid).

'Marinus Koster' (M. KOSTER & ZONEN, 1937); *griffithianum* ×; dark pink with paler spots.

'Marion' (FELIX & DIJKHUIS); *catawbiense* 'Grandiflorum' × 'Pink Pearl'; pink, large flowered.

'Mars' (WATERER, SONS & CRISP, before 1875); *griffithianum* ×; dark red.

'Max Sye' (FRETS, around 1935); 'Chevalier Félix de Sauvage' ×?; dark red with black marks, early.

'May Day' (A. M. WILLIAMS, 1932); *griersonianum* × *haematodes*; cherry red, in loose bunches.

'Merveille de Boskoop' (FELIX & DIJKHUIS, 1965); 'Mrs. C. S. Sargent' ×? 'Britannia'; dark pink with deep brown marks; 7 cm./2¾ in. wide, about 18 blooms together in compact cluster.

'Metternianum' (WADA; see page 72.)

'Mevrouw P. A. Colijn' (M. KOSTER & ZONEN); 'Madame de Bruin' × 'Mrs. G. C. Stirling'; dark carmine red.

'Mexico' (SEIDEL); ruby red with dark brown marks, middle late.

'Michael Waterer' (J. WATERER, before 1894); *ponticum* ×; dark red, flecked.

R 'Moerheim' (J. D. RUYS, 1950); *impeditum* hybrid; violet, flowers 3 cm./1 3/16 in. wide.

'Moerheim's Pink' (HOBBIE, 1965); 'Geneoveva' × *williamsianum*; rosy red.

'Moerheim's Scarlet' (HOBBIE, 1965); 'Earl of Athlone' × *forrestii repens*; blood red, flowers waxy.

'Monsieur Thiers' (JACOB-MACOY); bright red.

'Moser's Maroon' (MOSER & FILS, 1932); chestnut-red, darker markings inside; young leaves reddish brown.

'Mother of Pearl' (J. WATERER, 1925); mutation of 'Pink Pearl'; pale pink on opening, then becoming pure white.

'Mount Everest' (SLOCOCK, 1930); *campanulatum* × ?; pure white with brown markings; early; buds white.

'Mrs. A. T. de la Mare' (C. B. VAN NES); 'Halopeanum' × 'Sir Charles Butler'; white with green markings, scented.

'Mrs. Charles E. Pearson' (M. KOSTER & ZONEN, 1909); *catawbiense* 'Grandiflorum' × 'Coombe Royal'; pale lilac pink with brown markings.

'Mrs. Charles S. Sargent' (A. WATERER, 1888); *catawbiense* ×; dark carmine pink with yellow marks; edge waved.

'Mrs. E. C. Stirling' (J. WATERER); *griffithianum* hybrid; pale pink.

'Mrs. G. W. Leak' (M. KOSTER & ZONEN, 1916); 'Chevalier Félix de Sauvage' × 'Coombe Royal'; pale pink with purplish brown marks.

'Mrs. Helen Koster' (M. KOSTER & ZONEN); *catawbiense* 'Grandiflorum' × 'Mrs. J. J. Crosfield'; pale lilac with large purple-red fleck (Plate 19, 4).

'Mrs. J. C. Williams' (A. WATERER); white or pale red, red flecks.

'Mrs. Lindsay Smith' (M. KOSTER & ZONEN, 1910); 'Duchess of Edinburgh' × 'George Hardy'; white with small red markings.

'Mrs. P. den Ouden' (DEN OUDEN, 1912); 'Atrosanguineum' × 'Doncaster'; deep carmine.

'Mrs. Peter Koster' (M. KOSTER & ZONEN); pale pink, slightly deeper colour on the back.

'Mrs. R. S. Holford' (A. WATERER, 1866); salmon pink.

'Mrs. W. C. Slocock' (SLOCOCK, 1929); *campylocarpum* ×; apricot with yellow.

'München' (JOH. BRUNS, 1964); *williamsianum* ×; growth round, leaves medium large, flowers pink, large, overhanging.

R 'Myrtifolium'; *hirsutum* × *minus*; lilac pink.

'Naomi' (ROTHSCHILD, 1926); 'Aurora' × *fortunei*; pale pink with marked yellowish tinge, strongly scented.

'N. N. Sherwood' (SIBRAY); pale pink with yellow centre.

'Nobleanum' (A. WATERER, before 1835); *arboreum* × *caucasicum*; strong pink, very profusely flowering and early.

'Nordeney' (HOBBIE, 1947); this is a group of seedlings from 'Essex Scarlet' × *williamsianum*, from which the Oudijk's Sensation selection was made (*q.v.*).

'Nova Zembla' (M. KOSTER & ZONEN, 1902); red hardy hybrid × 'Parsons Grandiflorum'; dark red.

'Oldenburg' (HOBBIE, 1953); *discolor* × *williamsianum*, up to 2 m./ 6 ft. high; loosely wooded, flowers pale pink, on long stems, large, in loose bunches, beginning of May; shoots bronze.

'Oldewig' (SEIDEL); *catawbiense* hybrid; ruby red with paler centre, brown or yellowish green markings, late.

'Old Port' (A. WATERER, 1865); *catawbiense* ×; deep purplish red.

'Omega' (SEIDEL); *catawbiense* hybrid; clear ruby with brown or yellowish green markings.

'Ostfriesland' (HOBBIE, 1949); 'Madame de Bruin' × *forrestii repens*; scarlet, flowers in groups of 6–8.

R 'Oudijks Favourite' (LE FEBER, 1958); *augustinii* hybrid; pale violet, flowers about 4 cm./1 9/16 in. wide.

'Oudijk's Sensation' (grown by HOBBIE; named and introduced by LE FEBER, 1958); 'Essex Scarlet' × *williamsianum*; leaves broad and elliptical; base slightly heart shaped; flowers in groups of 5–7, 7 cm./2 3/4 in. long, broad funnel or bell shaped, dark pink, darker points inside, edge waved.

'Parsons Gloriosum' (grown by A. WATERER, introduced by S. PARSONS 1860); *catawbiense* ×; pale lilac pink.

'Parsons Grandiflorum' (grown by A. WATERER, introduced by S. PARSONS 1875); *catawbiense* ×; dark purplish pink.

'Peggy Bannier' (ADR. VAN NES); seedling of unknown hybrid × 'Antoon van Welie'; pink, edge waved, flowers up to 10 cm./ 4 in. across; in groups of 10–20 together, in large bunches.

'Pelopidas' (J. WATERER); *catawbiense* ×; clear carmine.

'Peter Koster' (M. KOSTER & ZONEN, 1909); 'Doncaster' hybrid × 'George Hardy'; carmine, edge paler.

'Picotee' (A. WATERER); white, edge dotted.

'Picturatum' (A. WATERER, before 1850); 'Altaclarense' × *maximum* hybrid; pink with chocolate brown markings.

'Pierre Moser' (MOSER & FILS, 1914); *caucasicum* ×; pale pink, early.

'Pink Brightness' (grown by HOBBIE, named and introduced by LE FEBER); leaves broad and elliptical, heart shaped; flowers in groups of 7–9, open funnel shaped, pink with darker edge.

R 'Pink Drift' (WHITE, Sunningdale); *calostrotum* × *scintillans*; lilac pink, very low growing, profusely flowering (Plate 16, 1).

'Pink Goliath' (P. VAN NES, 1961); origins unknown, dark pink with pale fleck, up to 10 cm./4 in. wide, up to 15 flowers together.

'Pink Pearl' (J. WATERER, 1897); 'Broughtonii' × 'George Hardy'. Pale pink, dark pink in the bud (Colour Plate 2, 2).

'Pink Perfection' (L. VAN HOUTTE); 'Duchess of Edinburgh' × 'Princess Alexandra'; pale pink with lilac tinge.

ponticum 'Imbricatum'; dwarf variety, with short shoots; leaves like rosettes on the shoots; flowers small violet,

ponticum 'Roseum'; see *R. ponticum* (= 'Maximum Roseum')

praecox, see page 74.

'Prince Camille de Rohan' (VERSHAFFELT, 1865); *caucasicum* ×; rosy red, centre dark brown, edge fringed (Plate 19, 5).

'Princess Elizabeth' (WATERER, SONS & CRISP, 1928); 'Bagshot Ruby' ×; dark carmine, strong growth.

'Princess Marijke' (FELIX & DIJKHUIS, 1948); clear pink, darker outside.

'Prof. F. Bettex' (DEN OUDEN, around 1912); 'Atrosanguineum' × 'Doncaster'; red (Plate 19, 8).

'Professor Hugo de Vries' (ENDTZ); 'Doncaster' × 'Pink Pearl'; pink, but darker than 'Pink Pearl'.

'Prof. J. H. Zaayer' (ENDTZ); 'Pink Pearl' × red *catawbiense* hybrid; bright red.

'Progrès'; *caucasicum* ×; lilac with purple fleck; somewhat darker than 'Prince Camille de Rohan'.

'Prometheus' (NOBLE); 'Michael Waterer' × 'Monitor'; scarlet.

R 'Prostigiatum' (MAGOR, 1916); *fastigiatum* × *prostratum*; violet.

'Psyche' (HOBBIE, 1950); 'Sir Charles Butler' × *williamsianum*; pink.

R 'Puncta' (GROOTENDORST, 1954); *ferrugineum* × *minus* ? Low-growing evergreen shrub, leaves oval to elliptical, 3·5–5 cm./1 3/8–2 in. long and 1·5–2 cm./9/16–3/4 in. wide, green underneath, but looking somewhat brown on account of its scales; with paler and darker scales, separated from each other by at least the width of their diameter; flowers clear pink, 2·5 cm./1 in. long, with just a few brown scales, June. Often known in Dutch nurseries as 'Rhod. punctatum'.

R 'Purple Willow' (J. STRENG, Boskoop, 1965); selection from *russatum*, lower and more compact than the type, leaves small, 2 cm./3/4 in. long, shiny, flowers violet, 3 cm./1 3/16 in. long.

Garden varieties

'Purple Splendour' (A. WATERER, before 1900); *ponticum* ✕; dark purple, blackish marks.

'Purpureum Elegans' (H. WATERER, before 1850); *catawbiense* ✕; deep purple.

'Queen Mary' (FELIX & DIJKHUIS, 1950); 'Marion' ✕ 'Mrs. C. S. Sargent'; pink.

'Raphael' (SEIDEL); dark ruby with dark brown markings.

'Record' (P. VAN NES, before 1958); seedling from 'Antoon van Welie' ✕ 'Prof. J. H. Zaayer' ✕ 'Annie E. Endta'; deep pink, some veins, becoming paler later, flowers in groups of 13–14, in large cones.

'Red Admiral' (J. C. WILLIANS); *arboreum* ✕ *thomsonii*; red; remarkable for the long young shoots with scarlet upper leaves.

'Red Carpet' (HOBBIE, 1966); 'America' ✕ *forrestii repens*; bright scarlet, early, end of April, profusely flowering creeper.

'Rijneveld' (grown by HOBBIE, introduced by VUYK VAN NES); garden hybrid ✕ 'Metternianum'; growth very compact, flowers coral coloured in groups of 6–10, hanging, appearing even on young plants.

'Robert W. Wallace' (M. KOSTER & ZONEN, 1915); *griffithianum* ✕; rosy red.

'Rombergpark' (BOHLJE, 1967); selection from *oreodoxa* hybrid 'Ronsdorfer Frühblühende'; white, profusely flowering, very early (Plate 16, 3).

'Romany Chai' (ROTHSCHILD, 1932); *griersonianum* ✕ 'Moser's Maroon'; reddish terracotta with brown markings.

'Ronsdorfer Frühblühende' (ARENDS); *oreodoxa* ✕ 'Doncaster'; pale pink to purple, grey.

'Rosamundi' (STANDISH & NOBLE); *caucasicum* ✕; pale pink.

'Roseum Elegans' (A. WATERER, before 1951); *catawbiense* ✕; rosy lilac.

'Rotenberg' (V. VON MARTIN); *williamsianum* ✕; leaves gleaming dark green, flowers pure white, exceptionally large.

'Roude de Mai' (D. J. HENDRIKSEN, Boskoop, 1961); 'Madame Jeanne Frets' ✕ 'Prof. F. Bettex'; pink, with dark brown markings inside, 6–8 cm./$2\frac{3}{8}$–$3\frac{3}{16}$ in. wide, 20–21 in cones.

'Royal Pink' (grown by HOBBIE, named and introduced by LE FEBER); 'Homer' ✕ *williamsianum* 1958; leaves broad and elliptical, almost heart shaped; flowers in groups of 5–6, open funnel shaped, pale pink, darker outside.

'Rubescens' (Origins unknown, but very old sort); very strongly growing, flowers small, red, extraordinarily early.

'Russellianum' (RUSSELL, 1831); *arboreum* ✕ *catawbiense*, carmine pink. ∧∧ (Plate 6, 4).

'Salute' (HOBBIE, 1964); 'Essex Scarlet' ✕ *forrestii repens*, deep blood red.

'Sappho' (A. WATERER, before 1867); white with large blackish brown fleck, growth very loose and shoots long (Plate 19, 2).

'Sarled' (INGRAM, 1942); *sargentianum* ✕ *trichostomum* var. *ledoides*, dwarf variety with very small leaves and small creamy white flowers; buds pink (Plate 16, 2).

'Scandinavia' (M. KOSTER & ZONEN, 1950); 'Betty Wormald' ✕ 'Hugh Koster'; cardinal red with black fleck.

'Scarlet Wonder' (grown by HOBBIE, named and introduced by LE FEBER, 1960); seedling from 'Elisabeth Hobbie', grex, particularly low growing; leaves dark green and a little wrinkled; flowers in groups of 5–6 together, 6·5 cm./$2\frac{9}{16}$ in. long, cherry red with not very noticeable markings, paler later, buds red-brown.

'Scharnhorst' (SEIDEL); dark ruby red with dark markings.

'Sir Charles Butler' (PAUL); pale lilac, scented; perhaps only a seedling from *fortunei*.

'Sonata' (REUTHE, 1949); *dichroanthum* ✕ 'Purple Splendour'; orange with purple tinge.

'Souvenir de D. A. Koster' (D. A. KOSTER, 1922); 'Charlie Waterer' ✕ 'Doncaster'; dark scarlet with darker markings.

'Souvenir de Dr. S. Edntz' (ENDTZ, 1927); 'John Walter' ✕ 'Pink Pearl'; somewhat darker pink than 'Pink Pearl', and with dark red markings.

'Souvenir of W. C. Slocock' (SLOCOCK, 1935); *campylocarpum* ✕; primrose yellow, but apricot on first appearing.

'Spitfire' (FLUIS, 1946); *griffithianum* hybrid; dark red with dark brown fleck.

'Stella' (A. WATERER, before 1865); *catawbiense* ✕; lilac with dark brown mark (= 'Stella Waterer').

'Strategist' (J. WATERER); *griffithianum* ✕; bright red.

'Suomi' (HOBBIE, 1953); 'Linswegeanum' ✕ 'Metternianum': grex; bright red, edge occasionally darker, flowers in clusters of 8–12.

'Susan' (J. C. WILLIAMS, 1930); *campanulatum* ✕ *fortunei*, pale violet, edge and veins darker, markings deep purple.

'Tangerine', see 'Fabia Tangerine'.

'Temple Belle' (KEW, 1916); *orbiculare* ✕ *williamsianum*; pale pink and bell shaped, low growth.

'The Bride' (STANDISH & NOBLE, 1850); *caucasicum album* derivation; white with green points.

'Unique' (SLOCOCK, 1934); *campylocarpum* ✕; clear yellow with salmon.

'Unknown Warrior' (C. B. VAN NES, before 1922); 'Queen Wilhelmina' ✕ 'Stanley Davies'; clear red, early.

'Van den Broeke' (DEN OUDEN, 1912); 'Charles Dickens' ✕ 'Lord Roberts'; carmine.

'Van der Hoop' (DEN OUDEN, 1912); 'Atrosanguineum' ✕ 'Doncaster'; dark carmine.

'Van Nes Sensation' (C. B. VAN NES); 'Sir Charles Butler' ✕ 'White Pearl'; pale lilac, centre white, scented.

'Van Weerden Poelman' (DEN OUDEN, 1912); 'Charles Dickens' ✕ 'Lord Roberts'; carmine.

'Virgo' (P. VAN NES, before 1959); 'Antoon van Welie' ✕ 'Prof. H. J. Zaayer' ✕ 'Annie E. Endtz'; white with large fleck, edge curly, buds and new flowers pale pink, in groups of 17–18 flowers, in cones.

'Von Oheimb Woislowitz' (SEIDEL, 1929); *catawbiense* hybrid; pale pink, yellowish green markings, late.

'Vulcan' (WATERER, SONS & CRISP, 1938); *griersonianum* ✕ 'Mars'; bright red.

'Wega' (HOBBIE); 'Mrs. Butler' ✕ *williamsianum*; growing to more than 2 m./6 ft. high, flowers large, overhanging, pale pink.

'Westfalenpark' (BOHLJE, 1967); selection from *oreodoxa* hybrid 'Ronsdorfer Frühblühende'; pink, profusely flowering, very early (Fig. 43).

'White Pearl' = 'Halopeanum'.

'Wiekoff' (HOBBIE, 1947); 'Mme de Bruin' ✕ *williamsianum*; medium growth, loose, leaves pale green, buds red, flowers dark pink, in groups of 5–8 together, early.

'Wilgen's Ruby' (VAN WILGEN, 1951); dark red outside, a little paler inside, dark brown markings.

'William Austin' (J. WATERER, before 1915); *catawbiense* ✕; dark carmine, flecked.

'Willbrit' (grown by HOBBIE, named and introduced by LE FEBER, 1960); 'Britannia' ✕ *williamsianum*; leaves broad and elliptical,

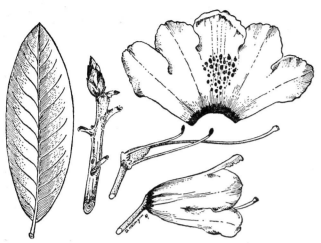

Fig. 43. R. *'Westfalenpark' an* oredoxa *hybrid.*

with small points, almost heart shaped; flowers in groups of 5–8 together, bell shaped, fleshy dark pink, a little paler inside, with darker points, edge paler.

'Winsome' (ABERCONWAY, 1930); *griersonianum* × 'Humming Bird'; low, cherry red, very profusely flowering (Plate 16, 4).

'Zuiderzee' (M. KOSTER & ZONEN, 1936); *campylocarpum* hybrid × 'Mrs. Lindsay Smith'; creamy yellow, red markings inside.

(*b*) Azaleodendrons

This small group consists of crossings between evergreen and deciduous rhododendrons, or, to put it horticulturally, between azaleas and evergreen rhododendrons. These are seldom seen in gardens, but most collections include one or two. In appearance, they look halfway between the parents; their leaves are normally only winter green, being shed the following spring.

R. *azaleoides* DUM.-COURS. (DUMONT DE COURSET, 1811); R. *ponticum* × R. *nudiflorum*; lilac, edge waved. Unknown whether this is still in cultivation.

R. *fragrans* PAXT. (PAXTON, CHANDLER & SONS, 1843); R. *catawbiense* × R. *viscosum*; pale lilac, paler in the centre; hardly cultivated nowadays (Plate 19, 7).

'Galloper Light'; *Azaleodendron* clone ROTHSCHILD; pale salmon pink with dark yellow eye (Plate 18, 2).

'Glory of Littleworth' (MANGLES, before 1911); *Azaleodendron* clone; lemon yellow with deep orange fleck.

'Govenianum' (METHVEN, 1868); *catawbiense* × *ponticum* × Azalea; Azaleodendron; pale purplish pink, scented.

(*c*) Deciduous Azaleas

Unlike evergreen varieties, deciduous azaleas have for a very long time been classified by nursery catalogues under their particular grouping; this book is therefore following this now fairly general usage.

All azaleas which shed their leaves are completely hardy in our

climate, even without winter protection. There follow a few notes on the most important groups of azaleas.

Ghent: (= Ghent hybrids of *Gandavense* sorts). These originated in Belgium and Holland, particularly during the period 1830–40, from crossings of American wild varieties (R. *calendulaceum*, *roseum*, *viscosum* and others) with R. *luteum*; flowers with long tubes, some sorts filled.

Knap Hill sorts: English cultivations, whose origins are not quite clear (including probably R. *gandavense* × *molle*, R. *calendulaceum* and others). Named after Knap Hill Nursery (ANTHONY WATERER) in Surrey, where they originated. Flowers large, very open, in clusters of several blooms, some sorts half filled. LIONEL DE ROTHSCHILD undertook the work of further cultivation in Exbury, and these then came on to the market as 'Exbury Azaleas'; however, these are not given a separate entry in the *International Rhododendron Register*. C. FLEISCHMANN in Germany has done further work on these, with the result that the flowers are becoming even larger. R. *japonicum*, R. *kosterianum*, cf. *Mollis* sorts.

Mollis sorts: this classification of the *International Rhododendron Register* is now firmly entrenched in the gardening world, and it is therefore best to stick to it. It includes also selections (clones) from R. *japonicum*, R. × *kosterianum* (= 'Mollis' × 'Sinensis'), as well as crossings.

Occidentale sorts: Achieved in England in 1864 and 1901 and later in Holland from R. *molle* × R. *occidentale*; flower corona wide open, white to pale pink, scented.

Rustica sorts (= R. *mixtum*); chiefly in Belgium around 1880 through crossing of the filled *gandavense* sorts with R. *japonicum*; All *Rustica* sorts have filled flowers.

'Admiral de Ruyter' (before 1855); Ghent; orange red with yellow fleck, late.

'Advance' (M. KOSTER & ZONEN, 1954); *occidentale*; pink with golden fleck, middle late.

'Aida' (VUYLSTEKE, 1888); Rust.; filled, with lilac tinge, middle early.

'Alphonse Lavallée' (LOUIS VAN HOUTTE, 1873); *japon.* clone orange with pink, markings paler orange.

'Anthony Koster' (M. KOSTER, 1892); *kosterianum* ×; yellow, bronze in the bud; shoots deep yellow.

'Antilope' (FELIX & DIJKHUIS, 1963); *viscosum* × (Mollis); flowers, narrow, tube or funnel shaped, scented, white with dark pink middle line, yellow fleck on the top lobe, 5 cm./2 in. wide, 4 cm./$1\frac{3}{16}$ in. long, flowers usually in groups of 10 together.

'Arpège' (Proefstation Boskoop, 1965); *viscosum* × Mollis; shrub thickly wooded, flowers deep yellow, 4–4.5 cm./$1\frac{9}{16}$–$1\frac{3}{4}$ in. wide, strongly scented, not appearing until end of May to beginning of June; about 10 flowers together.

'Aurora' (ROTHSCHILD, 1947); Knap Hill; salmon pink with orange and yellow, pink stripes, paler yellow fleck, reverse side darker, similar to 'Brasil', but better.

'Babeuff' (KERSBERGEN, 1918); Moll.; salmon red with orange tinge.

'Ballerina' (ROTHSCHILD); Knap Hill; pure white with yellow dot-marking and curly edge.

'Balzac' (ROTHSCHILD); Knap Hill; reddish orange with orange markings; flowers in groups of 12–15, scented, excellent.

'Baron Constant Rebecque' (L. VAN HOUTTE, 1872); *japonicum* clone yellow with pale orange markings.

'Bartholo Lazzari' (J. RINZ, before 1869); Ghent; orange yellow, double.

89

Garden varieties

'Basilisk' (ROTHSCHILD); Knap Hill; dark creamy white with yellow markings; flowers in groups of 12, young leaves brown.

'Bataaf Felix' (FELIX & DIJKHUIS): *kosterianum* ×; 'Anthony Koster' × red japon.; seedling yellow.

'Beauté Céleste' (before 1882); Ghent; pink with orange, scented, only 2·5 cm./1 in. wide (= Cardinal).

'Berryrose' (ROTHSCHILD); Knap Hill; rosy red with yellow fleck, very large flowered, scented, young leaves brownish.

'Bouquet de Flore' (VERSCHAFFELT, before 1869); Ghent; salmon pink with orange yellow markings, darker towards the centre.

'Bouquet d'Orange' (M. KOSTER & ZONEN, 1876); Moll.; *japonicum* clone orange-red.

'Brazil' (ROTHSCHILD, 1934); Knap Hill; orange-red fairly small flowered, vigorous growth, edge of flowers curly.

'Bullfinch' (KNAP HILL, 1949); Knap Hill; cinnamon with orange fleck.

'Buzzard' (KNAP HILL, 1947); Knap Hill; straw yellow with pink, scented.

'Byron' (VUYLSTEKE, 1888); Rust.; white, filled, lobes slightly tinged with red (= 'Garteninspektor C. Ohrt').

'Cardinal' = 'Beauté Céleste'.

'Catharina Rinke' (M. KOSTER, 1962); Moll.; 'Floradora' × seedling 213; crab red, with brown flecks on the upper lobes, 10 cm./4 in. wide, 9–10 flowers in a cluster.

'Cécile' (ROTHSCHILD, 1947); Knap Hill; salmon pink with yellow tinge; buds deep pink, very large flowered; similar to 'Berryrose' but better.

'Chanel' (FELIX & DIJKHUIS, 1961); *viscosum* × (Mollis); flowers narrow tube or funnel shaped, scented, amber yellow, with pinkish tinge outside, inside having deep yellow fleck, 6 cm./2⅜ in. wide, in clusters of 8–10.

'Chevalier de Réali' (L. VAN HOUTTE, 1875); *japonicum* clone; corn yellow, becoming paler later, 4 cm./1⅜ in. wide.

'Christopher Wren' (ENDTZ); orange yellow, dark orangey brown markings, large flowered (= 'Goldball').

'Coccinea Speciosa' (SÉNÉCLAUSE, before 1838); Ghent; glowing orange red, still one of the best and best known sorts (Colour Plate 4, 2).

'Comte de Gomer' (L. VAN HOUTTE, 1872); Moll.; orange red, 6 cm./2⅜ in. wide (= 'Consul Cérésole').

'Comte de Kerckhove' (from Belgium); Moll.; orange red with pink, markings orange, 6 cm./2⅜ in. wide.

'Comte de Papadopoli' (L. VAN HOUTTE, 1873); *japonicum* clone; salmon pink.

'Consul Pêcher' (L. VAN HOUTTE, 1873); *japonicum* Klon; salmon orange with orange markings.

'Corneille' (BUYLSTEKE); Ghent; pale pink, rosette like, filled, becoming paler later.

'Coronation Lady' (WATERER, SONS & CRISP); Knap Hill; 'Cécile' × pink seedling; pink with carmine fleck, flowers in groups of 11 together.

'Daviesii' (Is. DAVIES, about 1840); Ghent; *molle* × *viscosum*; viscosepalum clone; creamy white to white, yellow markings; foliage markedly bluish green.

'Devon' (SLOCOCK, 1952); Knap Hill; rosy red.

'Directeur Moerlands' (BINKEN, Boskoop); *kosterianum* ×; 'Anthony Koster' ×? golden yellow, darker inside, markings olive brown (= 'Golden Sunlight') (Colour Plate 4, 4).

'Domino Scassi' (L. VAN HOUTTE, 1873); Ghent; salmon pink.

'Dr. Charles Baumann' (before 1882); Ghent; carmine with golden yellow fleck; late; edge curled (= 'Anna Louise', = 'Julda Schipp'?).

'Dr. H. Colijn' (FELIX & DIJKHUIS, 1950); Moll.; orange yellow with red, yellow fleck.

'Dr. Reichenbach' (KOSTER & ZONEN, 1892); *kosterianum* ×; pale salmon; markings yellow.

'Eisenhower' (FELIX & DIJKHUIS, 1950); Moll.; orange red, darker veining on outside, orange markings.

'Evening Glow' (M. KOSTER & ZONEN, 1920); *kosterianum* clone; bright dark red.

'Exbury White' (ROTHSCHILD): Knap Hill; pure white with orange yellow markings, outside of tubes slightly reddened, large flowered.

'Ex quisita' (M. KOSTER & ZONEN, 1901); *occidentale*; creamy white with amber tinge, tube shaped, edge curled.

'Fanny' = 'Pucella'.

'Fénélon'; (Ghent); apricot yellow with orange-red tips; filled (Colour Plate 4, 1).

'Fireball' (ROTHSCHILD, 1951); Knap Hill; deep red, first class!

'Firecracker' (WATERER, SONS & CRIST); Knap Hill; currant red, growth rigidly upright, young leaves bronze.

'Firefly' (ROTHSCHILD, 1947); Knap Hill; dark carmine pink with orange tinge, very large flowered.

'Fireglow' (Knap Hill, 1926); Knap Hill; orange cinnamon; markings pure yellow, richly flowering.

'Flamingo' (Knap Hill); Knap Hill; carmine pink, darker outside, orange markings, curly.

'Floradora' (M. KOSTER & ZONEN, 1910); Moll.; *kosterianum* clone; clear orange with red fleck.

'Franklin D. Roosevelt' (FELIX & DIJKHUIS, 1950); Moll.; cinnamon with orange markings, large flowered.

'Frans van der Bom' (M. KOSTER & ZONEN, 1892); Moll.; *kosterianum* clone; apricot coloured to salmon.

'Fraseri' see page 65.

'Freya' (VUYLSTEKE, 1888); Rust.; salmon pink with yellow tinge, filled.

'Furnivall's Daughter' (Knap Hill); pink with darker red markings; 15 flowers in a cluster.

'Gallipoli' (ROTHSCHILD, 1947); Knap Hill; orange with pink and red, very large flowered.

'General Trauff' (before 1874); Ghent; clear violet-pink, paler veins with tinge of yellow, edge white, small flowered.

'George Reynolds' (ROTHSCHILD, 1936); Knap Hill; dark yellow, verging to green in the centre; markings deep yellow. Rothschild began improving the Knap Hill sorts with this variety; still excellent today.

'Gibraltar' (ROTHSCHILD, 1947); Knap Hill; glowing orange with pink, fringed, buds carmine.

'Ginger' (ROTHSCHILD, 1947); Knap Hill; glowing orange with pink, dark orange markings, buds deep orange-carmine; similar to 'Balzac'; but the reverse side is more yellow in colour; scented.

'Gloria Mundi' (SÉNÉCLAUSE, 1846); Ghent; orange with darker markings; fringed, 6 cm./2⅜ in. wide.

'Glowing Embers' (ROTHSCHILD); Knap Hill; orange red with orange markings.

'Gog' (Knap Hill, 1926); Knap Hill; brownish orange.

'Gold Dust' (ROTHSCHILD, 1951); Knap Hill; deep yellow.

'Golden Eagle' (Knap Hill, 1949); *calendulaceum* clone (?); orange with red, profusely flowering, but growth fairly weak.

'Golden Girl' (ROTHSCHILD, 1951); Knap Hill, yellow with darker markings.

'Golden Horn' (ROTHSCHILD, 1947); Knap Hill; deep golden yellow, more ivory coloured later, with pink tinge and orange tips, scented.

'Golden Sunset' (ROTHSCHILD, 1848); Knap Hill; yellow with orange markings.

'Goldlack' (HESSE, 1900); golden yellow.

'Graciosa' (M. KOSTER & ZONEN, 1901); *occidentale*; clear pink with orange markings, red strips outside.

'Grandeur Triomphante' (L. VAN HOUTTE, before 1872); Ghent; dark violet pink.

'Harvest Moon' (Knap Hill, 1938); Knap Hill; amber yellow with paler fleck, faintly scented.

'Heureuse Surprise' (before 1869); Ghent; white with pink shadows.

'Homebush' (Knap Hill, before 1925); Knap Hill; half filled, pink, in dense bunches.

'Honeysuckle' (ROTHSCHILD, 1933); Knap Hill; pale pink with orange (Colour Plate 2, 5).

'Honneur de la Belgique' (VERSHCAFFELT, before 1855); Ghent; orange with yellow markings.

'Hortulanus H. Witte' (M. KOSTER & ZONEN, 1892); *kosterianum* clone; clear orange yellow with yellow markings.

'Hotspur' (ROTHSCHILD, 1934); Knap Hill; red, very similar to 'Balzac' but a little paler.

'Hotspur Red' (ROTHSCHILD); Knap Hill, red.

'Hugh Wormald' (ROTHSCHILD); Knap Hill, deep golden yellow with darker fleck.

'Hugo Hardijzer' (JARDIJZER); Moll.; clear red.

'Hugo Koster' (M. KOSTER & ZONEN, 1892); Moll.; *kosterianum* clone; poppy red.

'Ignaea Nova' (before 1876); Ghent; carmine with golden yellow marks.

'Il Tasso' (VUYLSTEKE, 1892); Rust.; rose with salmon, filled.

'Irene Koster' (KOSTER & ZONEN); *occidentale* ×; pure pink with small yellow fleck, scented (Colour Plate 4, 5).

'J. C. Van Tol' (VAN TOL); red; 7 cm./2¾ in. wide.

'J. Jennings' (ROTHSCHILD, 1947); Knap Hill; carmine; beware of bad types sometimes sold.

'Joseph Baumann' (before 1875); Ghent; blood red.

'Kathleen' (ROTHSCHILD, 1947); Knap Hill; clear salmon with large yellow markings; buds darker; large flowered.

'Kestrel' (Knap Hill, 1952); Knap Hill; probably hybrid with *calendulaceum*; orange-red.

'Klondyke' (ROTHSCHILD, 1947); Knap Hill; creamy yellow with deep orange; centre green, very large flowered, buds orange yellow, scented, profusely flowering (Colour Plate 4, 3).

'Koster's Brilliant Red' (KOSTER & ZONEN, 1918); Moll.; glowing orange red.

'Koster's Yellow' (KOSTER & ZONEN, 1920); Moll.; *kosterianum* clone; yellow.

'La Surprise' (from 1898); Ghent; fleshy pink with yellow and orange, very open and upturned, very late and particularly attractive.

'Lenonora' (WEZELENBURG, 1912); Moll.; apricot yellow, with pink tinge outside, pale colour, not very beautiful.

'Magnifica' (KOSTER & ZONEN, 1901); *occidentale* hybrid; creamy yellow later pale pink, orange fleck.

'Marion Merriman' (Knap Hill); Mollis; pale yellow with large orange markings; middle early.

'Mécène' (VUYLSTEKE, 1888); Rust.; creamy white with pale yellow, filled.

'Mephistopheles' (Knap Hill); Knap Hill, red.

'Mevrouw G. van Noordt' (VAN NOORDT); *kosterianum* clone; salmon with orange yellow; large flowered (= Jeanne Oosthoek').

'Milton' (VUYLSTEKE, 1888); Rust.; creamy white, later filled with white, 5 cm./2 in. wide.

'Mrs. A. E. Endtz' (ENDTZ, 1900); *kosterianum* clone; yellow with orange, buds orange.

'Mrs. Peter Koster' (M. KOSTER & ZONEN, 1953); *kosterianum* clone; dark red with orange fleck.

'Murillo' (VUYLSTEKE, 1888); Rust.; carmine pink with salmon, filled.

'Nancy Waterer' (A. WATERER, before 1876); Ghent; glowing golden yellow, large flowered.

'Narcissiflora' (L. VAN HOUTTE, before 1871); Ghent; clear yellow, filled; 4 cm./1⁹⁄₁₆ in. wide, scented (Plate 18, 5).

'Nicolaas Beets' (M. KOSTER & ZONEN, 1892); *kosterianum* clone; apricot to corn yellow.

'Norma' (VUYLSTEKE, 1888); Rust.; rosy red and salmon, very lively colour, filled.

'Orange Glow' (VERWAY, Boskoop, 1956); Moll; selection from 'J. C. van Tol'; pillar box red, central line of upper lobes has darker veining and bright red fleck, 8 cm./3³⁄₁₆ in. wide.

'Pallas' (before 1875); Ghent; orange red with yellow fleck, 6 cm./2⅜ in. wide.

'Persil' (Knap Hill); Knap Hill; white with yellow fleck, edge not waved.

'Phébé' (VUYLSTEKE, 1888); Rust.; sulphur yellow, filled.

'Phidias' (VUYLSTEKE, 1888); Rust.; clear orange yellow, buds more reddish, filled, 4 cm./1⁹⁄₁₆ in. wide.

'Pink Delight' (ROTHSCHILD, 1951); Knap Hill, dark pink, yellow fleck, profusely flowering, but only medium sized flowers.

'Pink Mimosa' (FELIX & DIJKHUIS, 1965); *viscosum* × (Mollis); flowers narrow tube or funnel shaped, pink, scented, 4 cm./1⁹⁄₁₆ in. wide, 3 cm./2⅜ in. long, in groups of 6–8 together.

'Polly Claessens' (M. KOSTER & ZONEN, 1954); *Kosterianum* clone; pure orange.

'Prominent' (Proefstation Boskoop, 1961); Mollis; 'Antony Koster' × 'Alphonse Lavallée'; wide funnel shaped, pink with not very apparent yellow fleck; 8 cm./3³⁄₁₆ in. wide, 7–10 flowers together.

'Pucella' (Ghent); dark carmine pink with orange markings; tubes reddish brown on outside (= 'Fanny').

'Queen Emma' (WEZELENBURG); Moll.; *kosterianum* clone; dark orange with salmon.

'Quentin Metsys'; Ghent; dark pink, filled.

'Racine' (VUYLSTEKE); Rust.; pale pink, filled.

'Radiant' (KROMHOUT); *kosterianum* Klon; dark orange-red.

'Raphael de Smet' (before 1889); Ghent; pale pink, filled.

'Réplique' (FELIX & DIJKHUIS, 1965); *viscosum* × (Mollis); white with pink tinge, dark yellow markings above, narrow tube to funnel shaped, scented, 6 cm./2⅜ in. wide, 5 cm./2 in. long, in groups of 8–11 flowers together.

'Red Indian' (Knap Hill, 1951); Knap Hill; *calendulaceum* derivation; orange-red, yellow fleck.

'Roi des Feux' (before 1873); *gandavense* Klon; red, 5 cm./2 in. wide, late; shrub growing very high and upright.

'Rosata' (Proefstation Boskoop, 1965); *viscosum* × Mollis; growth widespread and upright; flowers dark carmine with red stripes, strongly scented, not appearing until end of May to beginning of June, 4·5 cm./1¾ in. wide, 10–11 blooms together.

'Royal Command' (ROTHSCHILD); Knap Hill; scarlet.

'Royal Lodge' (ROTHSCHILD, 1947); cinnamon red with long pistils, very late, fast growing.

Garden varieties

'Salmon Glow' (DEN OUDEN); *kosterianum* clone; dark salmon.

'Salmon Queen' (P. VUYK); *kosterianum* clone; apricot yellow with pink edge, later salmon pink.

'Samuel Taylor Coleridge' (KERSBERGEN); *kosterianum* clone; pale pink with yellowish brown markings.

'Sandpiper' (Knap Hill, 1941); Knap Hill; pale yellow with pink, orange inside.

'Sang de Gentbrugge' (L. VAN HOUTTE, 1873); Ghent, signal red, 4 cm./1$\frac{9}{16}$ in. wide.

'Satan' (Knap Hill, 1926); Knap Hill; dark carmine; small flowered.

'Seville' (Knap Hill, 1926); Knap Hill, orange, short tubes, very late (Colour plate 2, 4).

'Soir de Paris' (FELIX & DIJKHUIS, 1958); *viscosum* × (Mollis); narrow tube or funnel shaped, scented, pink with darker lines, and with pure orange fleck on upper parts, 5 cm./2 in. wide, 3·5 cm./1$\frac{3}{8}$ in. long, up to 7–9 flowers together.

'Spek's Brilliant' (JAN SPEK); *kosterianum* clone; orange-red with marked yellow anthers.

'Spek's Orange' (JAN SPEK, 1948); *kosterianum* clone; orange with greenish markings, late.

'Spinoza' (ENDTZ); Moll.; orange with pink, yellow in the centre.

'Strawberry Ice' (ROTHSCHILD, 1947); Knap Hill; fleshy pink with darker veins, dark orange markings, buds dark salmon.

'Sun Chariot' (ROTHSCHILD); Knap Hill; golden yellow, 8 cm./3$\frac{3}{16}$ in. wide.

'Superba' (M. KOSTER & ZONEN, 1901); Ghent; clear pink with orange fleck, fringed.

'Suzanne Loef' (M. KOSTER, 1962); Mollis; origins unknown; pink, with orange fleck inside, 8 cm./3$\frac{3}{16}$ in. wide; in groups of 8–9 flowers.

'Sylphides' (Knap Hill, 1950); Knap Hill, white with pink, yellow fleck, large flowered, early.

'Teniers' (Ghent); orange yellow with darker shadows; filled.

'T. J. Seidel' (M. KOSTER & ZONEN, 1892); *kosterianum* clone; salmon orange with darker fleck.

'Toucan' (Knap Hill, 1941); Knap Hill, creamy white to lemon yellow, edge tinged with pink, orange markings, very large flowered.

'Tunis' (Knap Hill, 1926); Knap Hill; pillar box red, orange fleck, scented.

'Unique' (before 1875); Ghent; yellowish orange, 5 cm./2 in. wide, long tubes; buds orange red.

Velasquez' (VUYLSTEKE, 1888); Rust.; creamy white, pale pink tinge, eventually turning completely white, filled.

'Virgile' (Vuylsteke, 1888); Rust.; pale yellow.

'Von Gneist' (P. VAN NOORDT & SON); *kosterianum* clone; orange red with salmon.

'W. E. Gumbleton' (L. VAN HOUTTE, 1872); Moll.; *japonicum* clone; yellow with pale greenish fleck.

'W. F. Raiffeisen' (P. L. BINKEN); Mollis; clear orange red, middle late.

'White Swan' (EXBURY, 1960); Knap Hill; creamy white, turning almost pure white later, but tubes gradually turning pink; corona often has 6–8 lobes.

'Whitethroat' (Knap Hill, 1941); Knap Hill; pure white, filled, almost like a Rustica sort.

'Willem III' (Ghent); orange yellow with orange red markings.

'Willem Hardijzer' (HARDIJZER, 1944); Moll.; signal red, very glowing (Colour Plate 4, 6).

'Windsor Lad' (Knap Hill); pale lilac with darker fleck.

'Winston Churchill' (FELIX & DIJKHUIS, 1949); *kosterianum* clone; 'Koster's Brilliant Red' × unknown seedling; mandarin red with dark red fleck.

(*d*) Evergreen Azaleas

Under this heading come all the varieties of the subseries *obtusum* and their hybrids (*R. kaempferi, kuisianum, mucronatum, obtusum, oldhamii, pulchrum, simsii, yedoense* and so on). The most important groups are labelled as follows:

'Amoena' Sorts; derivations from *R. obtusum* 'Amoena'; small flowered.

Kurume sorts; garden varieties from *R. kiusianum, kaempferi* and perhaps also *R. obtusum*; which originated through crossing and selection in Japan, but which were later achieved also in Holland and the United States. In 1917 H. Wilson took a selection of the best fifty varieties ('Wilson's Fifty') back to the States and gave them English names, under which they are normally sold in America (but not in Europe!). All varieties have small flowers; they are not usually wider than 2·5 cm./1 in.

Kaempfer sorts: have been developed in Holland from 1920 by crossing of *R. kaempferi* with 'Malvatica'; flowers large.

'Vuykiana' sorts: Dutch and (later) Belgian crossings of 'J. C. van Tol' with Kaempfer sorts and others; flowers usually very large.

'Glenn Dale' sorts: American crossings, developed from 1935 from varieties of the Subseries Obtusum, usually crossings of Kaempfer hybrids with *R. mucronatum, indicum, simsii* and so on. Large flowered, not very widely available in Europe.

Gable hybrids: American Hybrids, achieved by J. B. Gable in Stewartstown, Pennsylvania, from 1927 onwards, particularly from *R. kaempferi* × *poukhanense*; from 1933 onwards has been developed by Lionel de Rothschild, Exbury.

Arendsii hybrids; hybrids from *R. mucronatum* and Japanese azaleas, first achieved in 1927, named in 1951 and then put on the market. Grower Georg Arends in Wuppertal, Germany. All sorts named after regions in Germany.

'Addy Wery' (DEN OUDEN, 1940); Kur.; 'Flame' × 'Malvatica'; flowers funnel shaped in ones or twos, blood red with orange tinge, growth compact.

'Adonis' (FELIX & DIJKHUIS, 1952); Kur.; 'Truus' × 'Azuma-kagami'; flowers white, edge fringed, broad growth.

'Agger' (ARENDS, 1951); *mucronulatum* ×; lilac, very profusely flowering, hardy (Colour Plate 3, 4).

'Aladdin' (W. C. HAGE & Co.; 1943); Kur.; red.

'Amoena'; Kur.; *obtusum* cultivation; originated in Japan, introduced in 1850 by Fortune; carmine lilac or violet-red, small flowers but profusely flowering, leaves very small, very shiny (Colour Plate 3, 1).

'Annamaria' (HOOFTMAN, around 1950); Kaempferi; white (= 'Frau Dekens').

'Anny' (C. B. VAN NES, 1922); Kaempferi; *kaempferi* × 'Malvatica'; orange red with pink.

'Aronensis' (G. ARENDS, around 1960); Kur.; 'Multiflora' × *mucronatum* evergreen, small leaved, very low growing, profusely flowering, in varying colour tones; known until now as 'Fumiko' (salmon carmine); 'Hanako (lilac pink), 'Haruko' (purple); 'Kumiko' (salmon carmine); 'Momoko' (pink) and 'Talako' (lilac pink). Distributed by G. D. Böhlje.

'Atalanta' (C. B. VAN NES); Kaempferi × 'Malvatica'; pale lilac.

'Beethoven' (VUYK VAN NES); Vuyk.; 'J. C. van Tol' × 'Maxwellii'; lilac with darker markings, fringed.

'Bengal Fire' (ROTHSCHILD, 1934); *kaempferi* × 'Oldhamii'; 5–6 cm./2–2⅜ in. wide, pillar box red.

'Benigiri' (introduced in 1910 by C. B. Van Nes from Japan); Kur.; simple, clear red.

'Betty' (C. B. VAN NES, 1922); Kaempferi; *kaempferi* × 'Malvatica'; pink with darker centre.

'Bigge' (ARENDS); *mucronulatum* × ; lilac, purple markings, large flowered.

'Blaauw's Pink' (BLAAUW, 1953); Kur.; salmon pink with lighter tones, early, completely hardy.

'Caldwellii' (B. S. WILLIANS, around 1880); *obtusum* 'Amoena' × 'Magnifica'; clear pink.

'Cameo' (GABLE); clear pink, 4 cm./1 9/16 in. wide.

'Chopin' (VUYK VAN NES, 1954); Vuyk; 'Schubert' × unknown seedling; glowing dark pink, darker markings, 6 cm./2⅜ in. wide.

'Christmas Cheer'; Kur.; pink, partly half filled, 4 cm./1 9/16 in. wide.

'Diana' (FELIX & DIJKHUIS, 1952); Kur.; salmon pink.

'Diemel' (ARENDS, 1951); *mucronatum* × salmon pink.

'Double Beauty' (VUYK VAN NES, 1965); Vuyk.; unnamed filled seedling No. 37 × 'Vuyk's Scarlet'; leaves clear green; flowers in pairs, pink with carmine tinge, 6 cm./2⅜ in. wide, double.

'Eder' (ARENDS, 1951); *mucronatum* × ; salmon pink.

'Ennepe' (ARENDS, 1951); *mucronatum* × ; salmon pink.

'Esmeralda' (KOPPESCHAAR); Kur.; pink.

'Favorite' (C. B. VAN NES, around 1920); Kaempferi; 'Hinodegiri' × *kaempferi*; dark pink, edge fringed.

'Fedora' (C. B. VAN NES, 1922); Kaempferi: *kaempferi* × 'Malvatica'; dark pink.

'Fidelio' (C. B. VAN NES, 1922); Kaempferi; *kaempferi* × 'Malvatica'; dark pink.

'Florida' (VUYK VAN NES, before 1958); Vuyk; unnamed seedling × 'Vuyk's Scarlet'; dark red, filled, evergreen azalea.

'Frau Dekens' = 'Annamaria'.

'Gartenschönheit' (C. B. VAN NES, 1922); Kaempferi; clear pink (= 'Garden Beauty').

'Gretchen' (C. B. VAN NES, 1922); Kaempferi; dark lilac with violet markings, 5 cm./2 in. wide.

'Hardijzer Beauty' (W. HARDIJZER, 1958); Kurume Azalea × *racemosum*; funnel shaped, pink, with darker specks above, 2–4 flowers together and about 5–8 such clusters occurring on pseudo-end of stem.

'Hatsugiri'; Kur.; purple-carmine.—From Japan.

'Helena' (FELIX & DIJKHUIS, 1952); Kur.; pure pink, double, richly flowering.

'Herbert' (GABLE, 1931); 'Hexe' × *poukhanense*; red violet, with dark markings, double, 4 cm./1 9/16 in. wide, edge fringed.

'Hino-crimson' (VERMEULEN, U.S.A.); Kur.; 'Amoena' × 'Hinodegiri'; red, small flowered.

'Hinodegiri' (Introduced by E. H. Wilson from Japan, under the labelling No. 42); Kur.; carmine red (= 'Red Hussar').

'Hinomayo' (imported from the imperial gardens in Tokyo by C. B. van Nes in 1910); Kur.; pale pink.

'Hino-scarlet' (H. M. PETERS, Boskoop, 1963); seedling from 'Hino-crimson'; carmine, double, 4·5 cm./1¾ in. wide.

'Jeanette' (C. B. VAN NES, 1920); Kaempferi; deep pink with darker markings; similar to 'Fedora'.

'Johann Seb. Bach' (VUYK VAN NES): 'J. C. van Tol' × 'Maxwellii' Vuyk; purple, 6 cm./2⅜ in. wide.

'John Cairns' (ENDTZ, 1940); Kaempferi; dark red.

'Joseph Haydn' (VUYK VAN NES); 'J. C. van Tol' × *mucronatum*; purple red with brown markings, 7 cm./2⅘ in. wide.

'Johann Strauss' (VUYK VAN NES); 'J. C. van Tol' × *kaempferi* hybrid; salmon pink with darker markings, 6 cm./2⅜ in. wide.

'Kathleen' (C. B. VAN NES, 1922); Kaempferi, rosy red.

'Kermesina'; Japanese azalea; rosy red, middle late to late, very hardy.

'Kerspe' (ARENDS, 1951); *mucronatum* × ; carmine.

'Kirin'; Kur.; double, coral pink, 2·5 cm./1 in. wide, ('Daybreak', 'Coral Bells'). Imported by E. H. Wilson from Japan as No. 22.

'Kokin-Shita'; *indicum*; creeping, salmony orange, June.—Japan.

'Koningin Wilhelmina' (VUYK VAN NES, 1941); Vuyk.; dark cinnamon.

'Ledifolia' see *R. mucronatum*.

'Lilac Time' (ENDTZ); Kaempferi; intense lilac coloured.

'Lilian Harvey' (W. HARDIJZER); *racemosum* × 'Hatsugiri'; 1966; white with pink, only 2 cm./¾ in. wide, funnel shaped.

'Lily Marlene' (VUY VAN NES, 1965); 'Little Ruby' × 'Dr. W. F. Wery'; growth broad and low, keeps its leaves well, flowers deep pink, double, often filled too, 4 cm./1 9/16 in. wide, usually in groups of 5, very profusely flowering, medium early, very hardy (= 'Marlene Vuyk').

'Lister' (ARENDS, 1951); *mucronatum* × ; salmon carmine.

'Little Beauty' (VUYK VAN NES, 1950); 'Amoena' × ; 'Amoena' hybrid × 'Favorite'; pure pink, double.

'Louise Gable' (GABLE, 1930); *indicum* × (*kaempferi* × *poukhanense*); salmon pink, half filled, 6 cm./2⅜ in. wide; generally regarded as Gable's 'best azalea'.

'Madame Loth' (W. HARDIJZER, 1965); Kurume azalea × *racemosum*; funnel shaped, pink, 2·5 cm./1 in. long, always 2–3 together, and 8–12 of these clusters forming a pseudo end-standing group.

'Mahler' (VUYK VAN NES, 1965); *obtus.*; seedling No. 37 Gl × 'Vuyk's Rosyred'; growth broad and low; flowers lilac, darker markings, 7 cm./2¾ in. wide, in 2–3 together, late, hardy.

'Malvatica' (KOSTER & ZONEN, 1910); imported from Japan among 'Hinodegiri' specimens; lilac.

'Maxwellii'; *pulchrum* form; carmine with darker markings (Colour Plate 3, 5).

'Mevrouw Hugo T. Hooftman' (HOOFTMAN, 1935); Kaempferi; pink fringed.

'Mimi' (B. BUNSCHOTEN, 1958); Kaempferi; origins unknown, winter-green; pale pink with darker markings.

'Mozart' (VUYK VAN NES, 1931); Vuyk.; 'J. C. van Tol' × *kaempferi* hybrid; violet, 6 cm./2⅜ in. wide.

'Multiflora' (G. ARENDS, around 1950 ?); accidental seedling, Kurume type; lilac pink; growth very small, only about 30 cm./12 in. high and 50 cm./20 in. wide (Colour Plate 3, 3).

'Myosotis'; Japanese azalea; violet; not attractive.

'Orange Favorite' (VUYK VAN NES, 1953); Kaempferi; mutation of 'Favorite'; orange red.

'Orange Beauty' (C. B. VAN NES, around 1920); Kaempferi; 'Hinodegiri' × *kaempferi*; clear orange.

'Orange King' (ENDTZ); Kaempferi; orange red.

'Orion' (FELIX DIJKHUIS); Kur.; dark pink.

'Palestrina' (VUYK VAN NES, 1926); Vuyk.; 'J. C. van Tol' × *kaempferi* hybrid; ivory white; growth erect.

'Pink Treasure' (C. B. VAN NES); Kaempferi; pure pink.

'Prins Bernhard' (VUYK VAN NES, 1945); scarlet red.

'Prinses Irene' (VUYK VAN NES, 1941); Vuyk.; clear red.

Garden varieties

'Prinses Juliana' (VUYK VAN NES, 1941); Vuyk.; pure orange.

'Psyche' (FELIX & DIJKHUIS); Kuruma; pink, small flowered.

'Purple Splendor' (GABLE, 1939); Gable; 'Hexe' × *poukhanense*; purple red, double, fringed.

'Purple Triumph' (VUYK VAN NES, 1951); 'Beethoven' × unnamed seedling, deep purple.

'P. W. Hardijzer' (VUYK VAN NES); Vuyk.; dark carmine pink.

'Ria Hardijzer' (HARDIJZER, 1958); 'Hinodegiri' × *racemosum*; magenta red, somewhat flecked, in tight clusters composed of 10–15 divisions.

'Rose Greeley' (GRABLE, 1940); [*mucronatum* × *poukhanense*] × ['Hexe' × *poukhanense*] × *kaempferi*; white with greenish fleck, double, 6 cm./$2\frac{3}{8}$ in. wide, scented, one of the most beautiful early white varieties.

'Sakata Red' (KOPPESCHAAR, 1952); Kur.; pillar box red, relatively small flowered, but profuse.

'Schubert' (VUYK VAN NES, 1931); Vuyk.; clear pink with darker markings (Colour Plate 3, *2*).

'Sibelius' (VUYK VAN NES, 1931); Vuyk.; 'J. C. van Tol' × 'Maxwellii', orange red with chocolate coloured fleck, 5 cm./2 in. wide.

'Silvester' (Proefstation Boskoop, 1963); Kur.; 'Aladdin' × 'Amoena'; rosy red, 3 cm./$1\frac{3}{16}$ in. wide.

'Snow' (imported from Japan before 1920 and brought into cultivation under this name); Kur.; white, greenish markings, double, 4 cm./$1\frac{9}{16}$ in. wide.

'Sorpe' (ARENDS, 1951); *mucronatum* ×; purple.

'Uelfe' (ARENDS, 1951); *mucronatum* ×; purple.

'Victorine Hefting' (ADR. VAN NES, before 1962); seedling from 'Hinomayo'; dark pink, 6–7 cm./$2\frac{9}{16}$–$2\frac{3}{4}$ in. wide, 2–3 flowers together.

'Vuyk's Rosyred' (VUYK VAN NES, 1954); Vuyk.; glowing rosy red.

'Vuyk's Scarlet' (VUYK VAN NES, 1954); Vuyk.; dark red to carmine.

'White Lady' (ENDTZ); *kaempferi* clone; white.

'Willy' (C. B. VAN NES); Kaempferi; clear red.

'Wintertime' (Proefstation Boskoop, 1963); Kur.; 'Aladdin' × 'Amoena'; flowers geranium red, 4 cm./$1\frac{9}{16}$ in. wide, (= 'Midwinter').

'Wipper' (ARENDS, 1951); *mucronatum* ×; lilac, much darker than 'Agger'; very large flowered, very late, not occurring until the beginning of June, profusely flowering and very hardy.

'Yodogawa' = *R. yedoense*; see Colour Plate 3, *6*.

'Zampa' (C. B. VAN NES, 1922); Kaempferi; clear orange.

Index

Index